NIETZSCHE: A GU

Guides for the Perplexed available from Continuum:

Adorno: A Guide for the Perplexed, Alex Thomson

Deleuze: A Guide for the Perplexed, Claire Colebrook

Levinas: A Guide for the Perplexed, B. C. Hutchens

Sartre: A Guide for the Perplexed, Gary Cox

Hobbes: A Guide for the Perplexed, Stephen J. Finn

Wittgenstein: A Guide for the Perplexed, Mark Addis

Merleau-Ponty: A Guide for the Perplexed, Eric Matthews

Gadamer: A Guide for the Perplexed, Chris Lawn

Husserl: A Guide for the Perplexed, Matheson Russell

Quine: A Guide for the Perplexed, Gary Kemp

Existentialism: A Guide for the Perplexed, Stephen Earnshaw

Kierkegaard: A Guide for the Perplexed, Clare Carlisle

Rousseau: A Guide for the Perplexed, Matthew Simpson

NIETZSCHE: A GUIDE FOR THE PERPLEXED

R. KEVIN HILL

continuum

Continuum International Publishing Group
The Tower Building   80 Maiden Lane
11 York Road   Suite 704
London SE1 7NX   New York
                                      NY 10038

British Library Cataloguing-in-Publication Data
A catalogue record for this book is available from the British Library.

ISBN: HB: 0826489249
       9780826489241
       PB: 0826489257
       9780826489258

Library of Congress Cataloging-in-Publication Data
Hill, R. Kevin
   Nietzsche : a guide for the perplexed / R. Kevin Hill.
      p. cm.
   Includes bibliographical references and index.
   ISBN-13: 978-0-8264-8924-1
   ISBN-10: 0-8264-8924-9
   1. Nietzsche, Friedrich Wilhelm, 1844-1900. I. Title.

B3317.H5355 2007
193 - - dc22

                                                    2006034099

Typeset by YHT Ltd, London
Printed and bound in Great Britain by
MPG Books Ltd, Bodmin, Cornwall

CONTENTS

CONTENTS

ABBREVIATIONS

I use the following abbreviations in this book, followed by section numbers rather than page numbers, to facilitate reference to both the original German and to multiple translations. In most cases (e.g., *Birth of Tragedy*) this is simple enough when the work consecutively numbers all sections; if this is the case and Nietzsche furnishes part numbers, I have ignored them. In other cases (e.g., *Twilight*), where the section numbers return to '1' with each new part and the parts are not themselves numbered, I have added a Roman numeral to indicate the part. Prologues, epilogues, prefaces and postscripts are stated in the reference, e.g. '(TI, Prologue)', and not counted as 'parts'. With the original German, I have simply referred to page numbers. For detailed publication information about Nietzsche's writings, see William H. Schaberg, *The Nietzsche Canon: A Publication History and Bibliography*, Chicago: University of Chicago Press, 1995.

KGW	*Kritische Gesamtausgabe (Werke)*, Colli, Giorgio (ed.), Montinari, Mazzino, approx. 40 vols. in 9 divisions, Berlin: DeGruyter, 1967–present.
PN	*Portable Nietzsche*, ed. and trans. Walter Kaufmann, New York: Viking Penguin, 1976.
BT	*Birth of Tragedy* (1872), in *The Basic Writings of Nietzsche*, ed. and trans. Walter Kaufmann, New York: Modern Library, 1992.
UM	*Untimely Meditations* (1873–6), trans. R. J. Hollingdale, Cambridge: Cambridge University Press, 1997.
HA	*Human, All Too Human* (1878–80), trans. R. J. Hollingdale, Cambridge: Cambridge University Press, 1996.

D	*Daybreak* (1881), trans. R. J. Hollingdale, Cambridge: Cambridge University Press, 1997.
GS	*Gay Science* (1882), trans. Walter Kaufmann, New York: Vintage, 1974.
Z	*Thus Spoke Zarathustra* (1883–5), in *Portable Nietzsche*.
BGE	*Beyond Good and Evil* (1886), in *Basic Writings*.
GM	*On the Genealogy of Morals* (1887), in *Basic Writings*.
CW	*Case of Wagner* (1888), in *Basic Writings*.
TI	*Twilight of the Idols* (1888), in *Portable Nietzsche*.
A	*Antichrist* (1888), in *Portable Nietzsche*.
EH	*Ecce Homo* (1888), in *Basic Writings*.
NCW	*Nietzsche contra Wagner* (1888), in *Portable Nietzsche*.
WP	*Will to Power* (1882–8), ed. Walter Kaufmann, trans. Walter Kaufmann and R. J. Hollingdale, New York: Random House, 1967. This text remains useful for historical purposes and ease of reference as long as one is aware of the controversy surrounding its construction. Additionally, Kaufmann's translation pre-dates the *KGW*, and so there are numerous small textual errors carried over into translation. For a chronological approach that post-dates the *KGW*, see *Writings from the Late Notebooks*, ed. Rüdiger Bittner, trans. Kate Sturge, Cambridge: Cambridge University Press, 2003.

PREFACE

Nietzsche, writing in the late nineteenth century, proved to be one of the most influential figures of the twentieth century. Though his prose is in many ways the most accessible of any German philosopher, this surface clarity conceals depths. Even now there is no consensus about how his texts should be understood and, lacking that, any evaluation of them becomes impossible. Broadly speaking, there are three approaches among philosophers, corresponding to three very different philosophical communities and traditions. Among so-called analytic philosophers, prominent in but by no means limited to the English-speaking world, Nietzsche is regarded as a kind of empiricist, a critic of metaphysics and (for many) a non-cognitivist critic of morality. He is also often regarded as holding views that are compatible with liberalism. Among post-structuralist philosophers, prominent in but by no means limited to the French-speaking world, Nietzsche is regarded as a literary figure, an avant-garde irrationalist and an alternative to Marx as a basis for radical social criticism. For others, Nietzsche is a traditional metaphysician and system builder not so different in many ways from other post-Kantians like Fichte, Schelling, Schopenhauer and Hegel.

Because the quantity of Nietzsche interpretations is now becoming overwhelming, we cannot hope to do justice to all of them. Bearing in mind that other 'analytic' interpretations tend to be relatively clear and accessible, I have tried to provide what I think will be of greatest use to the reader new to Nietzsche. Accordingly, after two chapters that introduce Nietzsche's life and writings, I offer my own interpretative sketch in three chapters, dealing with metaphysics, epistemology and ethics in an 'analytic' vein. Because

PREFACE

'Continental' readings pose the greatest difficulties for comprehension, I follow with one chapter on Heidegger's interpretation and another chapter on Derrida's, Foucault's and Deleuze's interpretations.

CHAPTER 1

INTRODUCTION

A PERVASIVE PRESENCE

This book introduces the philosopher Friedrich Nietzsche to the advanced undergraduate, early graduate student and educated lay reader. It cannot be the last word on a subject that has generated over a thousand books and countless articles in many disciplines. What it does try to do is orient the reader within the world of 'the Nietzsche phenomenon', a constellation composed of his context, works, evolving reputation over the course of a century, and the main competing interpretative strategies that have emerged among academic philosophers.

Nietzsche is unusual among philosophers in that many read him not only outside academic philosophy, but also outside academia altogether. In the United States, there are two mass-market bookstore chains that offer 'bestsellers' with small sections devoted to other categories. In most of these stores, there is a philosophy section, usually four short shelves, stocked with the bare minimum of steady sellers in the category. Typically, one finds Plato, Nietzsche, Russell (though usually his non-technical works), Sartre and Ayn Rand. Nietzsche is among the few philosophers read by people who do not read philosophy. This is partly because Nietzsche's writings on psychological topics contain both explanatory theory and advice which readers drawn to 'self-help' find attractive.

Nietzsche's name, like Wittgenstein's, is frequently dropped in literary contexts. 'One of her passing fixations was a term – from Nietzsche, I think – *traumhaft*, a sense that all beliefs – religion, love, the golden rule – were but a dream with no provable justification in morality or science. Our lives, Nietzsche claimed, our customs, were really no more than rote learning. We were, she said, actually afloat within sensation and otherwise unanchored, free but terrified, like the moonbound astronauts had been when they left their capsules and stood in space'. This passage appears in Scott Turow's novel, *The Laws of Our Fathers*,[1] but one could multiply such examples endlessly: Nietzsche is a fixture in the literary imagination, as much for what he signifies as for what he said. His unforgettable persona casts a longer shadow than his ideas; the work about Nietzsche ranked highest in sales on Amazon.com is a biographical novel, *When Nietzsche Wept*, by Irvin D. Yalom. Beyond this, Nietzsche is an atmosphere, a pervasive presence: though Amazon.com has indexed over 1,800 books about Nietzsche (as evidenced by his name in the title but not as the author), over 27,000 books mention Nietzsche. No philosophical or quasi-philosophical figure of the past two centuries is referred to more frequently except Marx (64,708 Amazon.com references) and Freud (52,729). Among philosophers that remain, only Plato, Aristotle, Augustine, Descartes, Locke, Hume and Kant are mentioned more often.

What accounts for this interest? To be sure, Nietzsche's ideas play some role. But first, it must be said that Nietzsche's life and work, and their subsequent reception, involve a fair amount of drama. Nietzsche himself came to believe that he occupied a crucial moment in history, that his writings would have apocalyptic effects on the world. 'I know my fate. One day my name will be associated with the memory of something tremendous – a crisis without equal on earth, the most profound collision of conscience, a decision that was conjured up against everything that had been believed, demanded, hallowed so far. I am no man, I am dynamite' (*EH* IV, §1). Nietzsche's conception of his own historical importance is bound up with his critique of Christianity. While many previous thinkers had criticized Christianity and championed secularism, Nietzsche thought such critiques never broke free from Christian moral commitments, even while secularizing them; for Nietzsche, if Christianity's morality is inextricably intertwined with its theology, then both stand or fall together. Only after his own work, he thinks, does the necessity of a moral revolution in conjunction with the modern trend towards secularization become apparent. But such a moral revolution, while not a simple inversion of our prior moral commitments, inevitably involves rebaptizing as good much of what we had regarded as wicked. This realization is terrifying. One can already see that Nietzsche, rightly or wrongly, saw himself and his importance in dramatic terms, and for the most part, others have seen him this way as well. Opponents of secularization naturally see him as a kind of devil. But many secular thinkers who do not want Nietzsche's moral revolution (and perhaps resent the implication that it becomes necessary absent religion, a claim many religious people might well agree with) see him this way too.

Nietzsche's life and work have contributed in other ways to the dramatic character of his image. First, though Nietzsche's writings display a wide range of styles, masterfully deployed, one of his most widely read works, *Thus Spoke Zarathustra*, presents his ideas in speeches offered by a fictionalized ancient sage loosely based on the prophet Zoroaster, written in a romantic and pseudo-biblical style. To some extent, Nietzsche intended a parodic performance, yet in the years since his death, an optical illusion has arisen. The historical Nietzsche in all his concreteness has become displaced in the popular imagination by Nietzsche-as-Zarathustra. To use a more mundane analogy, in the 1970s David Bowie parodied the popular image of the rock star with a fictional character, 'Ziggy Stardust'. Somewhere in this process, David Bowie the parodist became confused with the character, so that he really became a famous rock star. Something similar happened to Nietzsche/Zarathustra: in playing the prophet he came to get himself accepted as one. One senses that in both cases, this was quite intentional. Nietzsche had always insisted on the role that creative interpretation can play in transforming malleable artistic material (including the self), and that the highest form of art would be to 'work on' humanity and history as well. Does Nietzsche's importance lie in his thinking about the moral crisis we find ourselves in anyway, his *dramatis personae* as self-appointed prophet of the crisis, or his creating both the crisis, the prophet-mask, and its reception all at once? There may not even be an answer to that question.

However that may be, Nietzsche's life has also contributed to his reception for reasons that are almost certainly irrelevant to his importance as a thinker. As Nietzsche was completing his last writings, in 1889, he experienced a permanent psychotic collapse, and remained insane until his death in 1900. Scholars still disagree on the causes of his collapse: the majority view blames syphilis, while others consider bipolar disorder, schizophrenia, or even drug abuse. However, given the extremely personal and engaged nature of Nietzsche's writing, and the dramatic quality of the issues he grappled with, there has been a tendency from the very beginning of Nietzsche's reception to see his madness as integral to his thought and authorship. The simplest reaction was to dismiss his writings as the work of a lunatic. But madness carries a fascination of its own. It is tempting to think that in rebelling against morality, Nietzsche sold his soul to the devil, who then claimed and destroyed it a decade early. Or perhaps Nietzsche's madness was a noble psychological crucifixion: that he bravely sacrificed his sanity to think forbidden thoughts. It is ironic that a thinker concerned with naturalizing religious phenomena should find a purely medical misfortune imbued with this sort of meaning. Most contemporary Nietzsche scholars mightily resist these lines of thought, perhaps because any one of them risks collapsing into the simplistic, dismissive one. But it would be a mistake to ignore the powerful undertow of the image of Nietzsche Agonistes, martyr to his own irrationality and moral transgression. Though philosophy is perhaps rooted in the rhetoric of depersonalization, the influence of charismatic personae on its history cannot be overlooked, as Nietzsche and Wittgenstein illustrate. Nor is the philosophical imagination immune to the charms of martyrdom, as Socrates shows.

The final source of Nietzsche's reputation, one that engages the mind as much as his madness (while provoking vigorous denial from his advocates) is his connection with Nazism. Though Nietzsche died decades before the Nazis' ascent to power, and though there are very important incompatibilities between his thought and Nazism, the Nazis themselves claimed him as their prophet, ideologue and justification. Here the themes of historical crisis, self-appointed prophetic stance, repudiation of conventional moral commitments and madness dovetail almost irresistibly. Was Nazism's murderous ideology the concrete embodiment of the new values meant to replace Christianity and the tottering secular yet quasi-Christian ethos of the liberal Enlightenment? If so, must we not turn away from Nietzsche in revulsion? Perhaps this explains the terrifying quality of his thought, and even the sacrifice of Nietzsche's sanity? Or instead of collapsing under the weight of truths he could not bear to contemplate for long, was Nietzsche instead the first spiritual suicide bomber of fascism?

Most Nietzsche scholars reject such thoughts as absurdly insensitive to the content of Nietzsche's philosophy, and they are probably right. Nonetheless, such thoughts are important for explaining Nietzsche's reception and influence. Put crudely: no press is bad press. Ironically, being the object of debate over the extent to which one's ideas contributed to the Holocaust may be a more effective way of gaining an audience than writing clearly, temperately and uncontroversially. And while being tarred by association with totalitarianism is a bad thing, would we know Marx's name had it not been for Lenin and Stalin? Would we know Nietzsche's name if not for Hitler? In any event, Nietzsche's reception has occurred largely within communities that once fought over Nazism: the United States, England, France and Germany. The importance of that context for understanding his reception during the postwar era cannot be overestimated, even when accompanied by the dogged insistence upon that context's unimportance.

BIOGRAPHICAL SKETCH

Another peculiarity of Nietzsche's is that the world that produced him was so different from the world that ultimately came to embrace him. Nietzsche, whose reputation reached its current height only in the twentieth century, and who is more read now in the English-speaking world, was a product of Bismarck's Germany, and lived out his life in the late nineteenth century. English and American readers should consider that Nietzsche's emergence as a thinker occurred during the reign of Queen Victoria and the administration of President Lincoln. Several more specific contexts need to be kept in mind to understand what Nietzsche drew on and transformed.

First, the only job Nietzsche ever held was as a professor of classics ('philology') at a Swiss university. Nietzsche's training in classical literature had a decisive impact on his conception of what culture could be. For much of his life, ancient Greece represented a standard of cultural achievement that informed his hopes for, and judgement against, his contemporaries. The scholarly methodology his classical training gave him informed his sense of what it was to have an 'intellectual conscience' while helping him to associate this with essentially *historical* inquiries. His understanding of philosophy was shaped more by his reading of the pre-Socratics and Plato, whom he taught repeatedly, than by modern figures such as Descartes or Hume. Lastly, he took Greek tragedy to have an ethical significance that could give meaning to a life lacking Judaeo-Christian commitments.

Second, Nietzsche spent much of his young adulthood involved with what we might call the Schopenhauer–Wagner 'cult'. Though Nietzsche's discoveries of Arthur Schopenhauer and Richard Wagner occurred three years apart, an enthusiasm for Schopenhauer was one of the bonds that joined together Nietzsche and Wagner in friendship for a time. Though Nietzsche never fully agreed with Schopenhauer even in his earliest writings, he took from him a sense of what philosophical inquiry was for, and what its proper methodological toolkit was. For Schopenhauer, philosophy's central function is to explain the problematic character of the world and human existence, to vindicate the significance of art, morality and religion, and to offer a form of non-religious transcendence. The toolkit is Kantianism. Broadly speaking, all this remained true of Nietzsche's thought to the end, though he would define much of what he was to do with these Schopenhauerian themes by deliberate opposition to Schopenhauer's handling of them. What Wagner added beyond advocacy of Schopenhauer was his example as a creative individual, his forceful agenda of cultural reform and, in the librettos of his operas, the valorization of heroes who opposed oppression, not in the name of morality, but the oppression of morality itself in the name of 'life'. Nietzsche devoted so much of his authorship to opposing Wagner, his music and his handling of these themes, that this debt is obscured. Nonetheless, *Zarathustra*, in style and content, owes much to *Siegfried*.

Third, though Nietzsche's self-image, especially after giving up his university post, was always that of a philosopher, he saw himself as part of the republic of letters, strove for literary excellence in the creation of his texts, and for the most part achieved it. Oddly, his models were neither Greek nor German, but French: Nietzsche's first artistically successful work, *Human, All Too Human*, was as much the product of stylistic engagement with and emulation of Montaigne, La Rochefoucault, Voltaire and Stendhal, as it was the product of reflection on Nietzsche's own thematic concerns. In 1881, the now no longer Young Hegelian Bruno Bauer praised Nietzsche as the German Montaigne, Pascal and Diderot. It is tempting to dismiss this 'French' side of Nietzsche as merely a

6

product of a stylistic and ideological experiment abandoned when he began *Zarathustra*, and left far behind in his mature works. But attention to the style of the late *Twilight of the Idols*, as opposed to some of its more striking philosophical pronouncements, reveals that Nietzsche the aphoristic stylist, the master of concision whose goal remained *épater le bourgeois*, was a part of his performance to the very end.

Of Nietzsche's life itself, apart from the content of his books, very little needs to be said. Nietzsche was born in the small Prussian village Röcken in 1844 to a Lutheran pastor, Ludwig Nietzsche, and the daughter of another Lutheran pastor, Franziska Oehler. His younger brother Joseph died in childhood and his younger sister Elisabeth lived (mostly to plague and profit from him) well past his death. The turning point in Nietzsche's childhood was the death of his father in 1849, and the subsequent move of the family from Röcken to Naumburg in 1850. Our first knowledge of Nietzsche's writing and letters dates from around this time.[2]

Nietzsche's youth was noteworthy for his passion for music and writing, and the beginnings of the headaches (migraines?) that would plague him for the rest of his life. In 1858, he entered secondary school at Schulpforta, from which he graduated in September 1864 with strong marks in all subjects except for mathematics. In October, he began his university studies at Bonn.

The year 1865 would prove to be the next major turning point in Nietzsche's life. In his second semester in Bonn, early in 1865, Nietzsche changed his major from theology to philology, suggesting reservations about following in his father's footsteps as a minister. When he returned home during the Easter holidays, he announced to his family his unwillingness to take communion. That June, he wrote to his sister that '[genuine faith] does not offer the slenderest support for a demonstration of objective truth. Here the ways of men divide. Do you want to strive for peace of mind and happiness? Then believe. Do you want to be a devotee of the truth? Then inquire' (*PN*, p. 30). One consequence of the change in major to philology was that his coursework now brought him into contact with ancient Greek philosophy (especially Plato), and philosophy more generally. In his own future career in philology, Nietzsche would regularly teach Plato, who would also become a foil for his own views in his future writings.

At the end of the school year, learning that his philology

professor Friedrich Ritschl was leaving Bonn for Leipzig, Nietzsche decided to follow him there. Leipzig would be the focal point for the remainder of Nietzsche's education; Ritschl, impressed with Nietzsche's classical scholarship, would prove instrumental in obtaining a job for Nietzsche as a philologist. But one of the most important consequences of Nietzsche's move to Leipzig occurred in a secondhand bookstore shortly after his arrival: he bought a copy of Arthur Schopenhauer's *World as Will and Representation* and read it closely. Though by 1868 Nietzsche had disowned key elements of Schopenhauer's metaphysics, the work made a lasting impression on him. His youthful ambivalence about Schopenhauer would inform his mature conception of what a philosopher should and should not be.

The final influence came in 1868. After a period of growing infatuation with Wagner's music, in November 1868 Nietzsche met Wagner and began an ambivalent relationship that would mark him ever after.

Remarkably, with only four years of post-secondary education, Nietzsche was offered a position as assistant professor of philology at the university in Basel in 1869; the faculty in Leipzig in response conferred the doctoral degree on him without a dissertation on the strength of several academic journal publications. During the Basel period Nietzsche's early preoccupation with Schopenhauerian philosophy, Greek literature and Wagnerian music would bear fruit in the precocious, uneven masterpiece *Birth of Tragedy out of the Spirit of Music* (1872). During this period, Nietzsche also wrote the four essays collectively known as *Untimely Meditations* (1873–76). But it would also see Nietzsche's gradual disenchantment with both Wagner and philology; by 1876, Nietzsche had begun to conceive of a new, aphoristic mode of writing based on French models. Also in 1876, Nietzsche would see both the first performance of Wagner's *Ring* and Wagner in person for the last time. When Wagner finally saw what Nietzsche had been writing during the previous two years, with the publication of *Human, All Too Human: A Book For Free Spirits* in April 1878, the rift between them became complete and permanent.

Nietzsche's declining health led to his resignation from his academic post at the beginning of the summer of 1879. For the next decade, Nietzsche was a wandering, independent writer and philosopher, living on his disability pension.

Between 1878 and 1881, Nietzsche published three more collections of aphorisms, *Assorted Opinions and Maxims* (1879), *The Wanderer and His Shadow* (1879) and *Daybreak: Thoughts on the Prejudices of Morality* (1881), the first two of which would be reissued as a second volume to *Human, All Too Human*. In the summer of 1881, while residing in Sils-Maria, Switzerland, Nietzsche first conceived of the doctrine of the eternal recurrence, the notion that the history of the cosmos and, within it, the life of each individual, have already occurred and will continue to occur an infinite number of times. This idea struck Nietzsche with the force of revelation: it offered both the prospect of a naturalistic immortality, and a psychological test of one's fitness for it. (One wonders if the 'revelation' was a symptom of a mental condition akin to déjà vécu.) For if an individual's life were marred by self-dissatisfaction, the prospect of endless repetition would seem damnation; but if an individual could achieve a life worthy of affirmation despite its sufferings, its eternal recurrence would be salvation. The very act of contemplating this thought, in turn, could provide just the goad necessary to drive an individual to personal perfection; by contrast, the prospect of eternal recurrence would make any other secular or progressive goals meaningless. For example, working to ameliorate the human condition is pointless if one's efforts are undone in the course of the cosmic cycle. And if one's life seemed so bad that one yearned for death, hope for annihilation was vain: suicides too eternally recur.

During 1882, Nietzsche worked on his last aphoristic work, *Gay Science*, while cultivating an intense friendship with a woman, Lou Salomé, who he hoped might become either his wife or disciple. Relations with her were complicated by the attraction between her and his close male friend, Paul Rée, and by Nietzsche's sister Elisabeth's jealousy of the attention Nietzsche lavished on Lou. By the end of 1882, the various tensions in this quadrangle ruined Nietzsche's connections with all of them, leaving him isolated. Dejected and in the grip of the idea of eternal recurrence, in early 1883 Nietzsche began the work for which he is most famous, *Thus Spoke Zarathustra: A Book For All and None*, a lyrical account of an ancient prophet who discovers and teaches the doctrine. The book would appear in three published instalments, with a fourth part privately printed and distributed, occupying most of Nietzsche's energies from 1883 to 1885.

If *Zarathustra* was Nietzsche's most popular work, the subsequent works had the greatest influence. In 1886, Nietzsche produced *Beyond Good and Evil: Prelude to a Philosophy of the Future*. The new book superficially resembled the earlier aphoristic works, but in a new, energetic style and displaying a new coherence. In 1887, Nietzsche followed it with a book of three extended essays in the same style, *On the Genealogy of Morals: A Polemic*, while bringing out second editions of his previous books, notably adding an additional section of aphorisms to *Gay Science*. Towards the end of 1887, Nietzsche began a systematic work presenting his entire philosophy, but ultimately abandoned that effort; his sister published a collection of writings organized around a plan that dates from this period as if it were the masterwork, entitled *The Will to Power*.

1888 would be Nietzsche's final productive year. He would produce with breathtaking speed a succession of very short works noteworthy for their tautness and energy, yet marred by flashes of megalomania: *The Case of Wagner: A Musician's Problem*, *Twilight of the Idols: Or How One Philosophizes With a Hammer*, *The Antichrist*, *Ecce Homo*, *Dithyrambs of Dionysus* and *Nietzsche contra Wagner: Documents of a Psychologist*. *The Case of Wagner* is a polemic against Wagner's music, personality and cultural influence. *Twilight of the Idols* is a summation of Nietzsche's philosophical views with his comments on some contemporary writers and thinkers. *Antichrist* encapsulates his critique of Christianity. *Ecce Homo* is an intellectual autobiography and a summary of his previous writings. *Dithyrambs of Dionysus* is a collection of poems, most of which had appeared previously in *Zarathustra*. *Nietzsche contra Wagner* is a collection of previous writings on Wagner designed to rebut criticisms of *The Case of Wagner*. All these works appeared shortly after Nietzsche had made his final revisions, excepting *Antichrist* and *Ecce Homo*, whose publication was delayed several years.

But Nietzsche himself was done. On 3 January, 1889, in Turin, Nietzsche collapsed in the street while witnessing the flogging of a horse. After this, he sent a series of letters to friends unmistakably tinged with madness. Medical treatment proved unavailing, and the philosopher of personal independence fell to the care of his family for the next eleven years. During this period, control of his writings devolved to his sister Elisabeth, whose cultivation of his memory and advocacy for his writings helped to win the fame that had eluded him during his sane lifetime. On 25 August, 1900, Nietzsche died in Weimar, perhaps of tertiary syphilis, the probable cause of his madness. He is buried in the village of Röcken with his family.

NIETZSCHE'S MINOR PUBLISHED WRITINGS

As we saw, much of Nietzsche's life is simply the story of his authorship. It is not feasible to list every edition and translation of every work that has ever appeared under Nietzsche's name, but it is useful to have an inventory of the published writings and collected German editions. Since I discuss the major works in the next chapter, brief descriptions of minor published works follow.

Nietzsche's earliest published writings were academic philology journal articles and reviews. Between 1867 and 1873, he published seven articles in *Rheinisches Museum fur Philologie* and an index to vols. 1–24, one article in *Acta Societatis Philologae*, and eight reviews for *Literarisches Centralblatt für Deutschland*. Nietzsche also had privately printed the essays 'Homer and Classical Philology' (his inaugural lecture at Basel, 1869), 'Contributions Toward the Study and the Critique of the Sources of Diogenes Laertius' (which overlaps some of the journal articles, 1870), and 'Socrates and Tragedy' (a rough draft of a portion of *Birth of Tragedy*, 1871).

Apart from his principal works, Nietzsche also published a few minor and occasional pieces. In early 1873, he wrote a letter to the editor of the magazine *Im neuen Reich* defending Wagner's reputation. Later in 1873, he wrote a privately printed fund-raising pamphlet for Wagner entitled 'An Exhortation to the German People'. During his mature period, Nietzsche published a group of poems under the title 'Idylls from Messina', in the journal *Internationale Monatsschrift* (June 1882); these same poems were later added as an appendix to the second edition of *Gay Science* in 1887. He also wrote two letters to the editor of the journal *Kunstwart: Rundschau uber alle Gebiete des Schonen* in December of 1888. Lastly, Nietzsche composed classical music until 1874, when he wrote *Hymn to Friendship*. In 1882, Lou Salomé presented Nietzsche with a poem she had written earlier (in 1880) which he adapted as a new lyric for the older composition. Nietzsche published his score with Salomé's lyric as *Hymn to Life, For Mixed Chorus and Orchestra* in 1887.

EDITIONS AND TRANSLATIONS

Since Nietzsche's collapse in 1889, there have been several attempts to produce a collected works edition of his writings. His friend 'Peter Gast' (Heinrich Köselitz) began producing the *Gesamtausgabe* in 1892, but this was never completed. Elisabeth Förster-Nietzsche supervised the editing of the *Grossoktavausgabe*, which appeared in two editions, the first in 1894–1904 (15 volumes) and the second in 1901–1913 (19 volumes). These editions are noteworthy for containing the first appearance of the text *The Will to Power*, selected from Nietzsche's writings of the 1880s, presented to give the appearance of a completed book by Nietzsche; the second edition, which greatly expands upon and alters the arrangement of the first, contains 1067 notes, and has been frequently reprinted and translated as if it were one of Nietzsche's books. Various editions based on the *Grossoktavausgabe* appeared subsequently, most notably the *Musarionausgabe* (23 volumes) which appeared in 1920–1929. A more scholarly attempt, the *Historische-Kritische Gesamtausgabe*, was attempted between 1933 and 1942, but never completed. It covered only writings from 1854 to 1869 and four volumes of correspondence.

In 1967, Giorgio Colli and Mazzino Montinari began producing a definitive historical-critical edition of Nietzsche's writings and correspondence, the *Kritische Gesamtausgabe Werke* (*KGW*) and the *Briefwechsel: Kritische Gesamtausgabe* (*KGB*), to contain all correspondence to and from Nietzsche up to 1889. The *KGW* is the scholarly basis for all contemporary research on Nietzsche's thought. It consists of nine divisions, each of which contains several volumes. At present, it is for all practical purposes complete with regards to the text of Nietzsche's published works and writings, though several volumes of editorial material remain to be completed.[3] A paperback edition, the *Sämtliche Werke: Kritische Studienausgabe* in 15 volumes, contains the same material with different pagination, minus the juvenilia, the philological writings, and some of the editorial apparatus. An overview of the *KGW* provides a useful glimpse at the structure of Nietzsche's corpus.

Division 1: Notes [Juvenilia] (1852–1869)
    Volume 1: Notes (beginning of 1852–summer 1858).
    Volume 2: Notes (autumn 1858–autumn 1862).

Volume 3: Notes (autumn 1862–summer 1864).
Volume 4: Notes (autumn 1864–spring 1868).
Volume 5: Notes (spring 1868–autumn 1869).
Division 2: Philological materials (1867–1879)
Volume 1: Philological writings (1867–1873).
Volume 2: Lecture notes (1869–1869/70). Appendix: Postscripts to Nietzsche's lectures.
Volume 3: Lecture notes (1870–1871).
Volume 4: Lecture notes (1870/71–1874/75).
Volume 5: Lecture notes (1874/75–1878/79).
Division 3: Works and materials (1870–1874)
Volume 1: *Birth of Tragedy. Untimely Meditations* I–III (1872 – 1874).
Volume 2: Writings (1870–1873).
Volume 3: Fragments (autumn 1869–autumn 1872).
Volume 4: Fragments (summer 1872–end of 1874).
Volume 5: Postscript to Division 3
First half-volume: Critical apparatus: *Birth of Tragedy. Untimely Meditations* I–III. Writings (1870–1873).
Second half-volume: Critical apparatus: Fragments (autumn 1869–end of 1874).
Division 4: Works and materials (1875–1879)
Volume 1: *Richard Wagner in Bayreuth* [*Untimely Meditations* IV].
Fragments (beginning of 1875–spring 1876).
Volume 2: *Human, All Too Human*. First volume.
Fragments (1876–winter 1877/78).
Volume 3: *Human, All Too Human*. Second volume.
Fragments (spring 1878–November 1879).
Volume 4: Postscript to Division 4
Richard Wagner in Bayreuth.
Human, All Too Human I and II.
Fragments (1875–1879).
Division 5: Works and materials (1880–1882)
Volume 1: *Daybreak*.
Fragments (beginning of 1880–spring 1881).
Volume 2: *Idylls from Messina. Gay Science.*
Fragments (spring 1881–summer 1882).
Volume 3: Postscript to Volume 1 of Division 5.
Daybreak.

Division 6: Works (1883–1889)
Volume 1: *Thus Spoke Zarathustra. A Book for All and None* (1883–1885).
Volume 2: *Beyond Good and Evil. On the Genealogy of Morals* (1886–1887).
Volume 3: *The Case of Wagner. Twilight of the Idols.*
Writings (August 1888–beginning of January 1889): *The Antichrist. Ecce Homo. Dithyrambs of Dionysus. Nietzsche contra Wagner.*
Volume 4: Postscript to Volume 1 of Division 6. *Thus Spoke Zarathustra.*
Division 7: Materials (1882–1885)
Volume 1: Fragments (July 1882–winter 1883–1884).
Volume 2: Fragments (spring–autumn 1884).
Volume 3: Fragments (autumn 1884–autumn 1885).
Volume 4: Postscript to Division 7.
Volume 4.1: Fragments (July 1882–winter 1883/84).
Volume 4.2: Fragments (spring 1884–autumn 1885).
Division 8: Materials (1885–1889)
Volume 1: Fragments (autumn 1885–autumn 1887).
Volume 2: Fragments (autumn 1887–March 1888).
Volume 3: Fragments (beginning of 1888– beginning of January 1889).
Division 9: Transcription of the handwritten materials starting from spring 1885

A few comments about the structure of the *KGW* are in order. First, as an historical-critical edition, it is essentially chronological, and largely follows the conventional wisdom in dividing Nietzsche's authorship into stages: Juvenilia (to 1869, the date of the appointment to Basel), Philologica, 'early' Nietzsche (*Birth of Tragedy, Untimely Meditations*), 'middle' Nietzsche (the aphoristic works), *Zarathustra*, and 'late' Nietzsche. The only possible difficulties with this arrangement from a philosophical perspective are as follows. First, though 1869 may be a natural stopping point from a biographical perspective, Nietzsche's philosophical thinking really begins in 1865, with the reading of Schopenhauer; the notes between 1865 and 1869 are of interest and shed considerable light on the development of the early Nietzsche's thought; unfortunately, the paperback edition does not reproduce them. Second, as the editors are aware, the fourth *Untimely Meditation* on Wagner occupies an awkward position in the developmental sequence. On the one hand, it belongs with the other three essays by design, but it is comparatively late, overlapping the emergence of 'middle' Nietzsche, and in some respects appears not to embody Nietzsche's genuine views of Wagner at the time. Third, *Gay Science* in many respects straddles the line between 'middle' and 'late' Nietzsche. Nietzsche wrote it in the style of the other aphoristic works, but after the revelation of the doctrine of the eternal recurrence, and it contains the opening section of *Zarathustra* as the last aphorism of Part Four. After writing *Zarathustra*, Nietzsche added Part Five for the second edition, which contains aphorisms representative of his 'late' thought.

The material from which *The Will to Power* was constructed is set aside in Divisions Seven and Eight, in a total of six volumes, thus enabling the researcher to see this material in approximately the sequence and context in which it was written. Beyond this, Division Nine when complete will attempt to reproduce, page for page, the appearance of the notebooks and sheets from which the texts in Divisions Seven and Eight are derived, though in typeset form. In other words, examining these texts reproduces the experience of examining the original manuscripts, without the inconvenience of having to decipher Nietzsche's handwriting.

Many translations of Nietzsche's works into English are available, but a few are especially noteworthy. In the 1960s Walter Kaufmann (with the assistance in some cases of R. J. Hollingdale) produced translations of all the major published works (excepting *Human, All Too Human* with its two sequels, and *Daybreak*, though selections from these are available in his *Portable Nietzsche, Basic Writings of Nietzsche* and *Will to Power*). Hollingdale brought out rival translations of several of these works, and his own translations of *Untimely Meditations, Human, All Too Human* with its two sequels and *Daybreak* for Cambridge University Press. Between the two of them, all of Nietzsche's major published works are available in reliable translations. Cambridge University Press has since supplemented the Hollingdale translations with its own editions of the other works by other translators, including a selection from the late notebooks. Oxford University Press has also brought out several of Nietzsche's works by various translators (*Birth of Tragedy, Zarathustra, Beyond Good and Evil, Genealogy of Morals, Twilight of the Idols* and *Ecce Homo*). Stanford University Press is publishing a complete translation of the paperback edition of the *KGW* in twenty volumes, though to date only three volumes have appeared.

CHAPTER 2

NIETZSCHE'S WRITINGS

THE EARLY WORKS

Nietzsche's major early published works were *Birth of Tragedy* (1872) and four essays collectively entitled *Untimely Meditations* (1873–76). The posthumously published essays *Philosophy in the Tragic Age of the Greeks* (1874) and *On Truth and Lie in an Extra-Moral Sense* (1873) are also noteworthy. Of these, *Birth of Tragedy* overshadows the rest, and is in many ways unlike anything Nietzsche wrote subsequently. Though the book ostensibly addresses philological questions about the origin, development and decay of ancient Greek tragedy (and has had an enormous if contentious influence on classical studies ever since), the book contains far more than this. In it, Nietzsche also outlines a general theory of art (as stemming from the dialectic of the 'Apollinian' [*apollinisch*] and the 'Dionysian') and explains the tragic affect, thus directly competing with Aristotle's catharsis theory. These discussions are set against the backdrop of a highly unusual metaphysical theory inspired by Schopenhauer, and an implicit 'tragic ethics'. Beyond this, Nietzsche offers a compelling critique of modernity as having fallen prey to a destructive rationalism (which academic philology itself exemplifies) at odds with the spirit of tragedy needed not only to make genuine culture possible, but to render human life meaningful and satisfying. Finally, Nietzsche fuses these concerns with a polemic on behalf of Wagnerian opera, which he then believed possessed the sole means of making tragedy available to modernity.

To understand the argument of *Birth of Tragedy*, one must understand the metaphysical theory that Nietzsche had developed and that serves as its presupposition. For this, we must turn to

Schopenhauer's *World as Will and Representation*. Schopenhauer's metaphysics followed Kant's in broad outline. According to Schopenhauer, the empirical world is an illusion, a mind-dependent appearance of the mind-independent 'thing-in-itself'. Whereas for Kant the character of the thing-in-itself was unknowable, Schopenhauer argued that in the experience of voluntary action, we come to know ourselves from the inside. In this, Schopenhauer followed the lead of Kant's ethics. Kant had attempted to escape the free will-determinism problem and the threat it posed to moral accountability by suggesting that while appearances are deterministic by virtue of the structure the mind imposes on its sensations, the will might be a thing-in-itself, and thus perhaps free.

Schopenhauer's identification of the will with the thing-in-itself, however, had profound implications. First, for Schopenhauer the experience of willing essentially involves both an object willed (some goal in the world of appearances) and the desire to achieve that goal. Since the goals of willing are always given within the phenomenal world, the character of the thing-in-itself is objectless desire. Second, Schopenhauer took the individuation and plurality of objects given in phenomenal experience to be a product of the mind's organizing activity. Thus if we conceive of the thing-in-itself as that which exists apart from this activity, it must be an undifferentiated unity. This leads him to the remarkable conclusion that the world in itself is an undifferentiated desiring without object, and each human being's willing must be identified with it. Thus, individuality is a kind of illusion: in reality, we are all one. Furthermore, since every phenomenal appearance must be the appearance of the thing-in-itself, it follows that even non-human objects are expressions of this hidden, undifferentiated desiring, which he called 'the will'. The result is a kind of cosmic vitalism.

Unfortunately, this bodes ill for human happiness. From the perspective of the individual, we think that if we achieved the specific objects of our desires, we would be content. But if our essential nature is to desire, then this too must be an illusion. Human life, then, is an unsatisfiable craving sustained by the illusion that satisfaction is possible. Worse, since we are all in the same boat, human life (indeed all life) is an arena of ceaseless conflict. Not only is satisfaction impossible, but conflict of (apparent) interest is inevitable. Yet this result is perverse, in that each party to a conflict of interest is, metaphysically, identical. The world will is a cosmic, perpetually self-violating sadomasochist. Human beings, as manifestations of it, are only motivated by pointless egoism, lust, boredom and spite.

Given that human life has this character, what is to be done? For day-to-day life, Stoical self-restraint can mitigate the inevitable dissatisfactions of willing. But we achieve a more genuine ethical stance when we realize the underlying unity of all creatures, their inevitable suffering and the futility of our own striving. Such an insight makes possible an altruistic ethic of compassion and humility. Beyond this, ascetic practices may pave the way for a final self-annihilation of the will itself and our release into an ineffable nirvana.

Lastly, Schopenhauer, building upon a misunderstanding of Kant's aesthetics, believed that the experience of plastic and literary art was another vehicle for 'quieting the will'. In art experience, the veil of appearances loses its character as the sphere of practical activity, enabling us to see objects not as things to be craved, but as instantiations of Platonic Forms to be contemplated. By contrast, he speculated that music, an essentially non-representational art expressing the passions, is a vehicle for direct insight into the character of the world will itself. This last point made a tremendous impression on Wagner, and would be taken up by Nietzsche in *Birth of Tragedy*.

Nietzsche's modifications of this system affect its metaphysics, epistemology, ethics and aesthetics. First, while Nietzsche appears to have accepted the basic characterization of the world will, he emphasizes that it must not only be the sum of all the world's suffering, but its pleasure as well; this is implicit in the characterization of the world will as self-violating sadomasochist. Second, in Nietzsche's notes preceding *Birth of Tragedy*, he suggests that the world will not only expresses itself as the phenomenal world, but also contemplates or experiences its creation. Third, Nietzsche rejects the claim that we can have any experiential or argumentative path to the identification of the thing-in-itself. To think otherwise would be inconsistent with the basic Kantian assumptions Schopenhauer makes, though how this is to be squared with Nietzsche's seeming characterization of the world will itself is a bit of a mystery. Finally, Nietzsche rejects the suggestion that the only path to ethical perfection is self-denial, compassion and self-annihilation. Following the clues left behind in Schopenhauer's aesthetics, Nietzsche looks for a way to use art to make life worth living.

It is in this last context that Nietzsche turns to tragedy. Schopenhauer's characterization of the world as cosmic sadomasochist seems echoed in the puzzle of why the tragic affect is pleasurable when tragedy portrays the destruction of characters with whom we identify. The crux of Nietzsche's answer is that something in tragedy inspires the audience to adopt the perspective of the world will itself, for whom every agony is also ecstatic pleasure. If we can come to perceive in our own sufferings not individual failure but the ecstasy of the world will, we will experience an energizing rapture. Though Nietzsche does not dwell on the point, the ultimate individual failure is death, but the world will does not die. Thus for Nietzsche, the 'juice' of tragic affect lies in its approximation to a Bhakti-like ecstatic merging into the immortal oneness that lies behind appearances. By now it will be apparent that both Schopenhauer's and Nietzsche's account of the world are permeated with displaced sexuality.

Nietzsche begins *Birth of Tragedy* with the famous distinction between two aspects of art: the Apollinian and the Dionysian. These aspects, though linked to the cults of the gods who give them their names, are to be understood as timeless features of experience explicated in terms of the metaphysical theory.

The Apollinian is associated psychologically with dreaming, and metaphysically with the world as representation. It is that aspect of art concerned with the formal features of objects presented to the spectator for contemplation. It is best illustrated by the plastic arts, though it is also present in literature to the extent that literary description also inspires images. In the context of Greek history, though Nietzsche associates it with Apollo, it can be seen in most of the Olympian deities, and is best illustrated by sculpture and Homeric epic. Nietzsche's inspiration here is Schopenhauer's theory of the plastic arts and their reference to Platonic Forms, though in the 1870s Nietzsche appears not to have accepted the real existence of Platonic Forms, regarding them as products of the mind.

The Dionysian, by contrast, is associated psychologically with intoxication, and metaphysically with the world as will. It is manifested in that aspect of art involving intense emotion, expression, participation and identification. It is best illustrated by dance, music (though Nietzsche makes clear that there is such a thing as Apollinian music as well), and lyric poetry. Nietzsche associates it primarily with the cult of Dionysus, but also refers to the Titans as

'Dionysian' figures. Here too, Nietzsche is following (one might say intensifying) Schopenhauer's theory of music.

Nietzsche's account of the 'birth of tragedy' draws on the foregoing, combined with some historical claims found in Aristotle's *Poetics*. He argues that tragedy came about as a synthesis of Apollo and Dionysus: what was initially a musical dance ritual celebrating the destruction and renewal of Dionysus became split into audience, tragic chorus, and represented action. The represented action symbolically expresses the meaning of Dionysus' story through an Apollinian mask or representation. The audience then contemplates this representation just as it contemplates other Apollinian arts, while simultaneously identifying with the tragic hero. Like the members of the audience in the world as representation, the tragic hero is only an individual human being, but also like the audience in the world as will, he is the 'primordial unity', agonized yet ecstatic, torn apart yet eternally reborn. By contemplating the tragic hero as individualized Apollinian form, each audience member comes to feel that despite his own suffering and failure, he too is an appearance of Dionysus, ecstatic and indestructible.

Nietzsche attributes the death of tragedy to a third 'deity': Socrates, Euripedes' muse, whose excessive rationalism destroyed tragedy from within. Socratic rationalism is 'optimistic' in several respects. First, it supposes that we can make our lives more satisfying if they were directed by rationality, instead of the irrational drives of dreaming and intoxication. If we accept Schopenhauer's metaphysics of desire, this would be a pernicious error, because it promotes desires that cannot be satisfied. Second, it cuts us off not only from the world-denying asceticism that Schopenhauer had proposed, but Nietzsche's aestheticist alternative of a life of suffering made meaningful through beauty. Third, it promotes the epistemological delusion that scientific knowledge is attainable. In short, Socratic rationalism teaches us that the world and the self are both knowable and correctable, and that through knowledge and action happiness can be achieved. Once Socratic rationalism gained the upper hand, the perceived need for the tragic, and in the end the ability to produce it, withered away.

However that may be, Nietzsche considered the triumph of Socratic rationalism over tragedy to be not only a turning point for the history of ancient Athens, but for western civilization as a whole. In modern Europe, 'the Socratic', in the form of the

Enlightenment, has prevailed. Late antiquity's cultural problem is our own, for we have become an 'Alexandrian' civilization. One key expression of this pathology is our attitude towards antiquity itself, which now inspires historical research instead of emulation. Oddly, Nietzsche also sees our Socratism illustrated in the character of much modern opera, in which music has become subordinated to text.

Two tendencies of the modern age promise salvation. First, 'scientific consciousness', seen not only in science but also in classical modern metaphysics and epistemology, eventually culminates in Kantian critique, firmly limiting the pretensions of the human mind to empirical knowledge while intimating that beyond appearances lies something else that escapes its grasp. Second, the emergence of classical, and eventually Romantic, symphonic music opens us to the world will again. With Socratism chastened and our intimations of the world will reawakened, the remaining task is to synthesize this new Dionysian music with Apollinian drama for tragedy to be reborn. This task, of course, falls to Wagnerian opera. Interestingly, all these accomplishments take place in Germany, while the opposing tendencies are associated with Great Britain, France and Italy. Thus *Birth of Tragedy* can be seen as an expression of cultural German nationalism at a moment (the Franco-Prussian War) when Germany was also becoming more assertive and self-confident politically.

It is also noteworthy that the early Nietzsche's characterization of the Dionysian has a surprisingly Rousseauist flavour: Nietzsche links it to liberty, equality and fraternity. Since Nietzsche invokes Dionysus in his late writings while championing an anti-democratic elitism, it is worth quoting at length to get a sense of this:

> Under the charm of the Dionysian, not only is the union between man and man reaffirmed, but nature which has become alienated, hostile, or subjugated, celebrates once more her reconciliation with her lost son, man. ... Now the slave is a free man; now all the rigid, hostile barriers that necessity, caprice, or 'impudent convention' have fixed between man and man are broken. Now, with the gospel of universal harmony, each one feels himself not only united, reconciled, and fused with his neighbor. ... [M]an expresses himself as a member of a higher community ... (*BT* §1, ellipsis mine)

With such sentiments, early Nietzsche not only aligns himself with Rousseau but also expresses a form of liberalism that had been associated with German nationalism from the anti-Napoleonic Wars of Liberation until the emergence of the Second Reich. Nietzsche's attitude not only towards Wagner, but towards both liberalism and German nationalism, was to change radically and Rousseau, far from being a model, would become a nemesis.

The scholarly reception of *Birth of Tragedy* by classicists is too complex to do justice to here, but a few short comments are in order. The earliest reception was quite negative, in light of the lack of patient marshalling of philological evidence, the implied critique of philology itself as 'Socratism', and the controversial (and professionally inappropriate) championing of Wagner. However, during the 1890s a school of classicists in England, the so-called 'Cambridge Ritualists', influenced as much by Frazer's *Golden Bough* as by Nietzsche, argued with some influence that the roots of Greek drama should be seen in irrational, ecstatic Greek religion; representative figures include Jane Harrison, Gilbert Murray, F. M. Cornford and E. R. Dodds. Though the Cambridge Ritualists are no longer accepted uncritically, attempts to relate Greek tragedy to the cult of Dionysus and its peculiar characteristics have persisted.[1] Others, most notably Gerald F. Else, reject Nietzsche's (indeed, most classicists') reliance on Aristotelian data and regard the link between tragedy and Dionysus as almost completely adventitious.[2]

Nietzsche's other published work of this early period is the collection of four polemical essays, the *Untimely Meditations*. The first essay, *David Strauss, the Confessor and the Writer*, though largely an attack on Strauss's writing style, also contains some interesting substantive complaints about Strauss's thought that provide clues to Nietzsche's own positions. Strauss was a Young Hegelian. The Young Hegelians had taken as their point of departure Hegel's attempt to 'demythologize' Christian theology as the non-literal expression of Hegelian metaphysical truths. Hegel thought that the underlying truth of Christianity was contained in a panentheistic idealist metaphysics in which the world is the expression of a world mind undergoing historical development towards perfection. By contrast, the Young Hegelians had tried to preserve something of this position within more naturalistic metaphysical commitments. Strauss himself had taken the dual commitments to demythologizing and naturalism as requiring a more Enlightenment-type anticlerical stance towards to literal claims of Christianity. In his *Life of Jesus Critically Examined* Strauss inaugurated 'historical Jesus' research. This work probably had a profound impact on Nietzsche, and may even have been one of the main causes of Nietzsche's own abandonment of a theology major and pastoral career. Nietzsche's essay, however, attacks Strauss's later book, *The Old Faith and the New*, in which Strauss defends his naturalistic perspective as the basis for an ethics and a culture. In the first few sections of Nietzsche's critique, he focuses his attention on Strauss's 'philistinism', the complacency with which Strauss appropriates German literature and music as a source of edification for a post-Christian culture.

Nietzsche objects to Strauss's positions on substantive grounds, in terms of the values Strauss expresses, and the cultural consequences of accepting them. He defines culture as 'unity of style' and insists that despite its classics, Germany does not now possess, nor has it ever possessed such unity, its recent political unification notwithstanding. Strauss's complacency represents a broader philistinism which, even in the age of Goethe and Schiller, had served only to obstruct cultural achievement, allowing it to occur in only isolated, exceptional instances and not in the community as a whole. By citing these exceptions and Germany's appreciation of them as proof of the continuing vitality of German culture, Strauss thwarts the emergence of true 'unity of style' in the future.

Nietzsche's substantive disagreements with Strauss not only reveal his own commitments at the time, but foreshadow later themes. First, Strauss's naturalism is a form of metaphysical realism incompatible with the results of Kantian critique. Second, Strauss's Darwinism would appear to require an ethics valorizing 'the war of all against all' (note Nietzsche's own commitment to ethical naturalism here). But Strauss is content to issue contrary moral imperatives with no greater backing than an appeal to a normative (Aristotelian?) essence of human nature. Not only does this stance lack metaethical justification, but it also fails to come to grips with human diversity. Nietzsche implies (and will explicitly claim in the third *Untimely Meditation*) that if there is a normative essence, it will vary so much from one person to the next as to leave us without any general ethical guidance. At this juncture Nietzsche also announces that before one can make ethical demands, one must first better understand how 'goodness, compassion, love and self-abnegation, which do exist [can be explained given] his Darwinist presuppositions' (*UM* I, §7). Finally, Nietzsche objects to Strauss's Spinozist worship of nature and natural law as the 'source of all life, all reason and all goodness' when it is also the source of all evil (ibid). Interestingly, he takes great exception to Strauss's view that to wish the world other than it is, given the necessity of all natural phenomena, is nihilistically to wish that the world did not exist. Though he attributes this view to Strauss's residual Hegelian 'deification of success', Nietzsche himself would adopt a very similar position in less than a decade.

The second and third *Untimely Meditations* are interesting structurally in that they both appear to persist in the fourfold pattern present in *Birth of Tragedy*: three different life-affirming modalities are contrasted with a dangerously rationalistic modality particularly associated with modernity. Though the correspondences between the categories is far from neat, it is worth calling attention to them:

Birth of Tragedy	Untimely Meditation II	Untimely Meditation III
Apollinian	Antiquarian history	Goethean man
Dionysian	Monumental history	Rousseauian man
Tragic	Critical history	Schopenhauerian man
Socratic	History as science	University philosophy

The second *Untimely Meditation*, *On the Uses and Disadvantage of History for Life*, continues both the critique of philology in *Birth of Tragedy* and the opposition to Hegelianism that appeared in passing in the Strauss essay. Nietzsche's central claim is that an excess of historical understanding can stultify cultural development. To take our cultural tasks seriously, we need a measure of the unhistorical, the sheer forgetting of the past, and the right balance of three different types of selective, life-enhancing modes of appropriating it. What we do not need is history as a science, which is incompatible with both forgetfulness and selective, life-enhancing memory. At best, history as science will lead to a world-denying 'suprahistorical' wisdom which is incompatible with cultural striving; at worst, it will lead to an ironical, hyper-aware philistinism.

The three modes of selective appropriation are the monumental, the antiquarian and the critical. The monumental approach to history is that which celebrates great figures and great achievements. Though the monumental can present the possibility of greatness in the past as a model for emulation in the present, preoccupation with past greatness can overwhelm and thus discourage us, while its selectivity can distort the record of the past. The antiquarian approach to history is that which reverently preserves all the detailed characteristics of one's own culture's past as an end in itself. Though the antiquarian approach sustains a sense of identity, continuity and self-satisfaction, it is also indiscriminate, revering both great and small, and conservative in a way that stifles innovation. Because the antiquarian impulse is rooted in identification, it also distorts by focusing exclusively on one's own past, promoting a kind of parochialism. The critical approach to history, by contrast with the former two modes, reveals the past to condemn it. Nietzsche's attitude towards it is more favourable than towards the other two, emphasizing how such a stance frees one for innovation. But here too there is a risk of prematurely cutting oneself off from necessary resources and guidance. A too critical stance for one not capable of creative response is destructive.

History as science, in its commitment to objectivity at any cost, may correct the epistemic shortcomings of the other modes of historical appropriation, whose selectivity is guided, ultimately, by pragmatic considerations. But this comes at the expense of cultural achievement. It disillusions us, leading to a detached, playful attitude towards historical styles, weakening both individual and community. It promotes epistemic arrogance and pride while inducing an ironical self-consciousness incompatible with taking any action seriously. It creates the illusion that one is at the end of history, or worse, beyond it. (It is worth wondering what Nietzsche would have said about recent claims to have achieved 'post-modernity'.) Nietzsche takes the shortcomings of historical science to be most trenchantly illustrated in classical philology. The Greeks themselves – for Nietzsche the pinnacle of cultural achievement – were a people largely lacking a sense of history. They lived in the moment, and perfected it.

Nietzsche devotes much of the essay to a criticism of Hegelian ways of understanding history, a theme he had touched on in passing in the essay on Strauss. Two aspects of the Hegelian approach trouble him. First, to the extent that we strive to understand the past, we may come to think of ourselves as occupying the end of history. This can promote the teleological illusion that history is a now completed tale of progress. If we in the present are the goal of history, then we ought not to strive for further changes, but congratulate ourselves for our superiority over the past. Second, Hegel's cultural determinism regards individuals as functions of the cultural formations that allegedly produced them, leading us to denigrate greatness and make its repetition less likely. Both features of Hegelian thought (which Nietzsche illustrates with the peculiar Schopenhauerian–Hegelian eclecticism of Eduard von Hartmann) lead to comformism and complacency. If this is where history is leading, it leads, not to 'higher men', but to 'last men', as Nietzsche will put it later in *Zarathustra*.

The third *Untimely Meditation, Schopenhauer as Educator*, is widely regarded as among the most interesting of Nietzsche's early writings. The 'education' in question is not education by Schopenhauer's doctrines, but by his example. The essay begins by articulating a kind of individualized teleological ethic easily mistaken for existentialism: each human being has a kind of essence or 'true self' as a latent potential that it is our task to actualize. But the diversity of these essences means that there cannot be any one pattern of living that is normative for all human beings; to suppose otherwise would be to do violence to the specific requirements of each unique individual and thus inhibit self-actualization. Similarly, the needs of society, being general, inhibit the flowering of one's idiosyncratic nature. However, since self-actualization is difficult, conformity represents a perennial temptation to shirk one's highest duty: to become what one is. Nietzsche recommends recalling people one has genuinely admired as a way of stimulating the drive towards self-actualization. Such figures are symbols of the self we are striving, and should strive, to realize. Thus Nietzsche recalls his own hero, Arthur Schopenhauer, who is presented not as a set of views, but as a role model.

Nietzsche's recollection has more than just personal significance, he claims, for we are at a peculiar historical juncture requiring new efforts; it is in *Schopenhauer as Educator* that Nietzsche first articulates the theme of European nihilism, the problem he would later encapsulate in the slogan, 'God is dead'.

[M]oral energy is at . . . a low ebb . . . [N]o one who considers the influence of victorious Christianity on the morality of our ancient world can overlook the reaction of declining

Christianity upon our own time. Through the exaltedness of its ideal, Christianity excelled the moral systems of antiquity and the naturalism that resided in them to such a degree that this naturalism came to excite apathy and disgust; but later on, when these better and higher ideals, though now known, proved unattainable, it was no longer possible to return to what was good and high in antique virtue, however much one might want to. ... [The result is] a disorder in the modern soul which condemns it to a joyless unfruitfulness. (*UM* III, §2, ellipsis mine)

Nietzsche's response to this historical challenge, here as in *Zarathustra*, is to discern in nature a teleological tendency towards the production of higher human beings: artists, philosophers and saints, who realize a 'transfigured *physis*'. Schopenhauer as Nietzsche describes him is one of these ideal types of human being through whom nature reaches fulfilment.

But before Nietzsche enlarges on that theme, he devotes himself to a somewhat disingenuous portrait of Schopenhauer (as he himself admits many years later in *Ecce Homo*). Using a rhetorical device he would return to in the essay on Wagner, Nietzsche describes Schopenhauer's character in terms of four challenges overcome. To some extent he is really describing Schopenhauer's shortcomings! Three of the challenges are said to be universal, the fourth a peculiarity of Schopenhauer's time. First, alienation from society makes one 'depressed and melancholic' and can lead to resentment, explosiveness and nasty polemic (this was clearly not a challenge surmounted by the real Schopenhauer). Second, Kantian metaphysics and epistemology can lead to 'despair of the truth', that is, a lack of confidence in one's ability to discover significant truths about the human condition, and distraction by purely technical philosophical concerns (*UM* III, §3). It seems fair to say that Schopenhauer overcame this challenge. Third, personal incapacity to achieve a saintliness one yearns for can lead to cynicism and 'severing bonds that [tie one to the] ideal' (ibid). Here, Nietzsche's Schopenhauer surmounts what the real Schopenhauer did not. Finally, the peculiar inadequacies of one's contemporaries can lead one to misjudge the value of life. On this point, Nietzsche is forced into a bit of caginess. He suggests that if one is able to be just to life, one will render the verdict of Empedocles, a statement he admits is 'incomprehensible'. If we turn to Nietzsche's notebooks, we find next to the name 'Empedocles' the phrase 'love and kisses to the world!' (*KGW* III, vol. 4, p. 143). The implication is that Schopenhauer's pessimism about human life was due not to the universal features of human life, but to his discouragement over the inadequacies of his contemporaries. If instead he had lived with the ancient Greeks as contemporaries, he could have affirmed life instead and rendered the 'judgement of Empedocles'. We see here that Nietzsche's notion of promoting the artist, philosopher and saint is not just nature's goal that we must take on board, but is Nietzsche's answer to the problem of pessimism. Ordinary human life may very well have the character Schopenhauer described: if there are no extraordinary human beings, pessimism is justified; if there are, it isn't.

The rest of the essay goes on to discuss the relationship between the philosopher and modernity in light of the overarching goal of producing great philosophers. Modernity is characterized by its speed, unreflectiveness, complexity, secularization, science/disillusion, economic competitiveness, cultural failure, incipient violence, and fragmentation. In the face of this, modernity has valorized three types of human beings, whom Nietzsche identifies with Rousseau, Goethe and Schopenhauer. We see here a possible structural parallel with the history essay: the Rousseauist is a man of action, a rebel against constraint and artificiality; this parallels 'monumental history'. The Goethean is a collector of refined and beautiful experiences; this parallels 'antiquarian history'. The Schopenhauerian is the disillusioned critic, philosopher and truthseeker; this parallels 'critical history'.

Nietzsche's preference is for 'the Schopenhauerian man'. He argues, however, not that each individual has an obligation to become such, for he seems to recognize that these efforts will usually fail. Rather, he suggests that each individual has an obligation to contribute to a community from which such philosophers might arise. Here we also see for the first time a theme that would reappear in *Zarathustra*: the idea of a perfectionist ethics based not on the individual's achievement of perfection, but in the individual's facilitating of someone else's achievement of perfection. The ethic is in one sense communitarian: I am to help realize a certain kind of community whose member I am, and certain community projects. But instead of the creation and sustenance of the community as the final goal, the community is only a means to individual goods. Oddly, the individual is not intrinsically valuable and to be helped to fulfilment; Nietzsche's ethic is not a form of liberalism. Instead, the sheer existence of a few exemplars of a particular form of human being is the goal. The issue here is not egalitarianism versus inegalitarianism, for the good of the exceptional person is not good because it is good for the exceptional person. Rather, the features that make her exceptional are objectively and intrinsically valuable. This appears to be underwritten by the claim that the production of such people is nature's goal, and we simply must further it. Whether there is any reason to accept this even if it is nature's goal is doubtful, and whether nature has a goal at all is even more so.

Nietzsche wants an ethics that the ordinary person can comply with. Promoting cultural excellence, insofar as it does not require realizing it oneself, seems to fit that bill. Though Nietzsche does not address this point, it would appear that even those with essentially no cultural skills could 'promote', in some sense: if not as critics, then as audience, and if not as audience, then as knowing supporters, and barring that, there are always forms of unknowing support possible. (Consider: if it happened for some reason to be 'nature's goal' to put a human being on the moon, we could think of society as organized in concentric circles with Neil Armstrong at the centre and the taxpayer at the periphery.) Nietzsche's primary concern is with the role of the critic as facilitator of a higher form of productivity unattainable by him or her.

The critic will be concerned to combat those tendencies which prevent the development of the philosopher. Here, Nietzsche is concerned not only with obstruction of cultural excellence, but with the diversion into other channels of resources 'meant for' cultural excellence. He singles out capitalism, the state, cultural philistinism, science and scholarship (again) as the chief culprits. What we need is a reorientation of the goals of education from service to these false idols to the true god of cultural achievement.

Lastly, one might think that all that is called for to create 'Schopenhauerian' philosophers is the kind of training and support academia already makes available. Here Nietzsche argues, following Schopenhauer's own essay 'On the University Philosophy' in *Parergra and Paralipomena*, that academia not only fails to provide an environment for the cultivation of genuine philosophers, but that it is a prime site for the aforementioned diversion of resources. Nietzsche even goes so far as to suggest that academic philosophy is designed to thwart the development of genuine philosophy.

The fourth *Untimely Meditation, Richard Wagner in Bayreuth*, is in some respects the most difficult of Nietzsche's early publications. It is marked to an even greater degree than the other three by serious problems of organization, as Nietzsche swings back and forth between an attempt to describe Wagner's biography and an attempt to make sense of the significance of his art. But more than that, as a piece of propaganda for the Wagner cause, it suffers from the evident contrast with Nietzsche's later, highly critical writings on Wagner. The more fully we understand these, the more difficult it is to make sense of this earlier enthusiasm. Worse, the essay, compared to the contemporaneous unpublished notes, reveals the disingenuousness of the performance, for Nietzsche had already come to have serious reservations about almost every aspect of the Wagner phenomenon. Nor are these reservations fully concealed: they peek out from behind congested prose on almost every page, in rebuttals of arguments others might make, appeals to sympathy, and the strategy of the third *Meditation*: claiming that shortcomings were merely challenges overcome. In this, to quote the third essay, Nietzsche 'paint[s] imperfectly, that ideal man who, as his Platonic ideal as it were, holds sway in and around him' rather than the concrete Wagner himself (*UM* III, §5).

The biographical sketch, to the extent that it can be teased out of the analysis of Wagner's art, is simple enough. Wagner is said to have begun as an unpromising dilettante. Later, as he began to come into his own, he was driven by two conflicting drives: ambition and admiration for the value of loyalty. His ambition, coupled with a strong histrionic aptitude, led him to the theatre, and he decided to make opera his life's work. He tried to succeed in the world of conventional opera, using whatever devices he could to manipulate his audience, but in this he was unsuccessful. This in turn led him to criticize the modern audience as unworthy, and to sublimate his desire for power into pure creativity. His creative drive appropriated an enormous amount of learning, which was always subordinated to his artistic goals. At last he began to achieve some success, upon which he devoted himself to creating the proper vehicle for the performance of his work to guarantee its future. Throughout these biographical remarks, Nietzsche glances at, or past, Wagner's ambition, irritability and manipulativeness, though they stick out awkwardly at times.

Nietzsche's account of Wagner's art is more interesting, and largely conforms to the account given in *Birth of Tragedy*. Wagner's mission in essence is to appropriate the tradition of modern classical music and with it to reform European culture by reforming the theatre, thus reviving the culture of ancient Greece. Nietzsche claims that each aspect of European culture is so intertwined with all the others that Wagner's operatic work, once presented properly, should suffice not only to transform theatre, but life more generally.

At the same time, Nietzsche's account of what the purpose of art is, and why Wagner's own art is especially suited to modernity, seem to be at odds with the transformative goals claimed for it. Modernity is characterized by the great complexity of life, vast amounts of knowledge made available by the sciences, and the urgency of the practical goals foisted upon us. Above all, modern man suffers from 'looking into the face of reality' (*UM* IV, §7). Underneath all this is universal anxiety over 'death and time' (*UM* IV, §4). The function of art is to provide recuperation from and compensation for these stresses by simplifying the world and conferring a tragic meaning on it. Though Nietzsche explicitly disavows here what he would later claim – that Wagner's music is essentially narcotic and thus uniquely suited for relieving these stresses of modernity – it would seem that if Wagner's art were to succeed in transforming European culture, it could only do this by transforming these very conditions, and thus removing the very yearnings it is so suited to address. If we are to become, as the final words of the essay suggest, simpler, more passionate, more authentic, why would we allow modernity to continue to have features that are at odds with our need to be this way? And if we did not, what would happen to the need for Wagner's art? Nietzsche seems torn between visions of Wagner as revolutionary and Wagner as balm.

The means by which Wagner's reform of the theatre are to be accomplished are: (1) a new relationship between music and language, (2) a new relationship between music and drama, and (3) a revival of myth. Nietzsche briefly sketches an account of language as a set of conventions used to represent the world conceptually. However, when language takes on this abstract character, we become alienated from ourselves and each other. Language loses its more fundamental and more valuable purpose, which is to express feeling in communicable form. By contrast, symphonic music can express feeling, but in a way that separates it from its interpersonal communicative context. By transforming opera into something akin to symphonic music, personal speech becomes reanimated by inner feeling, and music becomes anchored in its proper communicative context. To accomplish this, Wagner needs to transform the poetics of his language into something more primordial, while developing further the Beethoven-derived tendency to push music towards pure expressiveness.

But opera is also a drama and here, too, Wagner is striving to eliminate a source of alienation, for the proper condition of human beings is that their actions flow from their inner feeling. In earlier drama, speech and action are outwardly represented, but not the inner feeling that should animate them, while in earlier music, feeling is expressed but no action is portrayed. To overcome the severance of feeling and action, we need 'music drama'.

Furthermore, Wagner (like Herder) sees the intelligibility of the world and experience as essentially historical-communal and not individual. The proper role of art is not to communicate with sophisticates, but to channel the wisdom of the community and its primordial experiences back to the community as audience. To do this, the artist must tap into myth as the repository for the community's primordial understanding of the world. Nietzsche seems to associate this aspect of Wagner's work with his earlier socialist politics and his later nationalism, but towards the end of the essay suggests that a better way to think about Wagner's relationship to community is to see him as the creator of a community of the future, shaped by and responsive to the characteristic concerns of his art. The idea of creating, rather than conserving, a people is one that Nietzsche would return to in *Zarathustra*, where, of course, it will be Nietzsche's teaching, not Wagner's, that creates the future community. In any case we can see that Wagner, according to Nietzsche, is concerned to unify or reunify various things that have become estranged from each other to bad effect.

Lastly, Nietzsche perceives in Wagner's thought an ethics which foreshadows Nietzsche's own later concerns; the mythic content of the plots could not embody communal wisdom if it was not in some sense wisdom about how to live. Simultaneously, it is the ethic of the future community that Wagner's art is helping to bring about.

Yet this wisdom seems on the face of it to be at odds with received notions of morality, for it teaches

> that passion is better than stoicism and hypocrisy; that to be honest, even in evil, is better than to lose oneself in the morality of tradition; that the free man can be good or evil but the unfree man is a disgrace to nature and is excluded from both heavenly and earthly solace; finally, that he who wants to become free has to become so through his own actions and that freedom falls into no one's lap like a miraculous gift. (*UM* IV, §11)

If the third essay strained against egalitarianism by implying that our duty to bring about cultural excellence puts those less fit for it at the service of those more so, the fourth essay adds to this the suggestion that authenticity and passion are in some sense more important than mere moral duties, and are likely to conflict with them. Here are our first indications of where Nietzsche was heading.

During Nietzsche's early phase, he had also thought about writing a companion to *Birth of Tragedy* about ancient Greek philosophy. We can speculate that as in *Birth of Tragedy*, Nietzsche would not only have celebrated the birth and death of the Hellenic, but would also have pointed towards its modern renewal, perhaps in Schopenhauer, perhaps in himself. Though this work was never completed, Nietzsche left behind two manuscripts in connection with it, *Philosophy in the Tragic Age of the Greeks*, and *On Truth and Lie in an Extra-moral Sense*.

Philosophy in the Tragic Age of the Greeks argues that 'the Pre-Platonics' (as Nietzsche calls the Pre-Socratics, while adding Socrates to their number) represent not only the greatest, but in essence all of the 'types' available to philosophy understood both as a conceptual system and as a way of life. Subsequent philosophers represent either pale imitations or hybrid forms of these better archetypes (unless they represent mere scholarliness, in which case they are not true philosophers). The manuscript begins with a general account of what philosophy at its best can be: an attempt to step beyond the orientation available from traditional religious conceptions towards metaphysics, a conceptual representation of the world and its significance as a whole, from which one derives a mode of living appropriate to the world so described. But Nietzsche contrasts this kind of conceptual representation with that of empirical science, which as far as it goes accurately portrays the empirical world. On Nietzsche's Kantian presuppositions, metaphysics, unlike science, is incapable of providing a true account of the world. Thus a part of the pathos of the great philosopher, to stand in the truth and to have unriddled the world, rests on an illusion. This illusion, which Nietzsche had seen as early as 1868, was one that even Schopenhauer, in his claim to have identified the character of the thing-in-itself, fell prey to. Consequently, new philosophers confront a dilemma that ancient philosophers did not: it is their task to produce such orientating conceptual representations while knowing that all they have really achieved is a kind of conceptual myth. Whether this is Nietzsche's last word on the status of modern philosophy, including his own, is a subject subsequently debated by Nietzsche scholars. After presenting these general thoughts about the nature of philosophy, Nietzsche then gives us sketches of Thales, Anaximander, Heraclitus, Parmenides and Anaxagoras, frequently shedding light on them by comparisons with Kant and Schopenhauer. We gather from other sources that had Nietzsche continued the manuscript, he would have treated Empedocles, Democritus, Pythagoras and Socrates as well. But 'from Plato on there is something essentially amiss with philosophers ...' (*KGW* III, vol. 2, pp. 303–4); as in *Birth of Tragedy*, Socrates represents the turning point. As Nietzsche says elsewhere, 'with Empedocles and Democritus the Greeks were well on their way toward assessing correctly the irrationality and suffering of human existence, but thanks to Socrates, they never reached the goal' (*KGW* IV, vol. 1, p. 183).

On Truth and Lie in an Extra-moral Sense gives us the early Nietzsche's neo-Kantian epistemology, also yoked to his aestheticist goals. Throughout the early Nietzsche's writings, the modern commitment to science and scholarship is criticized for its psychological and cultural effects; here Nietzsche argues that it is rooted in an epistemological illusion as well, for the sort of knowledge we think attainable eludes us once we reflect on the mechanisms which bring it about. Kant himself had restricted his critique to showing that rationalist metaphysics is impossible, while reassuring us that *a priori* knowledge of the empirical world is possible once we see that the empirical world is the product of the constructive activities of the human mind. Nietzsche by contrast takes the lessons of Kantianism to be entirely sceptical. If the world we know is a constructed world, and not how things are in themselves, then our cognitive claims rest on an illusion, since we take the empirical world as real and mind-independent, and our cognition as adequate to it. Ultimately early Nietzsche's purpose is to argue for the ethical and cultural superiority of devotion to art and 'tragic wisdom'. Not only can science not satisfy us in the end – science cannot even satisfy itself.

Nietzsche's critique is rooted in Kantian assumptions about the phenomenality of the world of experience and the constructive role of the intellect in structuring it spatiotemporally and categorically (like Schopenhauer, Nietzsche regards causality as the only category). He adds to this some startling claims about the nature of concepts and language. Concepts provide a false sense of type-identity between concrete things which are absolutely unique and incommensurable; at most there is an analogical relationship between things. Language is nothing more than a system of metaphors, anchored by arbitrary social conventions whose purpose is ultimately moral rather than epistemic. The moral purposes that compel us to seek the truth express only the social interest in punishing the dishonest for the parasitic advantages accruing to their disobedience of linguistic convention. There is therefore no real reason to prefer truth to lies, an insight available to the artist if not the scientist. As with the claim that metaphysics is mere conceptual poetry, Nietzsche scholars continue to debate whether the radical scepticism of *On Truth and Lie* was Nietzsche's last word on the subject.

In any event, Nietzsche never completed his 'Philosopher's Book', as he sometimes referred to the companion to *Birth of Tragedy*. Instead, he initially contemplated a continuation of the *Untimely Meditations* series; as late as 1876, we see plans in his notebooks for another nine essays. A glance at some of the titles of these unwritten essays ('The State', 'Woman and Child') reveals that this project was retained but transformed. Nietzsche had already discovered that he had certain difficulties in organizing his scattered notes on various subjects into unified essays. With one eye fixed on the French, he realized that he could polish these individual notes into aphorisms and distribute them under headings corresponding to the projected topics of the unwritten meditations. In this way, *Human, All Too Human*, and the middle phase of Nietzsche's authorship, was born.

THE MIDDLE WORKS

Though there is some controversy over the division of Nietzsche's works into early, middle and late, at the very least there is a startling stylistic change in the works after *Untimely Meditations*. Though the topics Nietzsche had intended to treat in further essays in the early mode remain much the same, Nietzsche abandons the unified essay in favour of collections of aphorisms and epigrams. The prose style of these epigrams is strikingly different from the Emersonian and Schopenhauerian mode of the *Untimely Meditations* in being much more concise and much more dispassionate. Eventually, in the sequels to *Human, All Too Human*, Nietzsche even abandoned the organizational principle of grouping aphorisms into titled parts with headings indicating their content, though the ordering of the aphorisms is not arbitrary even here. It seems that Nietzsche's intention was to create in the reader's mind a non-linear linking and cross-referencing of various topics, in addition to the narrative flow that was present in the chapters of *Human, All Too Human*. Nonetheless, using the latter's chapter titles as a way of organizing this material is quite helpful.

In the first editions of the middle works, *Assorted Opinions and Maxims* was presented as a 'supplement' to *Human, All Too Human*, while *The Wanderer and His Shadow*, *Daybreak* and *Gay Science* were presented as freestanding works. When Nietzsche brought out second editions of these works, he reorganized them, making *Assorted Opinions and Maxims* and *The Wanderer and His Shadow* into volume two of *Human, All Too Human*, while *Daybreak* and *Gay Science* continued to exist as separate works. Also, in the second editions, Nietzsche added new prefaces to each book, and a fifth collection of aphorisms to the original four of *Gay Science*.

The immediate source of the idea of a middle period comes from Nietzsche himself. The back cover of the first edition of *Gay Science* read

With this book we arrive at the conclusion of a series of writings by FRIEDRICH NIETZSCHE whose common goal is to erect a

NIETZSCHE: A GUIDE FOR THE PERPLEXED

new image and ideal of the free spirit. To this series belong: *Human, All Too Human. With a Supplement: Assorted Opinions and Maxims, The Wanderer and His Shadow, Daybreak: Thoughts about the Prejudices of Morality, The Gay Science.* Earlier writings by the same author: *The Birth of Tragedy out of the Spirit of Music, Untimely Meditations* [which are listed].

Clearly Nietzsche thought the 'middle works' expressed a unified project, involving some sort of break with the earlier writings, and coming to completion with *Gay Science*.

What does Nietzsche mean by 'a new image and ideal of the free spirit'? First, the word 'spirit' [*Geist*] in part has the sense of 'intellect', which suggests free thinking, and thus a connection to the European Enlightenment. This association is confirmed by Nietzsche's dedication of *Human, All Too Human* to Voltaire. It is also reflected in the middle Nietzsche's 'positivistic' commitments to the virtues of empirical science as our sole source of knowledge. Nietzsche even suggests that empiricism should regulate cognition in our personal lives as well. However, 'spirit' also has many other connotations, suggesting personality, style and drive; part of Nietzsche's intention is that as important as free thinking is to freedom, one cannot become free by cognition alone. A free spirit is someone who has certain attitudes and practical comportments as well, in particular a certain freedom from convention. If she acts according to convention it will be for reasons of her own rather than out of submission to its perceived legitimacy and authority. Furthermore, a free spirit will require a certain immunity from practical limitations. Like Hegel and Marx, Nietzsche does not regard freedom merely as freedom from coercion, but also as freedom from needs that would require compromise with those who have the economic power to meet them. The free spirit cannot be a slave to tradition, convention, the state or the economy.

Thus far, Nietzsche's 'free spirit' seems to embody desiderata not so different from that of other Enlightenment figures. In what way then does the free spirit require a 'new image and a new ideal'? The first divergence is cognitive. In the modern period before Kant, scientific thinking was thought superior to medieval modes of cognition, but also adequate to reality as it truly is. Nietzsche's Enlightenment stance is post-Kantian. He recognizes that naïve rationality, without a reflective appreciation of the role of the intellect in shaping experience, will lead to cognitive errors of various sorts. Now Kant famously recognized the need for reflective inquiry into the structure of our cognitive powers and their limits, but if we took account of this and limited ourselves to objects of experience, the claims for scientific method, thus restricted, could go on much as before. Nietzsche, however, does not discern a timeless, fixed structure to the intellect that is inherent in its nature. For him, part of what a proper Enlightenment stance requires is a thoroughgoing naturalization of our conception of the world, and the intellect too must be seen as a part of nature. Consequently, the ways in which the intellect conditions or even distorts our access to knowledge will be dependent upon evolved natural constraints, historical influences and psychosocial factors. Thus 'critique' cannot be a once-and-for-all preliminary to cognition, for these factors vary from individual to individual, and are constantly shifting and changing. Thus the reflective 'moment' in inquiry must be a partial, idiosyncratic and ongoing one. The results of any inquiry will be inevitably provisional.

Another contrast with earlier Enlightenment figures, Kant included, concerns the practical side of freedom, both personal and social. First, it is common for Enlightenment figures to be committed to some form of egalitarianism, since the intrinsic capacity for freedom is the same for each individual. Nothing could justify the liberation of some and not the liberation of all. This means that the project of liberation is an inherently political one. Nietzsche, by contrast, does not think that the kind of multifaceted freedom he wishes to champion is attainable by all people, and so the creation of a society in which all are free is not necessary to his project. Nor is it desirable, for subordination of a potential free spirit to mere political tasks is itself an impediment to personal liberation. In many respects, Nietzsche would leave society and state as they are, focusing his interest on a minority who will achieve liberation independent of politics. That is not to say that community plays no role in the life of a free spirit: there can always be, for example, 'the republic of letters' within the community. But if social conditions are not to be an impediment to even this minority's liberation, they must also be free of the economic and professional constraints that many others suffer from. In short, they must have leisure. Thus Nietzsche's free spirits take on a certain aristocratic quality, and we now see why in *Human, All Too Human* he aligns himself, not with

Rousseau, but with Voltaire. Unlike Marx, Nietzsche would not transform the conditions of modern life for all. So modern life as it stands serves as the backdrop to projects of liberation that are ultimately private. This is one of the most fundamental changes in Nietzsche's point of view since the early writings, which, under the influence of Wagner, had contemplated all sorts of reforms of the conditions of modern life. On closer inspection, however, the early Nietzsche's revolutionary zeal had always been aimed primarily at the cultural sphere; in the Wagner essay, he even seemed to suggest that cultural reform was needed precisely to render the conditions of modernity more tolerable; in other words, those conditions themselves were not to change. Nonetheless, there is a definite shift. One gets the impression that the early Nietzsche was demanding general assent to his claims and goals from the world of culture. In the middle period, while he continues to push for cultural changes, the 'elite' is not the world of culture itself, but a self-selected audience within it; Nietzsche seems to have lost his zeal for a broader acceptance of his goals. Thus the free spirit will be comparatively isolated even within the world of culture, an isolation mitigated only by informal networks of like-minded 'spirits'. With this in mind, Nietzsche crafts a persona for himself, 'The Wanderer' (*HA* I, §638; the opening and closing dialogues of *The Wanderer and His Shadow*), both expressing and exemplifying this isolation.

However, the most important aspect of Nietzsche's new free thinking and free acting that differentiates it from previous Enlightenment projects is his critical stance towards morality. Nietzsche believes, with some justification, that previous Enlightenment figures not only wanted equal freedom for all individuals, but that morality requires this. But just as the commitment to naturalism profoundly changes the character of cognitive 'critique', moral critique must become different as well. Prior figures either sought to make the world more moral, or sought to understand theoretically what morality requires of us and why. For middle (and late) Nietzsche, morality is itself a part of nature. Once that is grasped in all its contingency and historicity, it can never again be enough (for the free spirits) merely to try to promote it or provide a rational reconstruction of it. Morality itself, though an interesting, perhaps *the* most interesting, object of free-spirited inquiry, no longer has any authority for us. And this gives us the final sense in which free spirits are free: they are free from taking the demands of morality seriously in the way that others do. Since that guidance will be lacking, and yet a life must guide itself somehow, Nietzsche proposes that free spirits live 'experimentally', not just as cognitive but as practical beings. Successful experiments can become incorporated into the individual's evolving, idiosyncratic code; unsuccessful experiments, as in science, constitute a gain for knowledge.

Since the aphoristic mode 'giving [his thoughts] in fragments' makes it almost impossible to summarize the full contents of the middle works, it is helpful that at least the first entry, volume one of *Human, All Too Human*, is divided into named chapters, which give us some rough guidance to the range of topics the middle Nietzsche is concerned with. 'On First and Last Things' concerns his metaphysical and epistemological commitments. As we have already indicated, these are a kind of naturalized neo-Kantianism. Like Kant, Nietzsche thinks that whatever knowledge we are capable of can only be the result of empirical inquiry; neo-Kantianism is the source of his 'positivistic' commitments. Also like Kant (on some interpretations), Nietzsche regards the real nature of things as inaccessible to reason or experience. However, unlike Kant and Schopenhauer, Nietzsche rejects the idea that the character or even the very idea of the thing-in-itself has any important role to play in inquiry or in human life more generally. Kant had thought that the possibility of things beyond experience allows us to have faith that we have free will. We may never be able to prove that we do, but the possibility is enough to allow us to take moral accountability seriously. Nietzsche completely rejects this line of thought; whatever human agency may be, it is an entirely empirical phenomenon, accessible to scientific inquiry, and therefore completely deterministic. This gives Nietzsche's critique of morality its deepest foundation: as an incompatibilist, middle Nietzsche regards the commitment to naturalism as entailing the destruction of moral accountability. Nietzsche apparently thinks that if we reject any important role for the thing-in-itself, then we are restricted to empirical phenomena if we are to investigate anything at all. But at the empirical level, there is no evidence to suggest that humans are anything other than natural beings embedded in the world along with all the other natural beings which are objects of natural scientific inquiry. Such inquiry gives us our best empirical theories of nature, and these are all deterministic.

Like Kant and Schopenhauer, Nietzsche thinks that our

experience, both cognitive and moral, is shaped to a significant degree by the character of our own intellects. Like Schopenhauer, he thinks that our intellects are themselves a part of nature. Far from leading to a thoroughgoing scepticism, Nietzsche holds out hope that empirical inquiry into the character of our psyches is nonetheless possible. By shedding light on how they have developed naturally and historically, we can correct for some of the epistemic defects that their limited and contingent character cause.

However, the more important task for reflective inquiry is in understanding our 'practical' side. Nietzsche stresses that active people are only able to act by virtue of the various false beliefs they have about themselves and the world. Only the philosopher-scientist of the sort Nietzsche wishes to be can pierce these veils, though in the middle works he suggests that this means that a life of inquiry will be essentially contemplative and detached from the life of action. The inquirer need not be inactive, but activity can no longer serve its customary goals. It becomes instead a source of data in the pursuit of self-knowledge.

Much of the middle works are concerned with psychological investigations. These psychological investigations have a multiplicity of purposes. First, Nietzsche is concerned with 'the history of the moral sensations', and 'the religious life', as in his later *Genealogy of Morals*. The purpose of these investigations is partly a response to Schopenhauer, who had based morality on compassion, and explained compassion by appealing to the metaphysical unity of all things (and people) in the thing-in-itself. Nietzsche seeks to replace this sort of explanation and legitimation of morality with a reductive, naturalistic account, not only to further his own naturalistic explanatory agenda, but also to undermine the historical propensity of people to align 'evil' qualities with our natural aspect and 'good' qualities with our alleged supernatural aspect. This propensity is harmful not only in obscuring understanding of the good, but in promoting the tendency to think that explicable, natural drives and interests must be wicked simply because they are explicable and natural. Thus the genealogical investigations in the middle period have a therapeutic goal of promoting both self-acceptance and a more benign attitude towards the natural world. Furthermore, the persuasive power of Christianity, the central obstacle to enlightenment, depends upon the mystification of phenomena like that of the 'saint', and the conviction that such phenomena defy any naturalistic explanation. Remarkably, much of the discussion of these things in the middle works closely echoes the more stridently argued analyses of the later works; for example, the master/slave contrast is fully present as early as *Human, All Too Human* (*HA* I, §45). What differentiates the middle works is the much lighter touch. Nietzsche seems to think it sufficient to demonstrate the erroneousness of a supernatural or moral-realist account of these phenomena to discredit them. In the later works, he focuses as much if not more energy on displaying their repugnance as well. It is noteworthy that Nietzsche's concern with genealogy only seems to grow over the course of the middle works; by the time of *Daybreak*, the topic is the stated concern of the work.

The middle Nietzsche's attempt to naturalize these phenomena depends upon two commitments, both of which are far from original to him. First, he stresses the historical genesis of that which he would both explain and debunk. In this he follows closely a path marked out for him by Hume (in his account of the origin of justice) and Rousseau (in his account of the development of inequality). These models, in turn, appropriate social contract theories as inspiration (both positive and negative) for their historical hypotheses. Though Nietzsche's own hypotheses differ in detail from Hume's and Rousseau's, both in content and purpose, comparison with them, and with earlier social contract theories, shows that Nietzsche's thinking is embedded in a prior, ongoing discussion of the artificiality and historicity of normative phenomena. Like his predecessors, he assumes that what is artifice is contingent and mutable; this, however, is something his naturalism does not strictly require.

His psychological inquiries also presuppose either psychological egoism or psychological hedonism, and in this Nietzsche also follows well-worn tracks laid down by his predecessors. Middle Nietzsche seems to take it for granted that this too is inevitable given naturalism. Therefore the naturalization of self-sacrificing behaviours will involve tracing them to hidden and convoluted channels of selfishness (though Nietzsche is not entirely consistent here, and by the late works seems to have given up the presupposition in the wake of the complex phenomena he uncovers using it as a heuristic). Unlike some previous psychological hedonists, however, Nietzsche's analyses do not merely accuse the altruist of hypocrisy. The analyses depend largely on error, self-deception, and even unconscious thought processes.

Nietzsche's analyses here are not all aimed at criticizing morality, though many of them are. He devotes a fair amount of energy to understanding the psychology of artistic creation, another subject which he thinks prior metaphysical theories such as Schopenhauer's have mystified. This has led not only to misunderstanding, but to the overvaluing of art's significance for life. Nietzsche prefers that we devote our attention instead to scientific inquiry, though he continues his interest in exploring the conditions for the creation and preservation of 'high culture', understood now to include a strong cognitive component. He is also concerned to expose the complex psychological pitfalls that both life in society and life in solitude pose, especially for the would-be free spirit. His discussions of vanity, timidity, compassion, revenge, and so on belong here. We also see Nietzsche's discussion of relations between the sexes, which, while not tainted by the vitriol of his later writings, largely involve cautioning the would-be free spirit against the entanglement and distraction that marriage involves.

Last, Nietzsche discusses politics, both to get a better cognitive handle on it, and to help discourage would-be free spirits from being seduced by it. When Nietzsche's concerns subsequently turn them to the public sphere, there is a fair amount of continuity with the earlier writings: Nietzsche is still not very happy with the public world of modernity, whether this concerns politics, economics, journalism, or anything else. However, as stated above, Nietzsche does not wish to combat it, let alone reform it, as much as to furnish an understanding of it sufficient to induce detachment and indifference. Unsurprisingly, Nietzsche rejects all the political ideologies on offer, from left to right, as delusions, 'convictions' with no foundation. That said, he also offers some perceptive analyses of political phenomena (his suggestion that economic liberals will eventually join forces with religious conservatives, or that socialism, if ever fully achieved, would be tyrannical and violent, though not entirely original, are among the more prescient of his comments, and each is the product of a far from obvious causal analysis).

Throughout the middle works, Nietzsche's concern with creating the conditions of cultural excellence and promoting the cause of the self-creation of the exceptional individual – concerns which also animated the early works – persist and occasionally emerge as the junction point of all his inquiries, with the forces of morality, religion, society and politics as their impediments. Nietzsche perhaps

expressed this best in the 'catechism' which concludes Book III of
Gay Science:

> What makes one heroic? – Going out to meet at the same time
> one's highest suffering and one's highest hope.
> In what do you believe? – In this, that the weights of all things
> must be determined anew.
> What does your conscience say? – "You shall become the person
> you are."
> Where are your greatest dangers? – In pity.
> What do you love in others? – My hopes.
> Whom do you call bad? – Those who always want to put to
> shame.
> What do you consider most humane? – To spare someone
> shame.
> What is the seal of liberation? – No longer being ashamed in
> front of oneself. (*GS* §§268–75)

But by the time of *Gay Science*, other, more dramatic themes are
being sounded. First, Nietzsche's opposition to Christianity, one of
his connections to the Enlightenment, begins to darken. Though
Nietzsche never backs away from his belief that the decay of
Christianity is in the main good news, he begins to realize that as
this process becomes more widespread, the foundations of western
civilization will weaken, with potentially devastating results; *Gay
Science* contains the first explicit reference to 'the death of God'
(*GS* §108, §125), though the sense of this as a potential catastrophe,
a crisis of nihilism requiring a more profound response than the
Enlightenment has been able to muster thus far, is one which we
saw was obliquely present even in the early works. Second,
Nietzsche abandons not only the Greeks as an adequate model to
return to, but also the Socratic life of inquiry and self-knowledge (in
marked contrast with the other middle works' celebration of
Socrates) (*GS* §340). Finally, in the midst of writing the middle
works, Nietzsche had 'discovered' the doctrine of the eternal
recurrence. With that he returned to his earlier practice of grand
world-interpretation, and the idea that life requires something akin
to tragic affirmation if the exceptional individual is to attain perfection and the paralysis brought on by the death of God is to be
overcome (*GS* §341). Nietzsche thus confronted a problem of both

style and synthesis: how could he combine his renewed tragic wisdom with the passion for inquiry, psychological insight and critique of morality that had become the watchwords of the middle works? The latter-day German disciple of Voltaire and author of La Rochefoucauldian aphorisms would not suffice. Nietzsche needed '[a]nother mask! A second mask' (*BGE* §278) different from that of the Wanderer; in response he invented Zarathustra (*GS* §342).

ZARATHUSTRA AND THE LATER WORKS

Thus Spoke Zarathustra is Nietzsche's most widely read work, and is generally thought to usher in the final phase of his work. It represents a major generic and stylistic departure. First, the work is structured as a narrative, with an imaginary setting and fictional characters, the central one being of course Zarathustra himself, who acts as Nietzsche's mouthpiece. Second, the style of writing, which consists in the main of speeches given by Zarathustra articulating his philosophical positions, is lyrical and declamatory, in marked contrast to the tight, epigrammatic and aphoristic style of the middle works.

The work is divided into four parts, though Nietzsche's intentions wavered over time. Initially, he had intended it to consist of only three parts, and it is the first three parts which he himself published. He had later thought to add additional parts; the current part four, 'The Temptation of Zarathustra', seems to have been conceived as an interlude to be followed by additional parts. Nietzsche printed this part privately but then requested its return from the friends to whom he distributed it. Nietzsche finally abandoned the plan of extending the narrative, but after his insanity the fourth part and eventually all four parts together were brought out as a unified and complete text. It is in this form that we have it today.

Nietzsche's choice of the historical Zoroaster as his mouthpiece is peculiar, given that the work clearly addresses issues relating to modernity. His own explanation for this is that the historical Zoroaster's achievement was to interpret the cosmos as the battleground between two deities or forces (Ahura Mazda and Ahriman) who represent the moral contrast between good and evil. Human beings are thus called upon to choose freely which side they will take in this cosmic struggle of human history, at the end of which good will triumph apocalyptically over evil. Thus Zoroastrianism could be said to initiate a conception of human historical time as linear, with a beginning, middle and end. Zoroastrianism is arguably the source for these conceptions in Christianity. Zoroastrianism also teaches, however, that honesty is one of the highest virtues. Nietzsche's suggestion, then, is that commitment to honesty would compel a rejection of the entire dualistic, voluntaristic and linear conception as not up to critical scrutiny. It is only natural, then, that the most honest man, Zarathustra, should be the first to discover its falsity.

Though interpretation of *Zarathustra* typically focuses on the content of the speeches, the plot is not without importance, not only for the light it sheds on Nietzsche's thought, but the insight it affords into his life and development. The Prologue begins by telling us that Zarathustra began a sojourn of solitude in the mountains ten years before, during which he accumulated wisdom (presumably the wisdom contained in at least the discourses of part one). But Zarathustra decides, out of love of humanity, to descend to teach people his doctrines. Upon his return, he tells a crowd that 'man is something to be overcome' (*Z* I, Prologue, §3) in favour of the overman, a person or type of human perfection presented as a source of meaning and as an alternative to the absent God. The value of humanity as it is presently lies only in its contribution to this project. Here Nietzsche simply reiterates the views he had already expressed in *Schopenhauer as Educator* about the duty to promote the creation of 'Schopenhauerian men'. The alternative is that humanity will degenerate into complacency and become incapable of creativity or excellence, turning into 'last men'. The crowd rejects this teaching, thus inspiring a change in strategy for Zarathustra: instead of urging on the people as a whole, he will seduce disciples away from the larger fold to form a smaller community devoted to his own goals, and from this smaller community the overman will arise (to paraphrase the last discourse of part one) like a messiah from amidst a self-chosen people. Thus while the discourses of part one contain important elements of Nietzsche's own view, it is important to recognize that they may be partial and geared to the task of seduction.

The first part contains twenty-two brief speeches outlining Nietzsche's views on various subjects, criticizing virtuous mediocrity, metaphysics, asceticism, moral accountability and punishment, modern politics and the public sphere, compassion, conformity, vengefulness, and much else, contrasting these with a noble ethos yoked to the task of promoting the overman. Noteworthy among the discourses is the first mention of the will to power, in 'On the Thousand and One Goals', where he claims that underneath the diversity of moral communities is one drive. But while each community sets its moral goals in contrast to each other, Zarathustra suggests that what is needed is a goal for all of humanity, thus alluding both to the overman and suggesting that if humanity wills the overman, it will then constitute a unified community. Finally, Zarathustra enjoins his disciples to rebel against him to further their own development.

Part two begins with Zarathustra returning to the disciples. His doctrine is in danger because of the rebellion, which has not driven them to further heights towards the overman, but to backsliding and compromise. In the discourses that follow, Zarathustra continues his championing of a noble ethos and his critique of modernity. However, certain themes begin to come together. First, Zarathustra's critique reveals his own nausea with modernity, with 'the rabble'. Next, he reveals that the central political and moral doctrine of modernity, egalitarianism, is motivated by the same vengefulness criticized in part one; this may be the source of his nausea. Next, the concept of the will to power becomes generalized: not only is it useful for explaining moral phenomena, it also serves to explain philosophizing itself, as a will to master the multiplicity of the world by unifying it and rendering it thinkable. What is more, these philosophers are said to be responsible for creating the very values which guide their communities. Yet Zarathustra betrays that he too is a philosopher in proclaiming that all life is will to power: for the first time the idea is presented as a doctrine which unifies life and renders it thinkable. And we already know that Zarathustra would create a community through his disciples and that he teaches his own values. The urgency of realizing his goals is heightened in 'The Soothsayer', in which we get our first description of nihilism as the likely outcome of modernity's domination by the last men, for not only are their lives meaningless, but it is only a matter of time before this meaninglessness becomes self-aware; lacking some meaning-conferring project, life will sink into despair and immobility.

Finally, Zarathustra reflects on the nature of the will to power and the spirit of revenge and concludes that while willing liberates, obstacles to willing inspire the desire for revenge, and from this the morality Zarathustra wishes to overcome arises. But the propensity for revenge is deeply etched in the human condition, for the very structure of time itself places an insuperable barrier against the liberating, creative will: one can desire and create a future, but the past is inaccessible and unalterable. Thus seeing that overcoming the spirit of revenge may be impossible given the linear and irreversible character of time itself, Zarathustra 'discovers' the doctrine of the eternal recurrence, though this is merely implied. If time is a circle, forward-directed willing and creating bring about the past, thus opening it to our power and removing revenge as an ontological problem at least. Zarathustra conceals this doctrine, being unwilling to teach it. He says 'I await a worthier one', presumably the overman, whom we can now identify as the figure who knows about the eternal recurrence, but has a different attitude towards it and therefore can teach it. Yet as Zarathustra's interior dialogue shows, it is his task to teach it and thereby become a 'commander' and to 'rule'. From this point on, the overman drops away. Zarathustra can no longer displace the goal of achieving human perfection onto some possible future: he must achieve this himself to teach the doctrine which has come unbidden to him. His inability to teach it leads him to abandon his disciples and return to solitude.

In part three, we see Zarathustra travelling by sea, and in the midst of his journey he articulates the doctrine of eternal recurrence clearly for the first time, though only to the sailors. The need for affirmation of the eternal recurrence is presented in a parable of a shepherd who swallows a snake (echoing the association of the snake with revenge in 'On the Adder's Bite' in part one) and must bite it to save himself. Over the course of part three, Zarathustra makes his way back to his cave, where the book began, presenting various discourses and reflections along the way, culminating in 'The Old and New Tablets'. This discourse is addressed to the disciples, and represents something of a summary of Nietzsche's ethical critiques and admonitions. In the next section, 'The Convalescent', Zarathustra finally confronts his procrastination over teaching the eternal recurrence: he cannot demand that his disciples affirm recurrence because he cannot, filled as he is with nausea at the thought of the eternal recurrence of 'the small man'. Contemplating the recurrence of the small horrifies him to the point of collapse. Arguably, this nausea was linked to his earlier teaching of the overcoming of the small man in favour of the overman, an elitist variant on a doctrine of linear time and progress which condemns the present and seeks to escape it into a better future. In the remaining sections of part three, Zarathustra overcomes his nausea and comes to affirm all of life and its eternal recurrence, even that of the ignoble who cannot do the same. He has become so joyful that he wants his joy to recur eternally, no matter what the cost.

The final part begins many years later, and is organized around the theme of Zarathustra's pity for those who accept his teaching but do not adequately embody the ethical ideal he seeks to realize, the so-called higher men. This is said to be Zarathustra's temptation which he must overcome. He encounters seven types: abdicated kings, a scientist, a romantic 'magician' (seemingly modelled on Wagner), the last pope, a freethinker who has killed God, a mendicant escaping from civilization and Zarathustra's own shadow. The shadow recalls the similar character from *The Wanderer and His Shadow*, suggesting that this higher man, whom Zarathustra calls a 'free spirit', is Nietzsche's former self, the author of the aphoristic works. However, if we consider that Nietzsche himself was once a dutiful soldier, a practitioner of 'science' in the extended German sense of *Wissenschaft*, a devotee of Wagnerian romanticism (of course Nietzsche himself wrote the poem attributed to the 'magician'), a Christian and a mildly impoverished retiree who had escaped from the world into solitude, the hypothesis suggests itself that the higher men are former personae, shells Nietzsche has outgrown. This might go some distance towards explaining his reluctance to see part four published, and his attempt to collect the privately printed copies from his friends. However, this is not to diminish the value of seeing them as types subject to critique from a higher vantage point.

One by one, Zarathustra encounters the higher men and, feeling kinship and compassion for them, invites them up to his cave to join him in his solitude. In the end, though they are comforted by him, Zarathustra realizes that coddling higher men will not achieve his 'work' of refashioning humanity into perfect beings capable of life and world affirmation, even if indulging his compassion for them makes him happy. In the end, he disowns his pity, these types themselves, and proceeds to what he calls 'his work', the task of transforming humanity through his teaching.

If there is an autobiographical counterpart in Nietzche's life to Zarathustra's 'work', it is the remainder of Nietzche's post-*Zarathustra* writings. Initially he had thought this writing would take the form of a treatise, a *magnum opus* to be entitled *The Will to Power*, but instead, Nietzsche produced two extended works, *Beyond Good and Evil* and *Genealogy of Morals*, and then a rapid succession of shorter works that occupied him until his collapse in 1889.

Nietzsche explains (in *Ecce Homo*) that *Beyond Good and Evil* is the beginning of a negative phase of his work, following the positive phase of *Zarathustra*; it is meant to be a 'critique of modernity'. Like *Human, All Too Human*, it consists of short, aphorism-like, numbered sections, grouped into nine parts according to topic. In part one, 'On the Prejudices of the Philosophers', Nietzsche argues that philosophical thinking is psychologically motivated by the will to power. He goes on to debunk available philosophical positions other than his own: scientific research, Epicureanism, Stoicism, positivism, neo-Kantianism, post-Kantian idealism, materialism, psychological egoism, Darwinism, Cartesianism and Scho-penhauerianism. A theme running through this part is scepticism about the value of the possession of the truth and the fitness of past philosophers for attaining it.

In part two, 'The Free Spirit', he begins to sketch his conception of the future philosopher's psychology, presents his critique of the appearance–reality contrast, and provides the only published argument for the doctrine that the world is will to power. He concludes by distinguishing his own elitist conception of free thinking from that of the egalitarian Enlightenment.

Part three, 'What is Religious', points back to 'The Religious Life' in *Human, All Too Human*, and forward to the third essay of *Genealogy of Morals*, 'What is the Meaning of Ascetic Ideals?' The psychology of asceticism and its role in Christianity is the main focus, and Nietzsche announces for the first time the idea of philosophers as value-legislators. The principal danger of Christianity is said to be its cultivation of modern man as herd animal, which he also links to egalitarianism. Part four provides an interlude of epigrams.

In part five, 'The Natural History of Morals', Nietzsche returns to the psychology of morality, also pointing backward to the middle works and ahead to *Genealogy*. The concept of slave morality, first introduced in *Human, All Too Human*, returns, and Nietzsche declares that 'the Jewish people ... mark the beginning of the slave rebellion in morals' (*BGE* §195, ellipsis mine). In the end he declares that modern morality is 'herd animal morality'. Again this is linked to 'the democratic movement'.

In part six, 'We Scholars', Nietzsche shifts his attention from the moral–political to the scientific, and while giving due weight to the epistemic usefulness of the scientific type, criticizes its tendency towards psychological depersonalization. Nietzsche contrasts scepticism as a manifestation of hesitancy to make commitments and to act (which characterizes the scientific type) with scepticism as a willingness to attack conventional wisdom in the service of one's own goals. The scientific type among philosophers is merely a 'philosophical labourer', and is assigned the task of being a tool in the hands of Nietzsche's philosopher as value-legislator.

In part seven, 'Our Virtues', Nietzsche criticizes the altruistic streak in modern morality as expressing self-contempt (which seeks to mask itself by a fascination with history). In the end, compassion is rooted in timidity and hedonism, and is incompatible with honesty, which is rooted in cruelty. Nietzsche's praise of cruelty, which he seems to think of as masculine, is complemented by a series of anti-feminist remarks which, though evincing a fair amount of misogyny, are also of a piece with his critique of egalitarianism, insofar as feminism can be seen as egalitarianism applied to gender.

In part eight, 'People and Fatherlands', Nietzsche makes many sweeping generalizations about the Germans, the English and the French. Perhaps the only continuing interest in these remarks is that they clearly distance him from German nationalism, as most of his criticisms are directed against German culture. Nietzsche speaks highly of the French, to whom he attributes artistic excellence, psychological acuity and a synthesis of 'northern' and 'southern' sensibilities. By contrast, the English are credited with responsibility for the very Enlightenment ideas Nietzsche has persistently attacked thus far. The part concludes with a rejection of nationalism in favour of a supranational Europeanness which, surprisingly, he sees in Wagner (excepting *Parsifal*).

Part nine, 'What is Noble', begins with an extended account of master morality versus slave morality (*BGE* §§257–60). Modernity is opposed to the spiritual nobility Nietzsche wishes to champion. As Nietzsche sketches his conception of nobility, the descriptions appear to shade off into thinly veiled self-portrait. Nietzsche concludes with a sketch of Dionysus as philosopher, and then a mournful comment on the inexpressibility of his views in writing. The book concludes with a poem, 'From High Mountains', in which he reflects on the loss of the friends of his youth and hopes for 'new friends'; as things are, his only companion is Zarathustra, a fictional self-projection.

Beyond Good and Evil was followed by a companion book in 1887, *On the Genealogy of Morals*. The book consists of three essays Nietzsche describes as 'preliminary studies by a psychologist for a revaluation of all values' (*EH* III, *Genealogy of Morals*). The first essay develops further the account of the contrast between 'master morality' and 'slave morality' presented in *Beyond Good and Evil*. The second essay provides a proto-Freudian account of conscience as the internalization of aggression. The third essay concerns asceticism as an ideal, explaining its origin, functions and value. We will discuss this work in detail in chapter Five.

Nietzsche's final productive year, 1888, saw a rapid succession of short works which have been the subject of controversy largely because of their proximity to his final collapse. This is unfortunate, because several of them represent not only the clearest and most concise expression of Nietzsche's views, but also represent his greatest success as a prose stylist. The first, *Case of Wagner*, is a polemic in twelve sections, with two postscripts and an epilogue. Nietzsche begins with a rhetorical contrast between Bizet's *Carmen* and Wagner's operas; while *Carmen* is this-worldly both in its libretto's attitude towards eroticism and in its music's rhythmical properties, Wagner's operas are otherworldly in their librettos, which focus on the problem of redemption and are disembodied in their lack of rhythm. Nietzsche argues that Wagner's music manifests a kind of physiological decadence and appeals to listeners similarly afflicted. He goes on to criticize Wagner's audience for its susceptibility to the manipulativeness of this music. Nietzsche's emphasis on manipulativeness calls attention to the evident theatricality of Wagner's art, which he regards as dishonest, but this leads to further criticism of Wagner as a librettist regarding plotting and the psychology of character. Beyond this, Nietzsche takes exception to Wagner's theoretical writings as being essentially apologia for the deficiencies of his art. Nietzsche sums up his 'case' by saying that Wagner is an actor, and that 'the actor should not seduce those who are authentic' (*CW*, §12). The first postscript focuses on the intellectual corruption that Wagner's art encourages. The second postscript stresses that Nietzsche's objections to Wagner should not be misread as tacit endorsement of his competitor, Brahms. The epilogue reiterates Nietzsche's contrast between master morality and slave morality. Nietzsche takes exception to Wagner's ability to present both in a favourable light (for example, in the *Ring* on the one hand and in *Parsifal* on the other) as if there was no meaningful distinction to be made between them. In this, Nietzsche sees Wagner as symptomatic of a larger cultural confusion and decline. To rebut the suggestion that Nietzsche's views were purely personal in motivation or recent in vintage, later in the year Nietzsche brought out an anthology of his previous writings touching on Wagner (who in the original source aphorisms is often not named explicitly), including material from *Human, All Too Human, Gay Science, Beyond Good and Evil* and *Genealogy of Morals*. Beyond reviewing Nietzsche's evolving criticisms of Wagner, it serves as a striking summary of Nietzsche's more general views on art and its relation to life. The book concludes with an excerpt from the preface to the second edition of *Gay Science*, declaring Nietzsche's own identity as an artist: they would be the last words Nietzsche would prepare for publication before his collapse.

Throughout the 1880s, Nietzsche continued to think he would write a *magnum opus*, for which he accumulated thousands of notes. Instead, he produced two short works, *Twilight of the Idols* and *Antichrist*, which appeared shortly after *Case of Wagner*. Taken together, they represent a kind of summation and synthesis of Nietzsche's thought. Again following the format of *Beyond Good and Evil*, Nietzsche presents nine chapters of aphorisms, sandwiched between a preface and a collection of epigrams at the beginning, and a quote from *Zarathustra* at the end. The first six chapters present Nietzsche's theoretical views on metaphysics, epistemology and ethics. The most noteworthy chapter is 'How the "True World" Finally Became A Fable'. Here Nietzsche organizes his thought about the history of metaphysics around the notion of a two-world picture of valueless appearance given by the senses and valuable reality accessible by either reason or faith, and traces this picture to normative intuitions rooted in psychological weakness. These chapters are followed by a seven-section essay on German culture, a chapter of 51 aphorisms on various figures and topics bound together by the theme of a critique of modernity (in which Nietzsche again signals his intentions by calling himself 'untimely' just as he had referred to the meditations of his second book), and a final, short five-section essay on the Greeks in which he returns to the themes of *Birth of Tragedy* and aligns himself with Hellenic life affirmation.

Antichrist was originally conceived as just one part of a project entitled *Revaluation of All Values*, which would contain four parts: (1) 'The Antichrist', (2) 'The Free Spirit', (3) 'The Immoralist', and (4) 'Dionysus'. The first part was to deal with Christianity, the second with philosophy, the third with morality and the fourth with the doctrine of the eternal recurrence.

Antichrist, unlike *Twilight*, is one continuous argument; it is not an aphoristic work but an essay in 62 sections, culminating in the judgement that Christianity is 'the one immortal blemish of mankind'. After such a judgement Nietzsche regards Christianity as completely finished and even suggests, half-playfully, half-seriously, that we should therefore abandon the Gregorian calendar in favour of one which counts the year 1888 as the first year of the post-Christian era (*A* §62). Nietzsche begins by outlining his theses about the will to power as both psychological motive and a basis for evaluation. Assuming a naturalistic ontology, Nietzsche explains that Christianity, by adopting a non-naturalistic ontology, reveals itself as fundamentally dishonest, an expression of sour grapes and symptomatic of this-worldly failure. By promoting pity as a virtue, it further promotes and protects the interests of other this-worldly failures. By promoting faith, it undermines inquiry. Buddhism and Christianity both represent attempts to cope with pathological suffering, but whereas Buddhism originates among refined classes, is honest and therapeutically effective, Christianity originates among lower classes, is dishonest and only makes one worse. In particular, the troubled barbarians of Northern Europe to which Christianity was sold were 'tamed' by it, but not made happier or healthier. In this we see a certain strategic dimension to Christianity: it seeks to get the better of the stronger.

Much of the middle of the essay is devoted to an attempt to reconstruct the history of Judaism and Christianity. Though we cannot do justice here to Nietzsche's hypotheses and how they may fare in the face of current scholarship, a few comments may be of interest. Nietzsche's attitude towards the earliest form of Judaism, which he associates with the era of the kings and prophets, is entirely favourable. He speculates that at some point after ancient Israel ceased to be successful in the world, a priestly faction seized control of ancient Judaic culture and society and began imposing a new set of values on it appropriate to its reduced status. This is essentially the same account as that given in the *Genealogy*, but with more specific allusions to the historical circumstances within which this took place. It was at that time, Nietzsche claims, that the priests concocted the Old Testament as a means of legitimating their power.

It is interesting to speculate on whether Nietzsche was aware of the 'Documentary Hypothesis' as it was presented by Julius Wellhausen in 1886, two years before he wrote *Antichrist*. To a large extent it supports Nietzsche's view, and since variants of the Documentary Hypothesis remain the dominant view in biblical studies today, this consilience is worth noting. According to Wellhausen and later scholars, the Torah or Pentateuch, the first five books of Hebrew Scripture, result from the editing together of a patchwork of four source texts, generally referred to as 'J' (Yahwist), 'E' (Elohist), 'D' (Deuteronomist), and 'P' (Priestly).[4] Nietzsche's favourable account of the early Israelis as pre-moralistic, warlike masters tallies with the material Wellhausen identifies as coming from J and E, and though dating is tremendously difficult, most scholars agree that both precede the deportation to Assyria in 722 BCE. D and P are generally regarded as post-deportation, and moral and priestly concerns do seem to dominate them. Nietzsche's evaluations are of course another matter, but philologically he appears to be on solid ground.

Nietzsche then proceeds to offer a speculative portrait of the historical Jesus, modelled, he broadly hints, on Prince Myshkin from Dostoevsky's *The Idiot*. Much of this account is favourable in the same way that his account of Buddhism is. Though Jesus represents a pathologically sensitive type, he discovers and embodies a therapeutic praxis of eschewing resentment and revenge that actually heals and helps. Nietzsche's Jesus has no obvious theological commitments, apocalyptic expectations or social criticisms. Here, Nietzsche is on weaker ground, not because there are no prominent historical Jesus scholars who would agree with his portrait, but because there is no consensus. Even if we limit ourselves to secular scholars, the historical Jesus literature is vast, conflict-ridden over questions of method and disparate as to result. It is worth noting that Robert Funk, and implicitly the consensus of the Jesus Seminar, supports the picture that Nietzsche paints.[5] Unfortunately, it is difficult to make sense of how such an historical Jesus could inherit an exceedingly apocalyptic and social-critical Baptism movement, or indeed inspire enough animus in anyone to trigger his judicial execution. It is worth noting here that Nietzsche's account, like that of the Jesus Seminar, expresses what one might call the Protestant pattern of differentiating between an early, more praiseworthy Jesus or Jesus movement, and a later corruption of it. Projection is to be expected and scepticism advised.

This may not ultimately matter, since the historically decisive Christianity for Nietzsche is not Jesus', but Paul's, who transforms it into the phenomenon that Nietzsche finds so disastrous. Though it is certainly plausible to regard Paul as an innovator when it comes to notions like the Atonement, again, Nietzsche may be seeing far more discontinuity in terms of ethos, social criticism and apocalyptic expectation than was the case.[6] But this issue is hostage to the historical Jesus question, which we will not be able to resolve here.

Towards the end of the essay, Nietzsche suggests that Christianity has deprived European civilization of the valuable influences of Greek, Roman, Islamic and Renaissance culture. In *Ecce Homo*, he would add the Napoleonic era to the list.

After Nietzsche completed *Antichrist*, he added a concluding preface to *Twilight*, and then turned his attention to his autobiography, *Ecce Homo*. The style of the work is exceedingly jarring and difficult to convey, yet immediately recognizable: terse yet meandering, grandiose and sarcastic. Though many readers detected signs of Nietzsche's coming madness in it, it is nonetheless valuable for understanding Nietzsche's thought and his self-understanding. The provocative chapter titles convey the tone, but not quite the content: 'Why I Am So Wise', 'Why I Am So Clever', 'Why I Write Such Good Books', and 'Why I Am A Destiny'. The first point to understand here is that Nietzsche is engaged in a kind of publicity stunt; his works had not attracted nearly the attention he had hoped for and thought they deserved, and in light of Nietzsche's posthumous reputation arguably did deserve. It is useful to see the book as falling into two halves. The first two chapters involve the construction of a semi-fictitious persona in much the same way that *Zarathustra* did. Though auto-biographical, they are anything but confessional memoirs and conceal more than they reveal. We hear next to nothing about the traumatic effect of his father's and brother's deaths, his disappointments with Paul Rée or Lou Salomé, his ambivalence about Wagner or his deep bitterness towards his sister. The second half is an attempt to shape the reception of his writings more directly. 'Why I Write Such Good Books' is a description of what he has accomplished, and 'Why I Am A Destiny' of what he is trying to do. The former has some utility, though one must approach Nietzsche's own readings of his earliest writings with caution. The description of *Birth of Tragedy* seems to be a projection of his late interests on the text. Interestingly, though his interpretation of the third and fourth *Untimely Meditations* as veiled self-descriptions rather than portraits of Schopenhauer and Wagner may seem to suffer even more from the same fault, this is arguably insightful; both essays were charitable to a fault and certainly involved considerable projection.

The final chapter is a surprisingly useful and concise, if florid and strident, account of the basic opposition between his commitments and those of Christianity, concluding its penultimate section with a motto from Voltaire. If Nietzsche remained a critic of modernity throughout his authorship, his bottom line from *Human, All Too Human* to the end was his allegiance, however conflicted, qualified and ambivalent, to the European Enlightenment.

CHAPTER 3

NIHILISM, WILL TO POWER, AND VALUE

NIHILISM

Nietzsche frequently characterizes his thought as a response to an alleged crisis of nihilism. This notion is associated with the 'death of God', the idea that western cultures have founded all their normative commitments on belief in Christianity, and that in the wake of the discrediting of this belief, we face a lack of normative guidance and restraint. Given the epistemic sources of the discrediting of Christianity, trying to restore its influence is not available; it must be replaced with some alternative foundation for our normative commitments. This characterization, though popular and warranted by many of Nietzsche's texts, does not do justice to Nietzsche's conception of nihilism and the kind of response it requires, for two reasons. First, as most readers of Nietzsche quickly realize, the difficulty is not in finding a replacement foundation for our prior normative commitments, since Nietzsche thinks that in various ways they are specifically and inextricably tied to Christianity. Therefore, an alternative foundation for values would require a change in the character of our normative commitments themselves. Often he characterizes this change as a reversal or inversion. But more importantly, Nietzsche thinks that the problem is not just that Christianity's attractive values cannot survive the collapse of its metaphysical assumptions. Rather, once one understands the underlying character of Christianity itself, and the more general processes at work within it, its values themselves come to be seen as repellent.

What follows is an interpretative sketch, a synthesis of various things Nietzsche says that are germane to nihilism and its overcoming that illustrates just how general those processes are. Though Nietzsche thinks of nihilism and its overcoming as real historical concerns, this sketch is in some ways a rational reconstruction of the onset of nihilism. In that sense it could be replicated in other cultures and at other times in history.

Consider human beings in the most primitive circumstances. Like other living things, human beings have needs, interests and goals which may or may not be met. All living things, human beings included, are engaged in a kind of struggle to serve their interests, to obtain the things they value. However, it is a pervasive feature of life that all valued states and accomplishments are subject to destruction. For example, no animal solves its food problem once and for all; hunger eventually returns. Safety requires ongoing vigilance. Worse, any accomplishment is inevitably undone because of the pervasiveness of change. The most obvious example of this, of course, is death. No matter what a living thing does to survive, it will eventually fail. But Nietzsche's concern is more general than death, for in a broader sense, many accomplishments fail even apart from death and within an individual's life-span. Consider romantic love: no matter what a lover does to secure the first glow of romantic love, eventually the relationship changes to something else, or the relationship ends, or (in perhaps the best case scenario) even if the relationship were to retain its initial character and persist throughout life, it will still end in death. All living things are engaged in an ongoing yet losing battle with the forces of destruction. This is not because there is some demonic tendency at work in life; it is an intrinsic characteristic of the world that 'everything must pass'. Given temporality and the pervasiveness of change, destruction is the inevitable fate of any desired or desirable state of affairs. To be sure, destruction is the inevitable fate of undesirable states of affairs as well. But this is cold comfort, given the natural desire of all living things for longed-for states of affairs to persist stably.

Human beings are peculiar, not in the fragility of what they value, since this is true for anything which desires, but in our superior awareness of this fact. One human lifetime is sufficient to notice and generalize about the operations of destruction. And even if it were not, the human capacity to communicate would allow human beings to draw upon the experiences of others. Again, this is most obvious with death, but is not limited to it. Thus, human beings are confronted with a unique dilemma. Like other living things, we strive to realize desired states of affairs, and yet these are threatened by destruction. Unlike other living things (as far as we know) we are aware of the ultimate futility of this striving, insofar as it aims at the attainment and preservation of what cannot last.

Knowing this, human beings are uniquely troubled animals. The ability to continue to strive depends upon our ability artificially to create the sort of obliviousness that comes naturally to other animals. In short, we need to be 'in denial' to be able to continue to be at all. The same imaginative capacities that make us so adaptable also enable us to envision the futility of our efforts. The crux of the human problem has to do with the mutability of the things we value and our ability to envision this imaginatively. But, if instead of imagining the ways in which the world necessarily thwarts our wishes, we were to imagine the world in a quite different way, we might restore our confidence in life and our willingness to act. The solution, then, is to imagine that instead of one world, pervaded with 'becoming' and destruction, there are really two worlds: a world of 'becoming' and a world of 'being'. We envision this latter world as a world of permanence.

Clearly the mere fact, if it is a fact, that there is a world of permanence, stasis and immutability will have no importance if nothing that we value subsists within that world of being, and everything we value is still in the world of becoming. But if we can also imagine that what we value subsists in the world of being, we can imagine value preserved. Once we hit upon this solution, it will seem inadequate to locate only some of what we value in the world of being and some in the world of becoming. For whatever we leave behind is still vulnerable and our ontological condition is not as good as it could be. This places pressure on the human imagination to relocate everything we value in the world of being and to downgrade the world of becoming to worthlessness. If all things in the world of becoming are worthless, their destruction is a matter of complete indifference; if everything we value is safely harboured in the world of being, our satisfaction, at least in our imagination, will be perfect.

Since this imaginative gambit is fundamentally false and flies in the face of the genuine character of the world and the place of our needs and interests in it, we will still feel the pull of our tendency to value things in the world of becoming, and come to grief when they are destroyed. But we can come to regard this as something we should overcome. Perfect equanimity as a goal to strive for becomes something plausible, and failure to achieve it a shortcoming.

The most powerful way we achieve this realignment of our sense of our ontological situation is by rethinking the nature of appearance and reality. It is a common experience of human beings that we are occasionally misled by appearances, by false inferences drewn from the evidence the world presents us with. Being 'in the truth' is advantageous and to be striven for, at the very least as a means of realizing our other desires. (Nietzsche does not think that this is the only source of our interest in truth, but it is surely a component of it.) But striving to regard the world of becoming with indifference is difficult. It really is the only world there is and the only site for whatever satisfaction of our desires is possible. So striving to assign no value to that which is in the world of becoming and to assign all value to an imaginary world of being needs a 'boost', which it can receive from our quotidian desire not to be misled by appearances. For even from the perspective of the 'two-world picture', it certainly seems as if things we value exist in the world of becoming, that we rightly care about them and that they truly are vulnerable to destruction. One way to neutralize this tendency is to regard the entire world of becoming, the world given to us in experience, as an illusion, to take our tendency to regard it as real as a larger example of the propensity to make faulty inferences from the evidence the world presents us with. Following this line of thought, the world of becoming is seen as not only valueless, but as unreal, a mere deceptive appearance. By contrast, the world of being is conceived as a contrasting, hidden reality.

Though Nietzsche is broadly critical of the pattern of thought described above, it is important to realize two things. First, he regards this pattern of thought as quite general if not universal. Christianity is just one example of it, with its God, a hidden reality behind the world, the soul, a hidden reality behind the apparent body, and immortality, a hidden destination behind the deceptive appearance of bodily destruction. Other examples can be found in the history of almost all religions and are plentiful in the history of philosophy too. Second, Nietzsche's account is not one of a merely compensatory process; the world of being is not simply the opiate of the masses. For imagining it expresses a tremendous amount of 'artistic' creativity and opens the prospect for giving human life all sorts of reservoirs of hitherto unavailable meaningfulness. At the crudest level, it allows us to populate the cosmos with interesting gods whose activities give a human, intelligible face to otherwise random, meaningless occurrences, both good and bad. At the most sophisticated level, it licenses philosophical interpretations which do the same thing. But it also has its downside: to the extent that the world of becoming is given the rank of worthless illusion, it encourages us to neglect our needs, interests and desires, and to misdirect our powers away from their pursuit.

The 'two-world picture' is inherently unstable, however, given the way in which the appearance/reality and the valueless/valuable distinctions are aligned. It directs our interest in inquiry at the hidden, valuable, 'real' world. Though there are many premature efforts and failures, we eventually hit upon an effective way to do this: science. The more we learn about what the world is really like, the more demystified our conception of it becomes. At first, the desire to locate a valuable world elsewhere can use various strategies to fight a rearguard action. For example, there is the Kantian idea that the world investigated by science *is* the apparent world, thus leaving a hidden, valuable reality untouched by it. But the Kantian manoeuvre, with its associated critique of the powers of the intellect, is itself a part of a larger movement of turning our desire for truth in upon ourselves. Though Nietzsche does not explore this point in detail, several modern philosophers before Kant argued for a reflective account or 'critique' of our intellectual capacities, the better to use them in our pursuit of natural knowledge. But this very idea, coupled with a championing of natural-scientific modes of knowledge, makes it inevitable that eventually a scientific account of the psyche arises.

With a scientific account of the psyche, the underlying motivations of the 'two-world picture' are revealed. This has the effect of discrediting them and the picture, for they are rooted in psychological inadequacies. It is at this juncture that nihilism proper first emerges (though Nietzsche also uses the term to characterize features of the preceding stage). For given that we have located everything we value in a hidden world, and then come to see that this hidden world does not exist, we seem left only with the manifest world of becoming. But this history has changed our stance towards it: it is no longer a world in which our values are imperilled, but a world which we regard as essentially valueless. If it is the only world that there is, then nothing has any value at all. That is nihilism, and Nietzsche's organizing thought throughout his work is to try to understand this event, and to provide some sort of answer to it.

Staying in nihilism is intolerable. Conservative or reactionary responses, however, are clearly inadequate. If we return to the two-world picture, this is at the price of suppressing what we have already come to know about the world. This resolution is inherently unstable, since the two-world picture is linked to the 'will to truth', which culminates in its supercession, and trying to return to the original, troubled stance looks unstable as well, assuming no change in human nature. For this is only to restore the anxiety which naturally leads to the invention of the two-world picture in the first place. In Nietzsche's early works, he had suggested that the way to cope with the problematic nature of life was to veil it in aesthetically satisfying illusions, which are known to be illusions. Late Nietzsche sees this response as inadequate; he wants a resolution that will preserve the 'will to truth' rather than set limits on it. Thus something fundamentally new is required to overcome nihilism. Nietzsche's conviction that the problem is important and that he has provided the fundamentally new response it calls for accounts for his expansive claims for his own importance.

The beginning of this new approach lies in re-conceiving what it is that human beings value. Nietzsche sees the most basic human interest as the exercise of creativity, the exercise of the ability to transform those aspects of the world that impinge upon and restrain us. If so, then the longing for stasis that Nietzsche discerns in the first stage is symptomatic of a second-best solution. We want the products of our creative transformations preserved, but then want the process of 'work' to end once and for all. Unsurprisingly Nietzsche traces this attitude to exhaustion with the process of creative transformation, a feeling that we are not quite up to it. This exhaustion, not the fragility of what we value per se, is what is responsible for magical thinking that would imagine away creative struggle and process. Since the capacity to respond creatively to constantly changing circumstances admits of degree, Nietzsche feels justified in speaking of 'strength' and 'weakness' here.

If what we really want is to exercise our capacities for creative transformation on the world, we must reconsider how compatible with this a world of being would be. As Talking Heads put it, 'heaven is a place where nothing ever happens'. A world of perfect stasis might be a world in which some goods are indestructible, but the highest good, creative transformation, is impossible there. Creative transformation requires the destruction of existing configurations of the world in favour of new configurations. It turns out that a world of becoming is a condition of the possibility of our highest good after all. Once we realize that, we ought to celebrate the world as it is. We should accept that the instances of destruction that we might deplore (especially the unwinding of the products of our prior creative activity) are instances of a general feature of life necessary to the realization of our highest goods. We should therefore celebrate them also as signs of this general feature, even though they unravel those things that we care about. This 'tragic wisdom' of Nietzsche in some ways resembles that of his early phase, which is in part why he re-uses the term 'Dionysian' in his late works to characterize it. But it acquires a new, aggressive and elitist dimension as well. For not only should we celebrate the world and its destructive character, much in the same way as an athlete in competition must sometimes celebrate the possibility and actuality of losing as features of a game necessary to make the experience of winning available. The *capacity* to do this is a function of the individual's capacity for creative transformation itself. Embracing tragedy is symptomatic of strength, and magical thinking that denies life's tragic character is symptomatic of weakness. Though we might think that Nietzsche's praise of strength and disdain for weakness here are mere prejudices, and unattractive ones at that, it is important to see that he sees this stance as flowing directly from his assessment of creative transformation as the highest good. Not only do the attitudes and preferences of the 'weak' lose by their inadequate epistemic character; not only do they lose by their failure to connect with and support our highest interests; worse, the valorization of stasis and the de-valorization of flux make the realization of our highest interests more difficult, insofar as they contribute to the de-valorization of the conditions for their realization.

Nietzsche identifies the desire for creative transformation as our highest desire, because it is the desire to attain our highest interest. He calls this desire 'the will to power'. I have avoided this expression so far for two reasons. First, the 'power' terminology leads naturally to assumptions (not all of them wrong) about Nietzsche's attitude towards conflict, domination and exploitation that distract attention from his larger points about value and nihilism. Second, Nietzsche also believes that this desire has a surprising explanatory role to play in psychology. All our desires are in some sense expressions of the desire for 'power'. This claim is clearly independent of the claim that what we value most is power, or even the claim that we cannot help but value power most. If all desires are really desires for power, then that blocks the suggestion that we should value something else. Contemporary interpreters have struggled to make sense of this doctrine once it is interpreted as a claim within philosophy of action; however that discussion goes, we can still claim that creative transformation is our highest interest or concern and explore the implications of this claim for a response to nihilism. Third, the will to power doctrine is implicated in a broader explanatory project which Nietzsche said very little about in his published writings: that will to power is involved in all natural processes. Since this project is far less attractive to many contemporary readers, it is also best kept separate from his axiology. Finally, Nietzsche invokes the will to power doctrine in more narrowly philosophical contexts where it is bound to be controversial; for example, in claiming that the mind is best understood as similar to the Kantian experience-constructing subject, but that operations of synthesis are expressions of an attempt to 'overpower' sensory chaos and thereby 'overpower' a dangerous environmental milieu. Similarly, Nietzsche argues for a kind of panpsychism (that all natural processes have something akin to desires) that is linked to the concept of will to power, another line that contemporary readers are likely to find unattractive.

THE WILL TO POWER

The will to power appears in Nietzsche's published work primarily as a psychological and axiological doctrine, and these two roles are closely connected. As he says in *Antichrist*, 'What is good? Everything that heightens the feeling of power in man, the will to power, power itself. What is bad? Everything that is born of weakness. What is happiness? The feeling that power is growing, that resistance is overcome' (*A* §2). This dense declaration needs to be unpacked.

First, the expression 'will to power' itself needs to be clarified. The use of the word 'will' suggests some sort of relationship to action and choice. This conflicts not only with Nietzsche's apparent claims elsewhere that there is no such thing as free will, but that there is no faculty of agency either. (We could still think that there is something described by rational choice theory, but that its operations were deterministic.) Nietzsche's picture of the psyche as a bundle of conflicting and cooperating drives and affects seems incompatible with the idea of the self, or some part of the self, as a chooser. Though it may be that choosing supervenes on these underlying processes in some sense, I think that the better interpretation is to note that 'will' here (the German verb 'wollen') is akin to the English word 'want'. Nietzsche is neither committed to nor playing a rhetorical game with the concept of choice here. His concern is with 'the desire for power'.

But what is 'power'? The German word here is 'Macht', which is cognate with the English word 'make'. So it may be helpful here to consider the will to power as a desire to make (something). This links the expression both to creativity, as discussed above, and to the earthier political connotations of 'power'. The artist makes objects, texts, performances. The politician makes people do things. The first common denominator here is causal efficacy: I cannot make anything happen without being a cause of effects. It is true that Nietzsche elsewhere criticizes the concept of causality, but I propose that we set this aside by distinguishing between the idea of causality that involves lawful sequence and the idea of causality as a power of making. Though Hume famously criticizes both notions, Nietzsche seems not to follow Hume in criticizing the notion of causality as a power to bring about changes in the world, for those passages in the late writings which contain critical discussions related to causality seem primarily to address the shortcomings of our psychological propensities in generating adequate causal explanations. It is our explanatory habits and practices which are being criticized, not the very idea of causation. Indeed, Nietzsche seems to be saying that the problem with these psychological propensities is that they *cause* us to produce faulty explanations which fail to disclose the real causes.

The idea of causal efficacy, however, is too thin to support the various things that Nietzsche says about power. In the case of the paradigmatic billiard ball colliding with another billiard ball and knocking it into a pocket, it seems a mere metaphor to say that the first ball exercises power over the other. This seems to speak against any attempt to characterize power as nothing more than causal efficacy. Some interpreters suggest that the notion of the will to power is best understood as a dispositional concept, but it seems that causality is already in part a dispositional concept.[1] If we are to avoid a collapse of the notion of power into the notion of causality, something more than the disposition to bring about effects is needed. At the very least, some subset of the kinds of effects that causes can have needs to be identified. Other interpreters have focused on the notion of resistance to the cause which brings about the effect, stressing that power involves the overcoming of resistance.[2] This seems to add something extra to the notion of causality, since we can imagine causal forces which operate without any resistance at all, at least in very simple hypothetical scenarios. But while it seems that the psychological pursuit of power is usually carried out in the teeth of countervailing resistance, it seems just as possible that a person with a certain quantum of power could strive for a lower amount of power, also in the teeth of resistance. Suicide, for example, is not easily accomplished. If we define power as the overcoming of resistance, then it seems that the suicide is by definition more powerful once dead, simply because of the difficulty in achieving self-destruction. Not that power is extraneous to many suicides: the power involved may express itself in making an impression upon survivors, or taking one's own pain in hand and ending it. But we can imagine at least the possibility of someone who makes death their primary goal and achieves it in the face of obstacles. We would not say that for that reason alone the person is more powerful than before.

Similarly, it seems that we can imagine power without resistance. If there were such a thing as magical powers, we can imagine humdrum instances of, for example, political power, being achieved effortlessly. Perhaps such results, coming too easily, will not be very satisfying, but it would be perverse to say that as the satisfaction drops towards zero, the magician approximates powerlessness.

Finally, it seems that one can have power without always exercising it, and this suggests that there is a counterfactual dimension to power: it is not merely about what I make happen, but about what I *could* make happen. That seems to point us back to the notion of power as a dispositional property. It seems better, though, to characterize this as an ability rather than as a disposition; breakability is a dispositional property, but it would be odd to describe this as a *power*. By contrast, when we say that a certain animal species has night vision, it is not that if it were night the animal would see, but that it is *able* to see at night.[3]

The suggestion, then, is that to have power is to have abilities, and that abilities are more than mere causal properties: I have the causal property of dissolving in acid, but this is not one of my abilities. Interestingly, however, the possession of abilities is a separate matter from that of agency and mentality. A bacterium has the ability to digest food, but (unless bacteria are very different from our current understanding) has no desires at all. Does having an ability require at least being alive? It would appear not: some automobiles have the ability to accelerate from zero to sixty miles per hour in ten seconds, while others lack that ability. By contrast, an automobile's disposition to explode on impact, say, because its gas tank is near the front, is not an ability. It is, in computer parlance, a bug, not a feature. Thus it would appear that having abilities cuts across both the mental/non-mental divide and the living/non-living divide, without being equivalent to having a causal property. It does, however, entail having some causal properties.

In those cases where we describe something as having an ability, it seems that we are applying some sort of (non-moral) normative conception. Abilities, unlike causal propensities, can succeed or fail in their exercise. But success is an inherently normative notion. Eyes are supposed to see, which is why night vision is an ability; cars are supposed to transport passengers, which is why a certain maximum acceleration is an ability. Cars are not supposed to explode, so this is not an ability; we would not say that a car *succeeded* in exploding. Though it is tempting to say that the 'supposed to' here is mind-dependent (it is only by virtue of 'ascribed intentionality' that a car is supposed to transport people), this is a tendency I think we should resist. It makes perfect sense to say that eyes are supposed to see, and yet unless we regard them as divinely manufactured, making the normativity involved depend upon intentions will have the consequence that only animals capable of forming intentions to use their eyes for vision could be said to have eyes that are supposed to see. That seems counterintuitive.

Suppose, then, that having power is having abilities. It would appear that I cannot have power unless there are some activities or processes that have a better or worse way of playing themselves out. That means that the notion of power is itself already a normative notion. Thus it should not surprise us when we see Nietzsche characterizing power in terms of 'health' or success, and attributing it not only to human beings, but (at least in the unpublished notes) to non-human things as well, typically living things. (I will return momentarily to the question of why Nietzsche sometimes ascribes will to power to inanimate things which are not artefacts.) This in part explains why Nietzsche thinks that showing the relationship between power and something else has normative force for an addressee: power *is* good. This reading suggests grounds for thinking that Nietzsche is some sort of axiological (though not necessarily a moral) realist.

Is there anything good which is not an ability or bears the appropriate relationship to an ability? Impediments to the exercise of an ability are on the face of it bad (unless they help to strengthen the ability). The absence of such an impediment is a derivative good. Also, while a particular animal's night vision is good in one sense and its deliciousness is good in another, this is a derivative, relative good for the predator, not the prey. One might argue that what it is relative to is the phenomenal quality that the predator experiences while feeding (the pleasure, or perhaps the pleasure as an inseparable constituent of the specific phenomenal taste). But here too, looking at the biological design of the predator, the deliciousness of the prey appears to be about the successful exercise of its nutrition-detection and motivational equipment. It is hard to say that this is itself a good thing if, by some strange contingency, the predator had been modified so that it experiences pleasure when eating poison. For this reason, I am tempted to say that the good of the deliciousness of the prey is a derivative of the successful exercise of the predator's nutrition-obtaining abilities.

Abilities have other interesting characteristics beyond admitting of success or failure in their exercise. First, abilities can improve (or decline) over time. The clock speed of digital computers has increased over time, and we rightly and straightforwardly characterize this as an increase in computational power. So not only is it a good thing to have abilities, and a good thing to exercise them successfully (since I can have an ability but fail to exercise it for contingent reasons), but it is a good thing for one's abilities to increase in scope or intensity. I have the ability to run, but it would be good if I could run faster. Furthermore, some abilities are also meta-abilities, the ability to acquire an ability. Learning, for example, is an ability, but it is an ability to acquire further abilities. I have the ability to solve differential equations, but this ability is the result of the successful exercise of my ability to learn mathematical techniques. So not only is it good to have abilities and to exercise them successfully, it is also good to have and successfully exercise the ability to acquire and improve other abilities. Though this point is not immediately obvious, I think that these phenomena also cut across the living/non-living and mental/non-mental distinctions; there are self-modifying computer programmes which could be described in these terms.

Nonetheless, Nietzsche does not merely say that power is good, but that the will to power is good. At the very least, 'will' implies the presence of desires. Nietzsche also seems to think that 'will' involves something like trying or striving. This may be nothing more than saying that in the ordinary case, having a desire typically involves striving to satisfy it, though in 'degenerate' cases one can have a desire without striving. For example, I would strive to satisfy a particular desire, but see no available means of doing so, or know that such striving faces insuperable difficulties. I still have the desire in these cases, but inertly. That said, I think that such cases will still involve striving in some counterfactual sense: it would be odd to say that I have a desire which is not in conflict with any other desire and which is not impeded (or which I do not believe to be impeded) and yet make no move towards its satisfaction.

But however we characterize 'will' here, it seems inescapable that it involves a psychological component. Now why is it good to have a desire to have abilities? It is tempting to think that the normativity here enters the picture entirely by virtue of the desire itself, and that in the absence of desire there can be no normativity. On such a view, the good just *is* desire satisfaction. But we saw above that there is normativity built into the very idea of having abilities, and that abilities do not require the presence of psychological properties at all. Furthermore, on the account we are developing, the value of a desire for abilities depends on the value of having abilities. In the normal case, having a desire involves striving, and having a desire for a particular ability makes it more likely that I will come to have it.

But there is a problem. We said that normativity is 'built into' the notion of an ability, that abilities make no sense unless certain activities constitute their successful or failed exercise. But that kind of normativity does not tell us why it is good to have an ability in the first place, and hence why we should want to have one. To be sure, if I already have an ability that admits of improvement, and I desire the *improvement* of the ability, having that desire (given striving) makes it more likely that the ability will improve, and thus be exercised more successfully more often. Also, the successful exercise of a meta-ability will spawn subordinate abilities. But why have any abilities at all? Since abilities open the counter-normative possibility of their failed exercise, would it not make just as much sense to strive not to have abilities, the better to avoid failure? You cannot lose if you do not play.

This gets us close to the heart of Nietzsche's conception: the point of having abilities at all. It is not that having abilities is good because we better satisfy our desires, for two reasons.[4] First, we saw that the successful exercise of an ability is good for non-psychological or even non-living systems. Second, to roast a very old chestnut, it is far from clear that the satisfaction of desires is intrinsically good. On many contemporary accounts of rational choice, an action is the joint product of my beliefs and desires, where both of these have propositional content, bear inferential relations to each other, and so on. On this conception, a desire is like a sentence in the head, in the imperative mood. Suppose that I have a box on my desk filled with slips of paper, and every time I remove one I see inscribed on it some arbitrary command to bring about some state of affairs. Is there any reason, apart from anything else, why it is good for me to carry out the command? Is this deficiency remedied if I can install the box inside my head?

If we focus on the non-psychological biological context, abilities seem to have value because of some state of affairs they bring about when successfully exercised. It is tempting to say that in the end, the successful exercise of biological abilities leads either directly or indirectly to the preservation of the creature. Notoriously, Nietzsche rejects this. A contemporary picture is that 'the name of the game' is differential reproductive success. This is some improvement on the self-preservation account, because reproduction does not in the main enhance my prospects of self-preservation, whereas self-preservation for a time and up to a point enhances my prospects of differential reproductive success. Interestingly, Nietzsche (in his unpublished notes) sees reproduction as admitting of a 'power analysis'. In Nietzsche's philosophical biology, nutrition and growth are the clearest instances of the will to power at work: the organism incorporates matter from the environment and transforms it into its own body, not only preserving it but allowing it to expand by growth. Reproduction is initially difficult to see on this model, since it does nothing immediately obvious for the parent. But we can regard reproduction as just like nutrition and growth, if we regard a population of organisms of a common type as if it were a single organism. When 'cells' of this 'organism' replicate, the whole grows and spreads. Since many individual organisms are themselves multi-celled, we can regard the distinction between growth and reproduction as relative to whatever perspective we adopt, whether we regard something as an individual or as part of a greater whole.

But why is 'growing and spreading' good? Ultimately, I can see no other reason than that the thing growing and spreading brings about creative transformations in the world. But does this not bring us right back where we started? If transformation of the world is the bedrock good, it might seem that we are endorsing the initial hypothesis that power collapses into causal efficacy.

A digression to Schopenhauer's views may be helpful here. Recall that Schopenhauer regarded the thing-in-itself as 'will' or undifferentiated, objectless, constant, pointless desiring and striving. But part of his view is that this fact about the thing-in-itself is manifested in the phenomenal world, not just as various psychological phenomena, but at the biological level as well. The manifestation of this phenomenally is competition. Competition for Schopenhauer is only partly explained by the character of the thing-in-itself, for in order for the thing-in-itself to manifest itself phenomenally, it must not only become empirical data to be organized by a Kantian subject; it must also take some definite (Platonic) form. So striving in the world is always a striving to maintain something as the kind of thing that it is. This is why objectless desire becomes the desire for self-preservation; on the phenomenal level, what I desire is the continuation of myself as a particular form. This enables Schopenhauer to make sense of reproduction as well, because while reproduction seems altruistic, the relationship between it, sexuality and strong desire points the other way. It looks like it should have something to do with the will rather than the rejection of the will. This connection becomes clear if we think of reproduction as the bringing about of another instance of the same form that we ourselves embody. Thus for Schopenhauer, egoistic, sexual and parental desires are of a kind after all: they all involve a striving to make the world reflect more of the form that I (also) am. And clearly this is far more specific than merely bringing about lots of changes in the world.

Fragments of these notions seem to be at work in Nietzsche as well. In the early Nietzsche, the suggestion that we ought to work towards creating the genius even if we ourselves do not become geniuses is very difficult to make sense of unless we assume that there is something intrinsically valuable about the genius. No desire-satisfaction account of value can do justice to this feature of the early Nietzsche's thought, for Nietzsche could at most claim that if we adopted this peculiar desire, it would be good to set about trying to satisfy it. He seems instead to be saying that we should want there to be geniuses. From a Schopenhauerian perspective, however, this makes perfect sense. Everything in the phenomenal world is an instance of some Platonic Form, and these Forms constitute a hierarchy. Thus we would expect that human beings would rank high, and that extraordinary human beings would rank highest *objectively*. The problem is that early Nietzsche seems to be committed to there being no such things as Platonic Forms. Instead of suggesting that this is a fault in our interpretation, I will go out on a 'principle of charity' limb and propose that there is an incoherence in the early Nietzsche's account of value: He wants to have his Platonic cake and nominalistically to eat it too.

Oddly, this same problem seems to reappear in the late Nietzsche as well. For unless the idea of creative transformation is to collapse into the idea of being a cause, I see no way to make sense of it other than by thinking of it as being the cause of specific forms. We do not think, and Nietzsche would not think, that destroying the world with, say, nuclear weapons would make one the most powerful being in the world, though this would certainly involve bringing about very far-reaching effects. By contrast, Nietzsche does seem to want to say that the growing and reproducing organism achieves and expresses power as it creatively transforms its world. But what makes this a transformation is the replacement of one form (the form of rabbit) into another (the form of coyote).

But doesn't every causal impact involve changing something from one form into another in some sense? Two possibilities suggest themselves here. One is that a creative transformation is good if it converts a 'lower' form into a 'higher' form. This would give us an intrinsicist account of the value of creative transformation. We could speak here of degrees of organization, complexity, richness and so on. Another possibility is that a creative transformation is good if it converts an alien form into my own form. This would give us a relationalist account of the value of creative transformation. Nietzsche's texts would appear to support either reading. On the one hand, he writes throughout his authorship of the importance of 'enhancing the type man' as if this were simply something one should do. On the other hand, towards the end of his writing life he wrote increasingly of humanity as clay in his own artist's hands, as if transforming people into his own image was what mattered. My question here is: do either of these notions make sense without something akin to Platonic Forms playing some sort of role? If that is taken as a rhetorical question, the next question becomes: is Nietzsche's apparent reliance on Platonism a 'mask' to conceal and facilitate the furtherance of his own essentially arbitrary agenda? Or is it a deep mistake, an implicit reliance on precisely that which he thinks himself overturning? For when we began our account of nihilism, we had Nietzsche characterizing the invention of the two-world picture as a fantasy born of weakness. Platonism is his most central example. But while Platonism does arguably involve commitment to the two-world picture, this only bears on two features of Platonism: the separateness of Forms from the world of concrete individuals, and the permanence of the Forms in their separate world. Certainly we can modify Platonism in the first aspect; this would be Aristotelianism. But once the Forms are brought down to earth, it seems that the permanence objection falls away, for an Aristotelian need not be committed to the claim that any concrete individual permanently embodies an Aristotelian essence. To be sure, Aristotle's conception of essence, linked as it is to the notion of species, entails that a living thing will embody the same essence over the course of its life, and this might be regarded as a manifestation of the yearning for permanence. I see no reason why Nietzsche would need to follow Aristotle in either of these ways, for an essence could be re-conceived as a particular configuration, unique to an individual and even unique to a time-slice of the individual.

If the preceding account is in the main correct, then we can set aside several rival suggestions for understanding the will to power.

First, on the 'abilities' and creative transformation account of power, it is not necessary to regard power as the capacity to satisfy desires, thus leading to the suggestion that the will to power is a desire to have the capacity to satisfy desires. For as we saw, abilities need not be restricted to minds, though the desire for abilities would be. Second, the suggestion that the will to power essentially involves the overcoming of resistance, something mentioned in the *Antichrist* axiology, can be seen as derivative and not fundamental. For the exercise of abilities does not strictly require that there be any resistance to them, nor does the presence and subsequent dissolution of resistance necessarily imply the presence and exercise of an ability. Nonetheless, resistance and its overcoming will be a contingently widespread phenomenon given the plurality of systems exercising their abilities and bringing about creative transformations, as long as these various systems are at cross-purposes. For even if (contrary to fact) systems of a certain kind could exercise their abilities effortlessly in the absence of competition, the goodness of increasing one's abilities will eventually expand one's sphere of action until it intersects that of some differently constituted system, and cross-purposes are bound to arise. Of course, cooperation can also be the outcome of such an intersection. Nietzsche seems to think that cooperation will always have a dimension of subordination to it and, to be sure, if one of the systems is more powerful than the other, that may prove to be the case. But this also seems to be a contingent feature of cooperation: if the two systems are roughly equal in power when they 'collide' I see no reason why the outcome could not be cooperation and symbiosis. Nietzsche seems to see this too, though he would stress that the new, larger 'confederation' then proceeds to expand into other alien spheres. Finally, the notion that power involves in some essential sense control over something also seems a derivative rather than a fundamental phenomenon. When an artist imposes a form on some materials, she exercises control in two ways: first, in the handling and shaping of the material, and second in the continuing embodiment of the artist's imposed form on the object after it is completed. This latter kind of control seems to be control in an extended or attenuated sense. We speak of control, typically, in cases where ongoing maintenance activity is required. However, in a world of becoming and plurality, no creative transformation is maximally successful unless ongoing activities are performed, for it will inevitably unwind and fall prey to competing agendas. Maximal creativity requires continual activity, and thus control.

The remaining comments Nietzsche makes in the *Antichrist* axiology can be dealt with briefly. Nietzsche also says that happiness is the feeling that power is increasing, and that it is a good. We can imagine a kind of hedonist gloss on this, in which the ultimate good is happiness as a certain quality of feeling, and that this feeling is brought about by an increase in power. This, however, does not seem to be Nietzsche's intention. He writes elsewhere of 'narcotics', certain kinds of aesthetic and moral experiences, as creating a dangerously illusory experience of power. This suggests two things. First, though we value the feeling of power, it is not the bedrock source of value. If it were, an illusory feeling of power would be just as good as the real thing. The standard strategy used by hedonists and desire-satisfaction subjectivists is to say that what makes such experiences bad is their lack of fertility for bringing about further such experiences. However, I see no textual warrant for imposing this kind of view on Nietzsche. If that is right, then Nietzsche is only claiming that happiness (which equals the feeling that power is increasing) has derivative value as a *sign* that power is increasing. Second, the mere existence of 'narcotics' here shows that the feeling of power increasing is not invariably associated with it actually increasing. Striving for happiness, however conceived, cannot therefore be our most valuable pursuit. As Zarathustra says 'am I concerned with my happiness? I am concerned with my work' (*Z* IV, §20).

'AND NOTHING ELSE BESIDES!'

The account we have provided above is neither a narrowly psychological nor a broadly metaphysical one. We have focused most of our attention on living things (and, occasionally, on machines which resemble them in certain respects). In the unpublished writings, Nietzsche seems to hold the much stronger view that everything is will to power. Setting aside the difficulties that this may present as an apparently metaphysical doctrine in some tension with Nietzsche's perspectivism and repudiation of the idea of the thing-in-itself, there is still some question as to how we should understand these unpublished notes, and whether they shed any light on Nietzsche's 'official' views.

In the unpublished notes, Nietzsche not only claims that the world is will to power 'and nothing else besides!' (*WP* §1067), but makes use of this notion in many explanatory contexts, physical, biological, psychological and sociological. Many interpreters try to set these notes aside because Nietzsche chose not to publish them, and call attention to the fact that *The Will to Power* as we currently have it is an editorial confection supervised by his sister, who was not known for having an especially deep understanding of his thought. However, the will to power is present in his published writings as well. As we saw, it is central to his late axiological theory in *Antichrist*. Furthermore, the doctrine that at least 'life' is will to power is prominently displayed in *Zarathustra*. Finally, almost no one denies that it at least plays a role in psychological explanation in the published works. The question here is whether there is any sense in which Nietzsche uses the concept 'metaphysically', however that term is to be understood. Arguably he does, in *Beyond Good and Evil* section 36, in which he offers an argument whose conclusion is that '[t]he world viewed from inside, the world defined and determined according to its "intelligible character" – it would be "will to power" and nothing else – ' (*BGE* §36).

The first question this passage presents us with is whether Nietzsche takes it seriously. Arguably, the mere fact that it is published and was written late in his career suggests that he does. However, the argument is presented as resting on a supposition, which may suggest that he is not really committed to the conclusion.[5] That would be premature, for an argument resting on a supposition is nothing other than an instance of *modus ponens*, and the mere fact of using such a valid argument form is not generally thought to discredit the conclusion. What it does do is make the conclusion (assuming the argument is valid) depend upon the truth of the antecedent. Though there are indications that Nietzsche rejects the 'suppositions' in the argument, these indications are misleading.

First, to assess this argument, we have to know what exactly the conclusion of the argument is supposed to be. The claim that the world is will to power is glossed as 'all efficient force univocally [is] will to power'. Nietzsche seems to be assuming here that an adequate account of the world could be given that appeals only to efficient causality. One might think from various other things Nietzsche says that this alone impugns the argument, for Nietzsche also criticizes our conception of causality. However, the criticisms that Nietzsche offers are directed primarily at the notion of causal lawfulness. Though he borrows from Kant an account of causal lawfulness that involves the notion that causal laws are the product of some sort of mental construction, he does not regard this notion as a legitimate condition of experience so much as a useful fiction. He even goes so far as to say that this fiction is not only useful for orientating ourselves in the world, but plays a more questionable role in allowing us to escape from feelings of responsibility, and to project our democratic (rule of law) values on nature. Yet what makes it fictitious is not the idea that the natural order is necessary, for he affirms this (*BGE* §22). So in what sense is it improper to say that there are causal laws? It is not just because there is a psychological explanation for our arriving at the notion, however questionable the motivations cited in that explanation. That would be to commit a genetic fallacy. Rather, I think Nietzsche's opposition to the concept of causal law rests, not on a rejection of either the concept of necessity or the concept of efficient force, but on the *generality* of natural law claims. It is Nietzsche's suspicion that no two processes, events or entities are sufficiently alike to warrant their subsumption under a higher-level concept. We should regard such subsumption as a merely pragmatic affair, legitimate to the extent that it is useful, but not implying anything about the real natures of the things subsumed. Nietzsche also seems to be suspicious of our attempts to circumscribe an individual item and distinguish it from the larger context in which it is embedded. Such boundaries in thought are also of no more than pragmatic significance. But even if we cannot take boundaries or similarities between concrete items seriously, even if there are no Aristotelian substances or Platonic Forms, this is still compatible with the claim that items have a causal impact on other items, and that all events are causally necessary.

What about claims that Nietzsche sometimes makes to the effect that the very idea of efficient causation is a projection? He argues in *Twilight* that we misinterpret the phenomenology of action as involving an actor, 'the will' or 'the ego', and a separable action, a 'doing'. Taking that as our paradigm of a causal relation, we imagine that the world outside us should be similarly conceived. His objection is that we infer from a false belief about agency to a belief that other things are similar. But agency is not as we conceive it;

somewhat hyperbolically, he says 'there are no mental causes at all' (*TI* VI, §3). However, his use of 'mental' here refers to 'a surface phenomenon – of consciousness', that is, an object of introspection, which 'cover[s] up the antecedents of the deeds'. But what does this mean, 'antecedents'? If there are no 'causal' connections between the real antecedents and the real consequents, then the antecedents of a deed are strictly irrelevant to it, indicating nothing other than temporal priority, and there is nothing being covered up that is important to explanation. Indeed, Nietzsche cautions us that our misinterpretation of introspective evidence 'inhibits any investigation into the *real* cause' (*TI* VI, §4, emphasis mine). This point is made especially clear when Nietzsche says that 'Will [is] a commanding: but insofar as underlying the conscious act there is an unconscious one, we need to think of this too as effective' (*KGW* VII, vol. 2, pp. 109–10).

The best explanation of such passages is that Nietzsche is rejecting the reification of the agent as distinct from its acts, not that he is rejecting causal explanation altogether. For the phenomenology of agency does, at least sometimes, present us with the impression of something distinct that deliberates, culminating in a decision, followed by an action. If this impression is misleading, it is not because the efficacy of one complex configuration of forces in realizing a later complex configuration of forces is in question. Rather, it is the distinctness of an entity from its activity and the later configuration that arises out of it that is being questioned. I suggest, therefore, that we read such passages as rejecting 'cause *and* effect', but not as rejecting 'efficient force'.

Now in the argument of *Beyond Good and Evil* §36, Nietzsche does rely on 'our faith in' the 'causality of the will' whereas in sections 19 and 21, he criticizes our conception of the causality of the will. But the criticism in section 19 does not deny that there is something which the expression 'causality of the will' refers to. Rather, he insists, contrary to 'popular prejudice', that 'willing [is] above all something complicated' (*BGE* §19). Once we become clear about the complex forces, affects and processes at work that lead to what presents itself to consciousness as deliberation, decision and action, 'a philosopher should claim the right to include willing as such within the sphere of ... the doctrine of the relations of supremacy under which the phenomenon of "life" comes to be' (ibid).

In section 21, the initial focus is on the *freedom* of the will, not whether 'willing' occurs; Nietzsche denies that we have radical free will. To be sure, Nietzsche then proceeds to criticize determinism as well. First, he rejects 'mechanistic doltishness', because it reifies and distinguishes too sharply between cause and effect as if these were separable items, regards the bringing about aspect of causation in terms of the crudest of these we are acquainted with ('press and push'), and because 'rule of law' is a projection. None of this commits Nietzsche to denying that *bringing about* occurs. Second, he criticizes those who experience causal connection (which Nietzsche places in scare-quotes, thus indicating that he is referring to something, but that it is misleadingly named), as 'constraint, need, compulsion to obey, pressure, and unfreedom' (*BGE* §21). In short, he repudiates those who conceive of free will as a certain desirable faculty which we happen to lack. 'The "unfree will" is mythology; in real life it is only a matter of strong and weak wills' (ibid). Yet what Nietzsche says here is how things are 'in real life'. This makes little sense unless we suppose that there are such things as wills (whatever they are) which can be 'strong'. Elsewhere, he speaks of 'commanding and obeying' (*BGE* §19). I can attach no sense to the idea of a commander being strong in this context unless the commander is obeyed, and that commanding *brought about* the obedience.

So it seems that Nietzsche does not really reject either the idea of efficient causation or the idea of willing; he merely regards them as misunderstood. If that is right, then when Nietzsche appeals to our 'faith in the causality of the will' we need not regard this as facetious, but rather as a kind of shorthand for the much more complex analyses of these notions he offers elsewhere – indeed, that he offers but a few pages before. With this in mind, let us return to the argument of section 36.

The argument is meant to identify 'all efficient force' with 'will to power'. The first premise is that we have desires and passions. This is said to be (for the purposes of the argument) 'given', which may lead the contemporary reader to think of the 'myth of the given' and dismiss the argument out of hand.[6] However, Nietzsche is not committed here to foundationalism; he is not claiming that the fact that there are desires and passions is known with certainty or that the proposition is incorrigible. Rather, as the *modus ponens* form of the argument is meant to show, Nietzsche wants to put the burden on his opponent of rejecting the startling conclusion, and thus being forced, *modus tollens*, to deny that we have desires and passions at all. This is consistent with Nietzsche seeing the discussion as a hypothesis, an interpretation. Similarly, Nietzsche is not appealing to the peculiarly diaphanous character of consciousness or the coextensiveness of consciousness and mentality (which he elsewhere denies) to support such incorrigibility. For even if the claim that we have desires is not incorrigible and is not based on the evidence of a diaphanous consciousness, denying it will surely put Nietzsche's opponent in a tight spot. 'What, you mean we don't have desires?' An eliminative materialist could surely take such a line and accept the outcome of inferring *modus tollens* instead of *modus ponens*. But that would put the eliminative materialist in a tight spot indeed, for then the burden would be on her to explain where the misleading appearance that we have desires comes from.

Nietzsche's argument here could be seen as a more specific form of an argument from the existence of qualia. One need not argue that the claim that we have qualia is incorrigible, or that we have incorrigible knowledge of what our qualia are like. But it *seems* as if we have them, and if certain consequences follow from that which an eliminative materialist finds unwelcome, the eliminative materialist is under the obligation of explaining away the appearance of qualia; mere dogged denial will not do.

Nietzsche announces that his intention is in some way to explain 'the so-called mechanistic (or "material") world' in terms of these desire-qualia. He quickly points out that he does not mean to do this in the same way that 'Berkeley and Schopenhauer' (*BGE* §36) did. This could be read to suggest that Nietzsche is repudiating the claim that qualia exist at all. That suggestion is inapposite, for the conclusion of the argument is that Nietzsche's 'idealism' involves identifying efficient force with desire. Berkeley's and Schopenhauer's idealistic attitude to the material world was to regard it phenomenalistically, as a logical construction from sensations. This is enough to distinguish Nietzsche's from Berkeley's strategy.

Nietzsche signals why it is that he wants to make sure that the reader does not confuse him with Berkeley. '[T]he so-called mechanistic (or "material") world ... hold[s] the same rank of reality as our affect'. He seems to think that phenomenalism, regarding physical objects as either episodes within consciousness or as unrealized possibilities of such episodes, in some sense reduces the material world to a lower rank than that of our affect. Initially, it is difficult to see why: our affects might be thought to be no more or less episodes within consciousness as perceptual states. I suspect that Nietzsche has two things in the back of his mind here. First, the phenomenalist analysis – though Berkeley presents it as common sense – is deeply counterintuitive, for common sense regards these 'possibilities of perception' as independent, self-standing objects which resist both our imagination and our will. With this conception in mind, the thought that these items are more akin to paradigmatically mind-dependent items like dreams, hallucinations, episodes of imagination and so on, seems to degrade them to something both less substantial and less resistant to our purposes than they really are, while re-conceiving the self as a narcissistic, quasi-solipsistic centre of things. Whatever the metaphysical status of the physical for Nietzsche, it seems that he wants to retain some sense of its independence and resistance. This consideration is strengthened in light of the fact that for a phenomenalist, the body too must be one of these 'appearances' and thus seems to lose much of the importance we would otherwise assign to it.

It might be thought that such echoes of the pernicious two-world picture are out of place here, given that Berkeley completely rejects the idea of the physical object as something distinct from its appearances. But that leads to our second point: for Berkeley there is still something more substantial than these appearances: the minds or souls in which they inhere as properties or to which they are presented as phenomenal objects. Clearly the rhetorical force of Berkeley's position is 'bodies are not real; only souls are real'. Nietzsche, by contrast, rejects the simplicity and substantiality of the soul, and is suspicious of both the 'subject-object' and 'substance-property' models of the self, favouring instead a kind of bundle theory.

With these obstacles out of the way, we can see our way clear to a reconstruction of the argument. It appears that we have desire-qualia, and that desire-qualia play a role in efficient causal (albeit non-lawful, see above) processes bringing about changes in our (provisionally regarded as non-mental) environment. It also appears that efficient causal processes occur between items in our (provisionally regarded as non-mental) environment. If we suppose that the former are mental causes of physical effects, and the latter are physical causes of physical effects, then there are two basic kinds of causation, because there are two different kinds of item: causation between heterogeneous spheres and causation within homogeneous spheres. It is not parsimonious to assume two different kinds of item and two different kinds of causation if one will do. But the problem (essentially the mind-body problem as it arises from Cartesian assumptions) is more than just a matter of parsimony, as important as that might be. For we cannot really understand how mental causes can bring about non-mental effects at all. ' "Will", of course, can affect only "will" – and not "matter" (not "nerves," for example)'. Though Nietzsche does not say so, presumably the same incomprehensibility attaches to non-mental causes bringing about mental effects. Both action and perception become a mystery. Thus Cartesianism commits one to a metaphysics that makes no intuitive sense.

One possible response to this, perhaps the most popular response, is to adopt some form of materialism. This solves the problem of interaction and the problem of parsimony. But it leaves us with a profound violation of our most pervasive and deeply rooted experience, that of bringing about physical change through experienced desire. The materialist as Nietzsche conceives him must insist that desire-qualia do not exist at all, or else that they can be reduced without residue to blind, physicalistic processes. Nietzsche denies that such a reduction is conceivable. 'Physical explanation, which is a symbolization of the world by means of sensation and thought, can in itself never account for the origin of sensation and thought; rather physics must construe the world of feeling consistently as lacking feeling and aim – right up to the highest human being' (WP §562). Eliminativism, on the other hand, by rejecting phenomenology altogether, comes into conflict with our own interest in intelligibility. Any rival interpretation which preserves such a crucial aspect of our experience, showing how it fits seamlessly into the natural world as conceived by the natural scientist, while being competitive with the parsimony and explanatory power of the physicalist account, will be the stronger interpretation.

In any case, Nietzsche thinks that materialism suffers from its own difficulties. First, the materialist is committed to the existence of matter and force. However, Nietzsche takes it that matter can be eliminated in favour of repulsive force, leaving only an ontology of force. But what understanding do we have of what force is? There are only two possibilities. Either the concept of force is an artefact of the use of the concept of causal law, or it is derived from our first-person experience of 'forcing' things to happen. The first approach, which sees causal explanation as essentially a matter of lawful or necessary regularity, falls afoul of Nietzsche's complaint that there are no event types and hence no regularities in the relevant sense at all. Thus if we are to speak of causal explanation, we will have to appeal to the notion of force *simpliciter*, and we have to get this notion from somewhere. If our paradigmatic notion of force is from the first-person setting, then the materialist is ill-advised to ignore it. While it may make sense to protest against anthropomorphizing in our understanding of nature, it makes less sense to be troubled by anthropomorphizing our understanding of ourselves. Of course we could try to do science without either the concept of force or the concept of causal law; this, I take it, is Hume's position, and it is one that Nietzsche might have said more about.

Nietzsche's startling proposal, then, is that desire-qualia are not inexplicable danglers: our physical bodies are *composed of* desire-qualia. To put it another way, Nietzsche is adapting Schopenhauer's claim that we know the thing-in-itself is will by introspection, but without the dubious appeal to the distinction between Kantian phenomena and Kantian things-in-themselves, and without accepting any overly simplistic philosophy of action. Instead, he is arguing that 'seen from the inside' the body is composed of desire-qualia. Since desire-qualia and the body (however conceived) bring about changes in the world, and we observe that apparently purely physical systems bring about changes in the world, the most parsimonious and intelligible hypothesis is that all physical items are composed of desire-qualia when seen from within. Efficient causation which we observe outside us is fundamentally no different from the efficient causation to which we are witting parties.

Contemporary materialists will not be persuaded by these considerations in part because they implicitly regard desires from the third-person point of view. If desires are simply explanatory posits for understanding the actions we observe in other systems, then no deep metaphysical problem arises. Furthermore, since the explanatory framework in question applies to human beings and perhaps to higher animals, the incredibility of generalizing to other items need not arise either. But Nietzsche would insist that this more commonsensical approach is flawed even if inter-theoretic reduction of desires so conceived to lower levels of description is in the offing (which is far from assured). For this is to concern ourselves with everyone else's desires except our own. We do not merely observe our own bodies and interpret their movements as caused by desires; we *experience* desiring. The problem of incorporating phenomenology into a satisfying metaphysical understanding remains.

The key to understanding the argument, then, is to see it as an argument for panpsychism, and as motivated by the problems of Cartesian dualism and its classical modern competitors. Cartesian dualism is ontologically inflationary and cannot make adequate sense of interaction. Materialism is ontologically austere, but cannot make adequate sense of how our own phenomenology fits into our own bodies and the larger world of nature. Idealism and phenomenalism are too anthropocentric and cannot make adequate sense of how subjectivity seems to be embedded in a larger natural order. Panpsychism suffers from none of these difficulties.

Naturally, the mind reels. Panpsychism is the best of a set of bad options bequeathed to us by Descartes? This stone has thoughts and feelings? Nietzsche has two responses available. First, nothing about panpsychism requires that the phenomenology of non-human things resembles human phenomenology in all its particulars. Presumably cats, lacking language, do not have interior monologues; molluscs do not feel lonely, being asocial and so on. Though it may strain the imagination, if we understand that the panpsychist's answer to the question 'what is it like to be a stone' will be 'not much!' this may ameliorate some of the tension the position induces. As a flip-side to this point, the suggestion that we cannot make sense of how a physical body can have thoughts and feelings, the panpsychist's response is 'sure we can; we are (properly conceived, nothing but) such bodies'. It's like *this*.

Since very few people find such considerations persuasive, I think the second response is the more important one: Nietzsche thinks that his panpsychism has independent explanatory power, apart from whatever metaphysical cramps it may relieve. 'Suppose, finally, we succeeded in explaining our entire instinctive life as the development and ramification of one basic form of the will ... then one would have gained the right to determine all efficient force univocally as – will to power' (*BGE* §36, ellipsis mine). We can only briefly allude to the sorts of explanatory gains Nietzsche is envisioning here (most of which are explored in the notes). First, he notices a certain analogy between organisms and societies: both have parts arranged in systematic and hierarchical structures. With societies, we can understand how social structure arises in light of the competition, cooperation and subordination of agents, who are the paradigmatic cases of beings with desires. Nietzsche finds it difficult to make sense of how the kind of 'subordination' and hierarchical structure seen in complex organisms can be explained unless we see it as the outcome of strivings of the sort he finds in the human social world. Second, over time, many individual biological systems show a tendency to grow and improve their capacities, most of which seem to involve greater ability to control and use their environment in favourable ways. Third, over evolutionary time, more complex and able species emerge. Naturally, we are inclined to think that some combination of Darwinism with physics and chemistry will be sufficient to handle these sorts of explanatory challenges. This is why Nietzsche is at some pains to criticize Darwinism, though it is far from clear that these criticisms are apposite or successful.

Is Nietzsche's argument at all convincing once we set aside his attempt to compete with Darwin? We are still left with the Cartesian legacy that Nietzsche is struggling with. It seems that the most significant oversight in his argument is the possibility that desire-qualia are emergent properties supervening on purely physical systems. If so, then the various difficulties of Nietzsche's own position and those of the competitors he takes account of seem to disappear. It is puzzling that Nietzsche did not consider this possibility, for two reasons. First, Nietzsche seems to be aware of the possibility of emergent properties, as when he describes 'thought' as a relation between drives. Perhaps this is easier to imagine than feeling as a relation between fields of blind forces. Second, Nietzsche really does not need the will to power metaphysics for problems in the areas that concern him the most: psychology and value theory. What explains his attraction to it?

I think that Nietzsche's interest in it is ultimately driven by his concern with overcoming nihilism. If power and the will to power are the basis for understanding value, then only living things can realize value and only sentient beings can desire value. This consigns most of the vast, lifeless universe to being merely an oversized stage in which the adventure of value transpires. And if someday life were to cease (something not difficult to imagine) all value would disappear. By contrast, if the adventure of value infuses everything, the world, the cosmos, is blessed as friendly to and protective of value. To imagine the world becoming stripped of value is to imagine the annihilation of the universe itself.

ETERNAL RECURRENCE

Though Nietzsche presents the doctrine of the eternal recurrence as central to the theme of *Zarathustra*, it has received far less attention than his other ideas. Interpreters have tended either to set it aside or reinterpret it so that it is divested of some of its force. The first published discussion is in *Gay Science*, where it is presented as a thought experiment: suppose you learned that the world, and hence your life, eternally recurs down to the last detail? Would this strike you as a good thing or a bad thing? Clearly Nietzsche associates this idea with nihilism and its overcoming. First, those prone to nihilism will find their dissatisfaction with life intensified, since the doctrine not only increases the weight of whatever is the source of dissatisfaction, it multiplies it limitlessly. Furthermore, various consolations that would be available are ruled out by the doctrine. Since it presupposes naturalism, no life after death can compensate for the shortcomings of life in this world. Goals beyond the life of the individual (commitment to the welfare of future generations, for example) are also ruled out, because any future accomplishment is bound to be unwound into a condition like that preceding its accomplishment. Lastly, should one respond to the crisis of nihilism by taking comfort in one's own, or even the world's eventual annihilation? That too is barred, since recurrence implies that the world cannot be finally destroyed. By contrast, if one affirms one's own life, one can come to affirm it as worthy of infinite repetition despite the lack of this-worldly or otherworldly compensations.

In the unpublished notes, Nietzsche attempts to argue for the 'cosmological' claim that the world eternally recurs; these arguments need not detain us other than to note that they are instances of rationalist-metaphysical argumentation, hinging on the presuppositions that the world is in some respects finite (as to quantity of force or number of combinatorial states, for example) whereas time is infinite. It is important to note here that none of the premises in these arguments are empirical; indeed, they are all based on assumptions about the intelligibility of thinking various basic kinds of things finite or infinite, and in that respect, fit comfortably within the compass of those sorts of arguments which Kant rejected in the 'Antinomy' chapter of the *Critique of Pure Reason*. Accordingly, I shall refer freely to these arguments and the conclusion they are meant to support as 'metaphysical'.

These observations, coupled with the broad consensus that the arguments are invalid in any case, have led to rejection of what I would call the metaphysical (or 'cosmological') interpretation of the doctrine. This rejection is reinforced by the absence of such arguments in the published writings. Unfortunately, this has led many such interpreters to try to propose interpretations in which the metaphysical dimension of the doctrine does not matter.

We can distinguish several different interpretative stances. First, there are those interpretations which depend upon the metaphysical doctrine being true and believed if it is to have any force. Second, there are those interpretations which depend upon the metaphysical doctrine being believed to have force (though it need not be true). Lastly there are interpretations which depend neither on truth nor belief. The attraction of the last stance comes from the fact that many interpreters regard the doctrine as so obviously false that even the prospect of it having some force by virtue of being mistakenly believed holds little attraction.

Two different approaches within this group have become common: the 'Kantian' and the 'experiential'. However, these are more alike than different. The Kantian account likens eternal recurrence to the categorical imperative, and sees it as a test for action. However, whereas the categorical imperative asks the agent to imagine that the maxims underlying her choices become universal law, the eternal recurrence asks the agent to imagine that the life composed of these choices becomes repeated an infinite number of times. In both cases, if the will would turn away from what it wills, this demonstrates some normative failing in the content of what is willed. Now there are various disanalogies between universalizing and infinitely repeating, but since Nietzsche evidently does not seek to recapture the content of Kantian ethics (on the contrary), we can set these aside. More important, it seems, is the motivational role of the test in both cases.

Can realizing that one's maxim is self-defeating by itself motivate one to want to act morally? Arguably not. One can easily imagine a prospective promise-breaker responding to the thought experiment with 'good thing my maxim won't become universal law, because then it would be self-defeating!' and proceeding to act in anti-Kantian ways. So what force does the test have? A Kantian would claim that universalizing reveals the irrationality of the maxim, and that the judgement that a particular maxim and its associated act are irrational carries some motivational force. But it remains to be seen whether the failure to universalize shows that the maxim is irrational, even if we assume that disclosed irrationality has some motivational force. For would it not be irrational to act in light of counterfactual conditions? Furthermore, the claim that it is irrational to act in ways that would be irrational (given an agent-relative conception of rationality) under counterfactual conditions raises the question: what is so special about these particular counterfactual conditions? I can imagine an ethical test that led to the conclusion that it is irrational to eat cherries because it would be irrational to eat cherries if all cherries were poisonous. There are infinitely many such counterfactual conditions which render a particular choice irrational if they obtain. So everything hinges on which counterfactual condition we choose as the basis for our test. Does Kant provide any reason for preferring universalization over some other imaginary scenario?

The only basis I can see for adopting universalization over possible competing tests is that it leads (let us suppose) to results which tally with prior moral intuitions. This is to lend the prior intuitions a great deal of normative authority. However, it does nothing to show that these particular intuitions are peculiarly *rational*. It would appear, then, that the motivational force of the categorical imperative rests, not on its allegedly distinctive rationality, but instead upon these moral intuitions and whatever motivational force they already have.

With this in mind, let us see how things stand with the eternal recurrence. It would appear that the same motivational flaw is present here as well: if I suppose that my life would in some sense appear 'bad' to me if, counterfactually, I eternally recur, but not if I do not, shouldn't the right response be 'good thing I don't eternally recur!' and then get on with what might for all that seem to me the best possible life under existing circumstances? What possible motivational force could thinking about recurrence have here? It would appear that it depends upon some prior normative intuition that the thought of recurrence highlights. This is bad enough in the

Kantian case, where appeal to universalization risks the appearance of begging the question in favour of Kantian morality. In Nietzsche's case, the intention seems to be to revise our normative commitments in important ways. How could the thought of eternal recurrence conjure up new normative intuitions if it is counterfactual? And if it does not conjure up new normative intuitions, it would appear at most to highlight some pre-existing ones while encouraging us to suppress others. But again, assuming that it draws upon some prior intuitions while suppressing others, what motivational force could it have for us in encouraging this suppression if it is counterfactual? Suppose that I have only naturalistic cognitive commitments, and I have some normative intuitions, some of which tally with Nietzsche's (such as the importance of joyful self-creation, the overcoming of resistances and so on) and some of which do not (caring about the suffering of future generations). I try to find a way of living that balances these conflicting concerns as well as possible. 'The demon' in *Gay Science* asks me to imagine that my life eternally recurs, and as I contemplate this scenario, I judge 'if I eternally recurred, I would care more about joyful self-creation and less about the suffering of future generations'. The next thought should be 'but I do not eternally recur, and my existing balancing of the weights I assign to my competing normative concerns still strikes me as the best possible under existing circumstances'. Perhaps the demon can reply, 'ah yes, but your concern with future generations has the following unattractive but hidden psychological or historical characteristics: (insert some Nietzschean analysis)'. Unless there is some additional content to the test, it seems to have no motivational force whatsoever. But if it has additional content sufficient to generate motivational force, it would appear that the thought of recurrence is otiose.

Considerations like these render any counterfactual interpretation of the recurrence suspect. For whether we conceive of the test as a Kantian one, or as a test of life affirmation in some other sense, my attitude towards my own life is determined by how I believe my life is, not how it would be if it were different. If there are lives which could be affirmed if they did not recur but could not if they did, it seems that the proper response to the thought of recurrence is an indifferent shrug. And it may be no coincidence that, unlike Nietzsche, this is the overwhelming response of most people when they hear the doctrine.

I conclude that it is an inseparable part of the doctrine as Nietzsche intended it that the metaphysical doctrine be believed, and this belief be sufficiently robust to stand against criticism. In short, it must be a well-warranted belief – we must regard it as true. I think that the textual evidence suggests that Nietzsche regarded it that way himself.

A further question is whether we would still be indifferent to the eternal recurrence if we believed it was literally true. Here I think matters are far less clear. The first worry is whether there are sufficient conditions for me to identify with my past and future 'incarnations'. If not, I will not regard myself as recurring at all, even if we assume that the metaphysical doctrine is true. Given naturalism, the only thing I have in common with the other incarnations is exact similarity; we can regard my incarnations as if they were instances of a common type. But it is far from clear that I care more about someone the more closely they resemble me. Suppose that I learned that I had an identical twin somewhere else in the world. Though this fact might motivate me to want to meet that person, and even to care about his welfare, there would still seem to be an asymmetry between my concern for myself and my concern for my twin. If we were brought together and I was forced to choose between undergoing some great physical pain, or that the twin undergo it, morality aside, I presumably would prefer that the twin undergo it, even if this preference were weaker than a preference that a non-twin undergo it.

Lockean-Nozickian theories of personal identity suggest that the reason for this is that I identify with entities with which I have some psychological continuity.[7] Though the focus is usually on memory here, other kinds of psychological continuity might also be relevant (for example, knowing that the twin will act in the future on my present intentions). But such continuity is completely absent in the case of the twin, and by extension, with the recurrent self. This may be part of the reason why people often have an indifferent reaction to the idea of recurrence once it is called to their attention that you cannot recall past incarnations or influence future ones.

However, this may be too quick. Of the various kinds of anaesthesia available, one kind depends not upon suppressing contemporaneous awareness of pain, but upon erasing memory of it. Though patients seem to accept this readily enough, it seems significant that physicians do not *emphasize* the relevant facts. If some demon were to steal into your room and tell you that you would be tortured over and over, while under the influence of such an anesthetic so that you would not remember the torture (and thus never resist or complain about such treatment), would you be indifferent? Arguably not. This suggests that the Lockean notion of psychological continuity is overrated (though it may be that being able to recall events between episodes of torture would induce one to identify with the self undergoing the torture – it is still a continuing self, though not as continuous as we might like). If that is correct, it may be that our identification with and caring about the fate of some being depends, not upon psychological continuity, but upon our beliefs about our relationship with it. Another example to illustrate this is our caring about our own future condition as coma patients. We know we will not care when the time comes, and that we will have no psychological continuity with what we will become, but this does not seem to prevent us from caring (though it may be due to some confusion of 'intuitions' – we may be uncertain about whether we should care or not). If it is true that we do and should care, it may be sufficient to have a well-warranted belief in recurrence to find the doctrine transformative.

Another obstacle is temporal remoteness. We care less about events that have happened or will happen to us when they are temporally remote. This is why people borrow money. Even when we do not literally mean that we will be another person when the time comes, we still care less about what happens to us in the distant past and future. How much less, one would think, should we care about what happened one or more world-cycles in the past or the future? If this impression is added to uncertainty about whether it will be truly ourselves which recurs, this might reduce the interest in the doctrine to almost nothing.

Nietzsche does have a response to this: we are not conscious of the time that elapses between incarnations, and thus it is as if no time had elapsed at all between my death and my next birth. This idea seems to be in some tension with the objection from psychological continuity above. For while it may not seem as if any time elapses, it also does not seem as if I recur at all (given the absence of memory). So what am I supposed to care about? The way it seems, or the way it is?

This leads to a third objection, which is interestingly linked to the very idea of the metaphysical doctrine. The reason a 'proof' is needed to create motivational force is because a recurring and a non-recurring life are qualitatively indistinguishable, in much the same way that life as it is versus life as a brain in a vat are qualitatively indistinguishable. When Cartesian scepticism is first presented to students, they often react with indifference. Some of this indifference comes from their not being able to see any reason why it is true. Once persuaded to enter into the spirit of the proceedings, some change their mind and conclude that it matters to them whether they are brains in vats or not, but a residual number persist: if the course of my experience will be qualitatively indistinguishable in either case, what possible difference can it make? Similarly, my life is as it is, with or without inaccessible 'echoes' – why should I care?

Interestingly, in cultures where religious or metaphysical theories are widely believed, there is often a prevalent view that the world of experience is some sort of illusion. This tends to influence people's conduct (for example, by promoting detachment from worldly concerns). It might be that really believing the recurrence would affect at least some people analogously, encouraging a kind of deep concern with the quality of one's life and one's attitude towards the world. It is difficult to say whether this would be the case or not, since we seem to have available only one case of someone who actually believed the recurrence to be literally true: Nietzsche himself. As with the 'veil of illusion' doctrine, we might expect that many people would not care, and get on with their lives as before.

Though this is quite speculative, I want to suggest that the force of the recurrence doctrine, like that of the 'veil of illusion' doctrine, depends upon something more than even well-warranted belief. What may attract some to the latter is more than just a metaphysical or epistemological argument, but rather some phenomenological state of experiencing the life world as being tenuous, evanescent and insubstantial. Many mystics report coming to have 'veil of illusion' beliefs, not because of argument, but because of some inexplicable experience of life seeming 'dreamlike'. Whatever the source of this experience is (Nietzsche himself might suggest that it has its roots, or at least derives some of its strength, from wishful thinking), it seems different from assent to a proposition. Indeed, the experience itself might lead one to seek arguments that would make sense of such an abnormal experience.

Similarly, we can imagine a phenomenological state of experiencing the things of the life world as being familiar and repetitive. It is perhaps as widely shared as a transitory sense of the life world being dreamlike: we call it *déjà vu*. Perhaps in some people the strength, persistence and inexplicability of *déjà vu*-like states is much greater than it is for most. (Interestingly, there is a neurological disease with symptoms very like this.) This may be enough to lend force to the literal claim that everything you experience you have experienced before. And just as such an experience may lend credence to eternal recurrence, it may acquire some non-rational support from wishful thinking. For Nietzsche not only says that the doctrine is 'the greatest weight' and something 'crave[d]' by those with the strength to affirm life (*GS* §341) – he also says that it is a 'consolation' (*WP* §1065). For if I can affirm my life, would there not be something to be gained by rendering it immortal as long as it loses nothing of its other characteristics by virtue of which I affirm it?

One begins to suspect that the doctrine of the eternal recurrence is best understood as a replacement for the Christian doctrine of an afterlife of rewards and punishments. Recurrence is like a reward for those who live well and are strong, and a punishment for those who live badly and are weak. This also tallies with the impression that a merely counterfactual interpretation is inadequate, as it surely would be for the analogous Christian doctrine. To be sure, if recurrence is false then by craving it I fall short of full world affirmation, preferring a possible world in which I retain a certain permanence over the actual one in which my destruction is final. Beyond any concern with myself, I find myself preferring a world that is in an odd sense indestructible to one which is prone to destruction, for the form of the world persists through each world-cycle by virtue of identity and repetition. Of course, this cannot be 'token-identity', for Nietzsche's doctrine of becoming involves regarding everything that happens as prone to (intra-cycle) destruction. But the world cycle as a whole and as a type cannot be destroyed, and inter-cycle, no particular constellation of forces can be prevented from re-arising. If we are to say that anything is actually recurring here, it must be the types of things, not their tokens. What is more, caring about your own recurrence seems to require that you fix your identity by way of your (instantiated an infinite number of times) self-type, not your (finite and eventually destroyed) self-token. Though these types may not exist separately from their instantiations, we may again suspect that Nietzsche has not repudiated Platonism after all. And he says as much: 'That everything recurs is the closest approximation of a world of becoming to a world of being: high point of the meditation' (*WP* §617), and '[t]he two most extreme modes of thought – the mechanistic and the Platonic – are reconciled in the eternal recurrence: both as ideals' (*WP* §1061). Whether this is a strength or a weakness can be left as an exercise for the reader.

CHAPTER 4

PERSPECTIVISM

LOGIC

The preceding discussion presents broad features of Nietzsche's conception of the world 'naively', or from a third-person point of view. This may strike some readers as problematic, since Nietzsche is well known for his critical views about the very possibility of human knowledge, a cluster of themes usually bundled together under the rubric 'perspectivism'. Unfortunately, it is often far from clear what precisely these views are or how they interrelate. That said, if Nietzsche's views entail that knowledge is unattainable, or worse, that truth itself does not exist, this will undermine his worldview, or at least any literal interpretation of it.

Let us return to the 'two-world picture'. We said that this picture not only associates value with a hidden realm of permanence and the destruction of value with a manifest world of flux, but that the latter is regarded as in some sense an illusion. Nietzsche hoped to overcome this view in part for normative reasons. But did he also hope to overcome the distinction between hiddenness and mani-festness, or even between truth and falsity itself? 'Indeed, what forces us at all to suppose that there is an essential opposition of "true" and "false"? Is it not sufficient to assume degrees of appa-rentness and, as it were, lighter and darker shadows and shades of appearance – different "values", to use the language of painters?' (*BGE* §34). The first reason why it would seem insufficient is that the distinction between true and false is essential to our logical prac-tices. Assuming that one could represent a fact or state of affairs in a sentence, if the sentence is true, then its negation is false. If Nietzsche is serious in the incidental comment that we reject the opposition of true and false, he would seem committed either to rejecting or dramatically revising our logical practices.

This suggestion gains some support from a note.

> We are unable to affirm and to deny one and the same thing: this is a subjective empirical law, not the expression of any 'necessity' but only an inability ... Either [the law of contradiction] asserts something about actuality, about being, as if one already knew this from another source; that is, as if opposite attributes could not be ascribed to it. Or the proposition means: opposite attributes should not be ascribed to it. In that case, logic would be an imperative, not to know the true, but to posit and arrange a world that shall be called true by us. (*WP* §516, ellipsis mine)

Nietzsche's suggestion that the law of contradiction is normative and not descriptive is one shared by the later Wittgenstein, and by itself does not tell us that there is anything amiss in this. After all, Kant's categorical imperative is normative and not descriptive, and yet this does not render it optional for Kant. In the note above, Nietzsche goes on to say that we have the logical norms that we do for pragmatic reasons. That might be so, and yet it could be that no other normative commitments in this area are either possible or desirable. Nietzsche does sometimes suggest something like this, as when he says that 'rational thought is an interpretation according to a scheme that we cannot throw off' (*WP* §522). Though this seems like a daring suggestion, it is not clear that it is, for the daring seems to lie in the possibility of rival schemes. If there aren't any, then Nietzsche's remarks are merely a gloss on our logical practices, a reminder not to make more of them than they warrant.

That said, Nietzsche does seem to be saying something stronger than the Wittgensteinian gloss. First, Nietzsche thinks that classical logic wrongly privileges its norms as uniquely descriptive, when all it really does is 'carve up' the world according to syntactical schemata that represent just one possibility among many. We then reify these schemata (for example, seeing the world as composed of substances and properties because our language and thought are syntactically structured in terms of referring and attributive expressions). Mistaking the structure of syntax for the structure of the world in turn fuels the illusion that rationalist metaphysics can get a foothold in our cognition and provide us with a non-empirical form of knowledge. This epistemological belief then supports the two-world picture in terms of the two different forms of epistemic access they are susceptible to.

Second, does the idea of degrees of apparentness make any sense here? Though one should not expect modern logical sophistication from Nietzsche, since the early twentieth century logicians have been aware of the possibility of multivalued logic. Though initially these systems were limited to three-valued logics containing false-hood, some intermediate value and truth $(0, 1/2$ and $1)$, it is possible to construct a multivalued logic which contains values corresponding to 0, all the rational numbers within the interval between 0 and 1, and 1. Such a logic would allow truth itself, and not just warrant or belief, to admit of degrees. We can call such a system a 'fuzzy logic' (not to be confused with fuzzy set theory, in which set membership admits of degrees).

But even Nietzsche's suggestion that the law of non-contradiction need not constrain us is defensible. Traditionally, the obstacle to rejecting the law of non-contradiction, intuition aside, is that a contradiction licenses an inference to any sentence at all. However, one can construct logics for which this inference is not licensed, so-called paraconsistent logics. Such systems allow us to segregate the malign inferential effects of contradictions so that other inferences can proceed. Furthermore, both infinite multivaluedness and paraconsistency can be combined in a single system to yield a paraconsistent fuzzy logic. This shows us that Nietzsche might not only be offering the Wittgensteinian gloss, but that the norm 'use classical logic' can be intelligibly contrasted with alternatives, as in 'one ought not to use paraconsistent fuzzy logic; one should only use classical logic'. It would even make sense to say 'one should do this because it is more computationally tractable, being simpler, and this simplicity carries with it certain pragmatic advantages, though real degrees of truth and real contradictions may very well obtain nonetheless'.

Though our purpose in this logical digression is only to suggest that some of the more radical interpretations of Nietzsche's views on truth need not be dismissed out of hand due to a misguided attachment to classical logic, is there any reason why Nietzsche (or a rationally reconstructed Nietzsche) might find such a view attractive? One possibility suggests itself. A common view of our epistemic situation is that knowledge is true belief, plus some additional factor(s) (warrant, justification, Gettier properties above and beyond these, Nozickian tracking and so on). On such an account, we can imagine scenarios in which our beliefs possess this additional factor, but lack truth. Such an approach frequently underwrites scepticism of various kinds. Given Nietzsche's rejection of the Kantian thing-in-itself, he could be taken to be troubled by such a distinction between truth and (let us say) justification. On one popular interpretation of Nietzsche, his rejection of the thing-in-itself should be read as a rejection of any distinction between truth and idealized warrant or justification.[1] If we accept that there is such a distinction, the sceptical possibility arises that our best possible theories could be mistaken and we could never know this. However, simply denying that there is any meaningful distinction between truth and idealized justification still leaves open the possibility of gaps between truth and actual justification. It is difficult to see how we can plausibly continue to regard truth and justification as distinct in all but the idealized case, and not continue to have a picture of the world that involves, as it were, localized things-in-themselves. Thus there is some pressure, if we are to identify truth with idealized justification, simply to identify truth with justification itself, thus closing the gap between how things seem and how they are in every case. But justification is not a binary affair as truth, on the classical conception, is thought to be: it admits of degrees. Thus it might be thought that we could close the gap between how things seem and how they are by simply identifying truthlikeness with justification and allowing truthlikeness to admit of degrees, or 'shades of apparentness'. Though I am doubtful that this interpretation captures the historical Nietzsche's own intentions, depending as it does on concepts nowhere in evidence in his writings, it is a plausible extension of one popular approach.

PERCEPTION

Another theme in Nietzsche's reflections on truth and knowledge is his repudiation of the 'thing-in-itself'. Though this conception has its origins in Kant, Nietzsche seems to have understood it more broadly to include any item whose determinate character obtains mind-independently. It is important here to read 'mind-dependence' literally, as perceptual states could be said to be mind-dependent, and not in the sense that one finds in recent discussions of meta-physical antirealism, where the issue is the replacement of the concept of truth with the concept of warrant or justification.[2] In this latter sense, though Berkeley believes that physical objects are mind-dependent, he is not a metaphysical antirealist, for whether a mind-dependent physical object exists or not is a matter of fact independent of our beliefs and verification procedures. One recur-ring theme is Nietzsche's claim that a thing is the sum of the per-spectives bearing upon it. This suggests some form of idealism or phenomenalism. But as we saw in the previous chapter, Nietzsche has some reason to resist such views, for they are more anthropo-centric than his vision of human beings embedded in a larger natural order will allow.

There are three ways one can think about perception from a first-person point of view: direct realism, phenomenalism and representational realism. Nietzsche, however, seems to reject phe-nomenalism. 'To study physiology with a clear conscience, one must insist that the sense organs are not phenomena in the sense of idealistic philosophy; as such they could not be causes! Sensualism, therefore, at least as a regulative hypothesis, if not as a heuristic principle' (*BGE* §15). Nietzsche is asserting here that there are sense organs (studied by physiology) and that they play a causal role in the character of our experience. But we cannot claim that the world of experience is identical to the external world while maintaining this, because 'then our body [which includes our sense organs], as a part of the external world, would be the work of our organs! But then our organs themselves would be – the work of our organs! It seems to me that this is a complete *reductio ad absurdum*, assuming that the concept of a *causa sui* is something fundamentally absurd' (*BGE* §15). And Nietzsche does assume this, calling it 'self-contra-diction', 'a sort of rape and perversion of logic' and 'non-sense' (*BGE* §21). So the identification of the external world with the contents of experience seems ruled out, leaving only direct realism and representational realism as options.

Surprisingly, direct realism seems to be asserted in the latest of Nietzsche's late writings. '[The senses] lie neither in the way the Eleatics believed, nor as [Heraclitus] believed – they do not lie at all. What we make of their testimony, that alone introduces lies; for example, the lie of unity, the lie of thinghood, of substance, of permanence. "Reason" is the cause of our falsification of the testimony of the senses' (*TI* III, §2). This view is consistent with Nietzsche's repeated emphasis on the importance of interpretation. We could regard interpretation as an essentially intellectual or judgemental affair, operating with but not altering the evidence of the senses. This would seem to be contradicted by the following. 'Against positivism, which halts at phenomena – "There are only facts" – I would say: No, facts is precisely what there is not, only interpretations. We cannot establish any fact "in itself": perhaps it is folly to want to do such a thing' (*WP* §481). But this passage does not unambiguously assert that the senses are not reliable, for he goes on to say that '[i]nsofar as the word "knowledge" has any meaning, the world is knowable; but it is interpretable otherwise, it has no meaning behind it, but countless meanings – "Perspectivism" ' (ibid). This passage seems in some way to distinguish between knowledge and interpretation. One possibility is that 'knowledge' here means the evidence of the senses (though this is far from clear). This interpretation is supported by the following. 'There are no "facts-in-themselves," for a sense [*Sinn*] must always be projected into them before there can be "facts." The question "what is that?" is an imposition of *meaning* from some other viewpoint. "Essence," the "essential nature," is something perspective and already presupposes a multiplicity' (*WP* §556, emphasis mine). Notice that in this passage, the absence of facts is attributed, not to the interpretative work of the senses themselves, but to 'an imposition of meaning', a projected '*Sinn*'.

So how are we to explain the apparently phenomenalist theme of a thing being the sum of perspectives upon it? If Nietzsche were content to limit the idea of perspectives here to judgemental or intellectual perspectives, no problem would arise. However, in some places Nietzsche also seems to include perceptual properties – conceived as dependent upon the observer – within his notion of perspective, identifying the object with the sum of these mind-dependent perceptual properties. ' "In the development of thought a point had to be reached at which one realized that what one called the properties of things were sensations of the feeling subject: at this point the properties ceased to belong to the thing." The "thing-in-itself" remained' (*WP* §562). But '[t]he "thing-in-itself" [is] nonsensical. If I remove all the relationships, all the "properties," all the "activities" of a thing, the thing does not remain over ...' (*WP* §558). 'That things possess a constitution in themselves quite apart from interpretation and subjectivity, is a quite idle hypothesis: it presupposes that interpretation and subjectivity are not essential, that a thing freed from all relationships would still be a thing' (*WP* §560). Consequently '[a] thing would be defined once all creatures had asked "what is that?" and had answered their question' (*WP* §556).

If we take 'subjectivity' here to include perceptual properties (though it is far from clear we should), such a line of thought seems to involve a rejection of representational realism. For it is precisely representational realism, with its distinction between the object and the perceptual states it causes, that makes us question how we know that our experience resembles the object. Phenomenalist identification of the properties of the object with our perceptual states is usually a response to the sceptical threat that this distinction gives rise to. And we know that Nietzsche has some reason to be concerned with such a sceptical threat, for it is one of the vehicles driving us to the two-world picture. Yet Nietzsche does not want to abandon the underlying scientific account of perception, 'study[ing] physiology with a clear conscience' either, and phenomenalism seems in tension with such an account.

Here Nietzsche's panpsychism may afford him a way of avoiding the Scylla of phenomenalism and the Charybdis of representational realism. Seen from the third-person point of view, the scientific account of perception (a remote physical object causally interacting with the physical sensory apparatus) is correct. Usually it is reflection on such facts that motivates representational realism. However, these physical processes, for Nietzsche, involve struggles between systems of fields of force, whose expansive and repulsive relations with other fields of force in its environment has a first-person point of view aspect or dimension to it: what it is like to be an encroaching or defending field among others. When one field is impinged upon by another, it does not 'represent' some alien event within the alien field within itself: it directly experiences the impingement. The question of similarity between what is within the 'passive' field and the 'active' field does not arise. Consequently, a gap between the undergone experience and the 'real' world apart from it disappears, and with it any possible concern for what the world is really like apart from our experiences.

The irony is that Nietzsche seems to have traded one form of scepticism for another. For notoriously, classical modern ways of thinking about perception and mind-body relations leads also to the problem of other minds. And even if there is something that represents what it is like to be passive in relation to another field of force, how does one know (if one is such a field of force) that there is a corresponding 'what it is like to be active' experience in the encroaching field? It would seem that here Nietzsche has to rely on some sort of analogy between what the passive field experiences when it is, in other circumstances, an active field. Given Nietzsche's panpsychism, there will always be some sort of experience associated with being a field of force caught up in struggling interactions with other fields. Perhaps Nietzsche implicitly thinks that there is something about the experiences of encroaching and being encroached upon that are necessarily connected, so that one cannot understand the one without understanding the other? If that is correct, then the experience of being encroached upon would necessarily involve an understanding of what it is like to be the alien field that is encroaching upon one simply by virtue of the fact that it is encroaching upon one. Then there would in principle be no residue of unknowability in the world, and hence no basis for a two-world picture.

It is important to note in passing that whether Nietzsche is successful or not in rebutting some form of scepticism by metaphysically recharacterizing mind-world relations, scepticism in general cannot be rebutted by Nietzsche's strategy, by common-sense direct realism, or phenomenalism. The sceptic's concern is that we might be massively deceived while enjoying access to the evidence we have. But sceptical scenarios can always be generated within any metaphysical frame and any account of perceptual access to the world. Consider phenomenalism. Suppose that I mistakenly believe that physical objects are mind-independent, and that representational realism is true. I may suffer sceptical doubts. My neighbour Rudolf explains to me that physical objects are just logical constructions from perceptual states, and thus I cannot be mistaken in judging that the table before me is real. Thus reassured, I resume my life, which, unbeknownst to me, is the life of the character Truman in the film *The Truman Show*, a life in which almost everything I believe about matters of great personal concern is mistaken. Similarly for direct realism. After my neighbour Martin explains to me that I have direct perceptual access to (am 'open to') the life world in which I am embedded, I am reassured, not knowing that, again, I am in *The Truman Show*. It seems that we must either approach sceptical problems with something other than philosophical accounts of perception (perhaps by abandoning internalist or non-contextualist assumptions about justification that such strategies share) or resign ourselves to scepticism. And in any case, all such strategies will leave us still unable to escape fallibilism.

However, Nietzsche may not be troubled by these issues. For the normative concern that the two-world picture generates requires that we have some reason to think that the entire world available within experience can be plausibly contrasted with another complete world in which change is absent. Such an hypothesis appears to gain strength only from the kinds of scepticism that depend upon metaphysical considerations. Other forms of scepticism (*'Truman Show* scepticism', brain-in-vat scepticism), while being potentially wildly disorientating given the number of our beliefs they might undermine, do not give us reason to think that the contrasting world, the world as it really is, is a world of changeless, painless stasis.

KNOWLEDGE IN A WORLD OF WILL TO POWER

That is not to say that Nietzsche's metaphysics are without any epistemological implications. Though I have argued that Nietzsche does not reduce objects of cognition to actual and possible experiences of them – as in phenomenalism – this does not mean that objects have an intrinsic character. On the contrary, Nietzsche claims that the properties of an object are nothing other than its propensities to affect or be affected by other objects. Since objecthood itself is 'synthetic', it follows that objects are nothing but bundles of relations. Not only does Nietzsche reject the idea that the 'objects' of cognition have an intrinsic, non-relational character; he also rejects the idea that cognitive 'subjects' have disinterested cognitive capacities to apprehend such objects. But rather than seeing this state of affairs as crippling to the intellect, he sees it as empowering. Cognition will then involve mutually constituting and highly interest-laden relations between the subject and object. This suggests to him that we should reject a conception of objectivity in which subjective interests only serve as distorting biases, and that detachment is the royal road to knowledge. For such a conception urges us to reduce our relations with the 'object' and at the limit, know nothing about it. Rather, Nietzsche urges that we cultivate intensely interested, but very broad and diverse, relations with the object.

This conception is paralleled in the metaphysical conception of the object as constituted by the sum of its experiential relations with the rest of the world, with the sum of the 'perspectives' on it. Such a conception of the object identifies its full reality, at the limit, with all of these relations and given the will to power metaphysics, these relations will all be 'interested' ones. The more involved we are in the world the object is embedded in, the closer to full knowledge of the object we get. Nietzsche says that

> 'objectivity' [should be] understood not as 'contemplation without interest' (which is a nonsensical absurdity), but as the ability to control one's Pro and Con and to dispose of them, so that one knows how to employ a variety of perspectives and affective interpretations in the service of knowledge ... There is only a perspective seeing, only a perspective 'knowing'; and the more affects we allow to speak about one thing, the more eyes, different eyes, we can use to observe one thing, the more complete will our 'concept' of this thing, our 'objectivity', be. (*GM* III, §12, ellipsis mine)

This doctrine applies, in the first instance, to perception, to our literal eyes (and other senses), and dovetails with the claim that the senses do not lie. For given the scientific account of perception, perception is our most basic means of entering into commerce with objects and creating the mutually constituting experiential relations or 'perspectives' the will to power metaphysics suggests are characteristic of the world in any case. At what we might call the first level of the metaphor, 'more eyes' surely encourages rich and diverse perceptual commerce with the object and the accumulation of as much evidence about it as possible. But perhaps the more important metaphor is secondary: affectively driven, highly interested interpretations of the object. For these can be multiplied far more, and far more usefully, than the mere accumulation of evidence.

Nietzsche's enlightened empiricism, associated though it is with his questionable panpsychist metaphysics, gains plausibility from his abstention from any notion of incorrigible perceptual claims characteristic of classical modern empiricism, or of theoretical claims being vindicated by deductive inferences from such foundations. In this he resembles what has become the broad mainstream of contemporary empiricists since Quine. And as we have seen, the various 'perspectivist' themes, properly understood, do not undermine his metaphysics, but rather stand with it in various relations of mutual support.

CHAPTER 5

CRITIQUE OF MORALITY

NOBILITY

In what sense is Nietzsche a moral theorist? We saw in Chapter 3 that Nietzsche is committed to some sort of axiological realism, and is concerned to promote a conception of life in which creativity occupies a central place. Yet it might be thought that Nietzsche has no interesting positive moral theory to offer us, for two reasons. First, the recommendation 'be creative' is so general as to be completely uninformative. Second, a central part of Nietzsche's project is concerned with a critique of morality, and if this critique is itself sufficiently general, he may not have any basis for making any recommendations at all.

On the face of it, neither of these construals seem right. Nietzsche devotes considerable attention to very specific characterizations of the 'ideal' person though, to be sure, these descriptions do not take the form of rules for decision in the way that much modern moral theory does. Similarly, Nietzsche's critique of morality does not seem to target all possible forms of ethical life. Rather, he seems to be operating with certain richly imagined types of persons, which we can initially characterize as 'higher' and 'lower'. (I am deliberately avoiding characterizing them as 'master' and 'slave' here, concepts which play a crucial analytical role in the descriptive and explanatory account of morality, and which may or may not fully correspond to Nietzsche's own normative attractions and aversions.)

Nietzsche does not appear to have arrived at his characterizations of ideal human traits by constructing some composite from an independent account of these traits separately considered; on the contrary, he seems to have arrived at what insights he has into the individual traits by initially considering their presence in exceptional individuals. Though Nietzsche praises many historical individuals in various contexts, a brief glance at several reveals certain overlapping themes.

In *Beyond Good and Evil*, he singles out Alcibiades, Caesar, Frederick II and Leonardo as 'magical, incomprehensible, and unfathomable ones ... enigmatic men predestined for victory and seduction' (*BGE* §200, ellipsis mine). The first three seem to share noble class origins, military skill, boldness, ambition, shrewdness and a certain freedom from moral or religious constraint. Frederick is also noteworthy for what was said to be an insatiable intellectual curiosity. Leonardo, by contrast, does not display any military or political traits, was of middle-class origin, but displayed tremendous artistic skill, sensuousness and productivity and intellectual curiosity. Elsewhere in *Beyond Good and Evil*, Nietzsche calls attention to some exceptional modern figures: Napoleon, Goethe, Beethoven, Stendhal, Heine, Schopenhauer and Wagner (*BGE* §256). Since Nietzsche's attitude towards Schopenhauer and Wagner are complex, let us set them aside. Napoleon fits the mould of Alcibiades, Caesar and Frederick, but the other figures represent a different range of types. Goethe, whom Nietzsche mentions frequently with the highest praise, like Leonardo manifested extraordinary intelligence, curiosity and artistic-literary productivity. Like Leonardo, Goethe came from a middle-class background. His Enlightenment anticlericalism and pantheism are noteworthy. Lastly, he is famous for his succession of intense romantic attachments, which may partly explain why Nietzsche says elsewhere that 'love as passion – which is our European specialty – simply must be of noble origin' (*BGE* §261).

Beethoven, also from a middle-class background, is of course noteworthy for his extraordinary musical productivity, the complexity and passion expressed in the bulk of his work, but also for his initial sympathy with Napoleon and the republican ideals of the French Revolution. His religious attitudes remain a matter of controversy, but like Goethe he appears to have had both Enlightenment anticlerical attitudes and an attraction to pantheism. In our list so far, we seem to see two recurring types (with some overlap): the skilled and bold military-political figure, and the fecund artist. The figure of Napoleon seems to connect the two types among modern individuals. Napoleon, Goethe and Beethoven all seem to be of a piece in their participation (in various senses) in the upheavals of the post-Revolutionary period and their commitment (again, in various senses) to Enlightenment ideology and a kind of proto-Romantic passion manifested in their 'works'. All three are in important senses 'self-made' men, rising in the world more through talent and energy than through birth and inherited social advantages. Stendhal and Heine are crucially different, and one might hesitate to identify them too strongly with Nietzsche's ideal, though they contribute important elements to it not immediately evident in the other types. Both are of middle-class origin and were, though in a less spectacular way than Napoleon, 'self-made'. Both are noteworthy for their romantic-passionate side (Stendhal wrote a remarkable book, *On Love*, which remains one of the most interesting works on the psychology of falling in love), but this is tempered with a kind of cynicism, manifested in Stendhal's writing by his coldly clinical psychological descriptions, and in Heine's by his satirical streak. I mention them here because one would hesitate merely to assimilate them to Alcibiadean indifference to moral constraint, for acute psychological insight (and self-insight) seems to add something more.

If it were possible to construct a composite of these figures, we would see someone who is skilful, cunning, bold, energetic, ambitious, sensual-erotic, romantic, productive/creative, intellectually curious and honest, free from moral and religious scruple, psychologically perceptive and mocking. Of course, central to Nietzsche's conception of the best form of human life is the idea of life affirmation, but as this list suggests, affirmation of life is here a natural outgrowth of energy and success. Though Nietzsche himself often emphasizes the importance of suffering, it is far from clear that any of these figures (except Beethoven) could be described as great sufferers, though many of them stand out as unusually courageous, which of course has a conceptual link to suffering (the willingness to risk being exposed to it).

What this survey suggests – and I think this is borne out by Nietzsche's specific discussions of excellence of character where these are not linked to historical illustrations – is that Nietzsche's positive ethical sketch cannot be readily assimilated to a merely formalistic conception, in which those traits which enable one to 'become what one is', regardless of specific content, are valorized.

To be sure, the traits these figures share can be seen as having instrumental value. Great energy is usually if not always a means to accomplishing whatever it is one wishes to accomplish. But I think this is to see things backwards: Nietzsche seems to find value in the activity of such figures not because they realize the figure's interests or goals, but because of the energetic quality of the activity itself. In each case, there are strong desires and great abilities manifested. In short, in their different ways, they all demonstrate 'power' and 'the will to power'.

This is evident with ambition, skill, cunning and the like, and in a different way with great artistic productivity. But it is also manifest in the romantic-passionate impulse, which could be variously characterized as both a thirst for pleasure, experience and (though we should be wary of masculinist bias) sexual conquest. Intense intellectual curiosity, outwardly directed, shows an unwillingness to yield in the face of obscurity, as well as drive outwards towards experience. Psychological acuity can be a combination of this curiosity combined with an unwillingness to give in to wishful thinking about oneself, and an amoral perceptiveness about others, which could also be linked to ambition. Finally, freedom from moral or religious scruple can be seen not only as an expression of intellectual integrity, but as a refusal to sanction restraint on one's self-assertion.

Nietzsche's own accounts of human excellence add two other traits to the above picture which arguably played a limited role in the lives of some of these figures: solitariness and condescension. Because of the dramatic portrayal of loneliness in Nietzsche's own writings, it may be easy to miss the extent to which most of these figures were, if not gregarious, then at least thoroughly caught up in their social milieus. Indeed, great ambition usually makes little sense divested of a social context in which competitiveness can play out; war is one of the most 'social' things one can engage in. Again, Beethoven seems to be the only figure who fits the kind of alienation that Nietzsche found in himself and celebrated. Second, Nietzsche frequently mentions a kind of exaltation that seems akin to condescension (*BGE* §286). Alienation is a common denominator of both solitariness and condescension (*BGE* §284). However, he seems to have confused condescension (which could manifest itself in an insistence upon one's own nobility and the baseness of others) with the facility for 'command' that he associates with the martial figures. His account seems to pull in two different directions here. On the one hand, he praises a willingness to employ and direct others for one's own purposes without scruple over the harm that one might do to them. But this does not seem at all the same thing as a 'consciousness of difference' and superior value; on the contrary, it seems to lack the requisite reflectiveness of the latter.

Finally, one may wonder about the class and gender dimensions of Nietzsche's conception. Though the ancient and medieval martial figures are all to some extent associated with 'noble birth' (though this seems to matter little in the case of Napoleon given the low tier of nobility that Napoleon's family occupied, and the likely social disadvantages of being a Corsican in France) all of the modern non-martial figures are middle class. To be sure, Nietzsche does not simply identify attitudes with class origins, allowing that sublimated attitudes can become disengaged from their sociological matrix. But his emphasis in *Genealogy of Morals* on the importance of the experiences of social superiority and inferiority in shaping fundamental attitudes makes the pervasiveness of bourgeois origins in his most praiseworthy people seem curious. Indeed, it is far from clear to me that ambition of the consuming sort that Nietzsche finds praiseworthy is not more a trait of the precarious middle classes than it is of those confident in their inherited advantages (and the considerable social constraints and expected conformity that typically attend them). And while self-conscious condescension does not seem to characterize the people Nietzsche celebrates, it seems a trait one more readily associates with a bourgeoisie that has 'arrived' than with a stably dominant social group. When we turn to Nietzsche's account of the 'ignoble', one wonders whether condescension is not just the flip side of *ressentiment*, a trait more often found among the 'not yet arrived' bourgeoisie, whose expectations have outstripped society's ability to deliver, than among a stable 'peasantry'.

Another explanation, however, for the prevalence of middle-class exemplars emerges from within Nietzsche's own texts. In *Genealogy of Morals*, after he explains the distinction between master morality and slave morality, he says that the conflict between these two evaluative schemes 'has risen ever higher and thus become more and more profound and spiritual: so that today there is perhaps no more decisive mark of a "higher nature," a more spiritual nature, than that of being divided in this sense and a genuine battleground of these opposed values' (*GM* I, §16). How might one come to have both 'master morality' and 'slave morality' internalized within one psyche?

> In an age of disintegration that mixes races indiscriminately, human beings have in their bodies the heritage of multiple origins, that is opposite, and not merely opposite, drives and value standards that fight each other and rarely permit any rest ... [W]hen the opposition and war in such a nature have the effect of one more charm and incentive of life – and if, moreover, in addition to his powerful and irreconcilable drives, a real master and subtlety in waging war against oneself, in other words, self-control, self-outwitting, has been inherited or cultivated too – then those magical, incomprehensible, and unfathomable ones arise ... (*BGE* §200, ellipsis mine)

Setting aside the Lamarckist presupposition that ancestral experiences can be inherited, given that the middle class is more likely to be 'heir' to evaluative schemes originating from multiple sources, this could explain their prevalence among Nietzsche's exemplary individuals. That said, one can still question whether this is plausible or even necessary as an explanation. Given Nietzsche's willingness in the first place to trace evaluative schemes to social circumstances, it is striking that he assumes that such schemes could only originate among the nobility and peasantry. For Nietzsche, middle-class experience contributes nothing other than combining these sources and the difficulties flowing from that. It would seem that the peculiar class circumstances of the middle classes might generate distinctive values independently. For example, a certain sense of fairness might emerge from experience with commercial transactions, a value might be placed upon being 'self-made', on being ambitious and so on.

Beyond the question of how probative Nietzsche's explanation for the psychological preconditions of his ideal is, we might also ask whether his conception reflects class bias (ironically, not 'noble' but 'bourgeois' bias). Perhaps Nietzsche has laid too much emphasis on the value of creativity and ambition at the expense of other arguable goods that may more often be associated with 'masters' or 'slaves'. With the former, conservation of tradition, something Nietzsche himself associates with noble origin, may be being given short shrift. Nor need all the experiences that generate the evaluative perspective of the socially subordinate be associated with *ressentiment*, as Nietzsche seems to suggest. Hegel, for example, writes in the *Phenomenology of Spirit* about the value of the experience of mastery over nature through work and craft, and a distinctive kind of rationality that emerges from it.[1] It is easy to see how Hegel might be right about this. While it may also be true that the socially subordinate are unusually prone to *ressentiment*, these traits are logically distinct even if they have a common cause. Finally, one may question Nietzsche's hypothesis that social subordination as such generates *ressentiment*. For as Nietzsche himself emphasizes, it is not suffering that is hard to bear, but meaningless suffering (*GM* III). In this connection, I would suggest that Nietzsche has overlooked crucial components of the psychology of *ressentiment*, namely the role of expectations, the failure of the world to meet them, and changes in circumstances. Nietzsche seems to fail to notice the importance of low expectations and stable circumstances as coping mechanisms for the socially subordinate. If that is correct, it may also suggest that *ressentiment* belongs, in its origins at least, more among those whose fortunes and expectations are mutable – again, the middle class.

Whatever characterizes and explains Nietzsche's ideal, it is noteworthy that it seems, on the face of it, to have a certain masculinist bias to it. Calling attention to this appearance helps strengthen our case for Nietzsche's ideal being substantive rather than merely formalistic. It is difficult to see how a purely formalistic ideal of thin self-creation and thin preference satisfaction could generate any particular biases for or against distinctively 'masculine' ways of being (this point applies equally to any discernible class biases). On the other hand, if Nietzsche's ideal is somehow inherently masculine, this will raise the question of whether he really has grounds for saying (if that is what he is saying) that only men can attain the ideal, or that one can do so to the extent one resembles a man. And if the ideal he sketches is inherently masculine in some sense, this will also raise the question of bias: Nietzsche's account of the ideal may be overly restrictive due to his particular perspective (being a man).

Is Nietzsche's conception of the excellent human being sexist? Notoriously, Nietzsche's late texts seem to seethe with misogyny. One possible response to this is to attempt a de-gendered reading in which Nietzsche's tendency to align the 'master' and 'slave' distinction with 'masculine' and 'feminine' (thus inevitably identifying feminism as another form of 'slave revolt' to be despised) is simply set aside as a personal idiosyncrasy. On this approach, Nietzsche's ideal of human excellence as described above becomes available to men and women alike. Though this may seem the most superficial approach, it is worth considering whether we want to accept that skill, ambition, courage, shrewdness, freedom from undesirable scruple, creativity, productivity, curiosity, intellectual integrity and psychological perceptiveness are or should be considered 'masculine'. That said, Nietzsche would not be Nietzsche without his critique of 'slave morality' and its offshoots, Christianity and its modern secularized form of liberal and social egalitarianism. To affirm Nietzsche's vision while separating it of its gendered dimension may be coherent, but it would seem to require leaving behind a vision of feminism as a concern with the oppression of women, if we also accept that there is something 'slavish' about being concerned with oppression at all.

The thought that Nietzsche devalues the feminine in some more essential sense seems to me to mislocate the worry, however. Nietzsche undervalues certain traits which we may be tempted to identify as feminine, but this is a temptation we should resist. They are human possibilities which have no specific 'gendered' dimension unless we are determined to assign them. First, Nietzsche's emphasis on independence and competition fails to do sufficient justice to how these take place against a backdrop of multiple interdependencies which facilitate rather than undermine it. If we think of competition as game-like, even if the competitors are individuals, the game itself is a shared practice which all depend on and must partly support before there can be competition. Furthermore, much competition is itself the competition between cooperating group members. Though Nietzsche frequently valorizes war at least metaphorically, his vision of war itself is far too individualistic; or, to follow the game analogy, some sports are team sports. Second, Nietzsche's valorization of romantic passion stresses the pursuit of possession at the expense of the achievement of intimacy, mutual comprehension and even altruism. Though in our more cynical moments we take lightly the experience underlying the phrase 'I would die for you', the experience is real and valuable (it is, to use the Kantian expression, 'sublime', and echoes martial experience as well). It is doubtful that Alcibiades, if classical accounts are at all accurate, experienced intense intimacy, self-disclosure and the self-squandering of personal loyalty that romantic love makes possible, and if so, his 'soul' would be the poorer for it. Third, the experience of tending and nurturing – pleasures most commonly associated with parenting – cannot be assimilated to either compassion (which he criticizes), commanding or condescension (which he celebrates). It is simply something else, and something valuable. Little is gained and much is lost if we essentialize these values as 'feminine' and regard Nietzsche's ideal as perniciously 'masculine'. Rather, Nietzsche's ideal suffers from an excess of alienation from others and a narrowness of focus. If we reflect on these points, it will be seen that nothing in these criticisms depends upon begging the question in favour of the 'slavish' traits Nietzsche criticizes for their rootedness in *ressentiment*, since none of the traits mentioned appear to be so rooted.

GENEALOGY

Nietzsche has lately been celebrated more for his critique of morality and his 'genealogical method' than his positive ethical vision. In this section, we focus attention on this critique, drawing primarily on *Beyond Good and Evil* and *Genealogy of Morals*, both of which contain elements crucial to his project. What exactly is Nietzsche's purpose in these two texts? My suggestion is that he is not primarily targeting Christianity, which he thought was on the wane. Rather, his concern is with modern secular morality in western societies, what we might call 'Enlightenment ideology'. This ideology has two key components: a commitment to modern science as an expression of the 'will to truth', and a commitment to liberal or social egalitarianism.

Why is Nietzsche opposed to these two tendencies? In part the answer will have to wait until we have a complete account of the *Genealogy*, but the main contours can be expressed as follows. Recall that Nietzsche claimed that the higher type, which he exemplified with Leonardo, is the product of 'an age of disintegration that mixes races indiscriminately', which causes people in them to contain 'opposite [and often conflicting] drives and value standards' (*BGE* §200). Such an age produces many people, perhaps the majority, who are internally divided in this way. However, he believes that there are two fundamentally different ways that people can cope with such an internal division. One strategy is 'self-control, self-outwitting' which leads to the higher type: we can characterize such people (presumably in the minority) as those who respond to their internal chaos through a kind of artistic self-fashioning, thus making themselves into distinctive human beings of the sort Nietzsche values, and which we discussed above. The second response to internal chaos, however, is far more prevalent: it is an attempt to diminish as much as possible the intensity of the internal conflict by diminishing internal intensity itself as much as possible, in the pursuit of 'the happiness of resting, of not being disturbed, of satiety, of finally attained unity' (*BGE* §200). This diminution of internal intensity, however, is incompatible with the kind of energetic quality necessary to achieve excellence and to embody the ideal that Nietzsche has sketched. But precisely because the preconditions are the same for both types, there is an open question which way any particular case will tip.

It is in this setting that modern morality becomes surpassingly important for Nietzsche. For modern morality, or 'herd animal morality' as Nietzsche polemically characterizes it, valorizes beliefs and practices which tip towards the restful, mediocre state and away from the excellent, higher state. In short, most moderns are in an historically determined state of distress which can be resolved either through cultivating energy, excellence and self-creation, or through cultivating a 'fair, modest, submissive, conforming mentality' (*BGE* §201). But modern herd animal morality responds to this fence modern human beings sit on by pushing a normative claim aimed at all individuals, urging that one ought for moral reasons to prefer the latter to the former. Thus if we are to avoid '[t]he overall degeneration of man' we must undermine the persuasive power of this normative claim (*BGE* §203). And it is precisely the content of modern morality which finds expression in one component of Enlightenment ideology – liberal or social egalitarianism.

The second component of Enlightenment ideology is its commitment to truth as an end in itself, following the methods of modern science, detached from any pragmatic interests or overarching non-cognitive goals. Nietzsche argues that this commitment is an expression of what he calls 'the ascetic ideal'. This is a component of modern morality, which seeks and achieves detachment

NIETZSCHE: A GUIDE FOR THE PERPLEXED

and depersonalization, which are also incompatible with the engaged, energetic tendencies necessary to produce excellence. If Nietzsche can polemically undermine the persuasive force of modern morality, then he can to some extent thwart these developments and their likely effect on potential higher human beings.

One popular interpretation of Nietzsche's strategy is to see him as committed to some form of moral antirealism. If there are no such things as moral facts, this would undermine morality's claim to objectivity. Nietzsche's commitment to moral antirealism in some sense is clear. As he says, we must 'leave the illusion of moral judgment beneath [ourselves]. This demand follows from an insight which I was first to formulate: that there are altogether no moral facts' (*TI* VII, §1). On this sort of view, the agenda of the *Genealogy* would be to show that an explanation of moral beliefs is possible without appealing to the truth of these beliefs; thus the historical accounts provide us with causal (largely psychological) explanations for the genesis of these beliefs, undermining the plausibility of explanations that depend upon moral facts. Such an account would be needed because in many other settings the simplest explanation for why people have certain beliefs is that the beliefs are true. If they are true, then there are mind-independent truth conditions for them which play a role in the causal explanation for the emergence of the beliefs in question. And Nietzsche certainly does insist that many moral and moral-psychological beliefs are not true.

But we should be wary of inferring that Nietzsche is committed to any broader non-cognitivism about normative claims simply because he often insists that certain specific moral and moral-psychological beliefs are false. First, non-cognitivism is not the substantive claim that our moral beliefs are false; on the contrary, it is the metaethical claim that moral (and for most non-cognitivists, all evaluative claims) are not the right sort of thing to be either true or false. Thus the claim 'there are no moral facts', which entails that none of our moral beliefs are true, is apparently ambiguous: it could be the claim that all our moral beliefs are false, or the claim that all moral discourse is neither true nor false. It is doubtful that Nietzsche held the latter. First, the very idea of non-cognitivism emerges from a later philosophical context (the transition from G. E. Moore's intuitionism to later attempts by logical positivists to accommodate certain Moorean claims about morality without accepting either his moral realism or his intuitionist moral epistemology) that would be anachronistic to project back on Nietzsche. Second, to impute non-cognitivism to Nietzsche suggests that he would have regarded his own normative statements as merely expressing his own private preferences, thus giving them little or no 'binding' force on readers. It is possible simply to accept the latter consequence. But I do not think there are any texts which can decide this question one way or another. Non-cognitivism is not really a part of Nietzsche's context, and thus nothing he says will be likely to address it directly. Furthermore, we cannot appeal to the great force and vigour with which Nietzsche puts forward his own evaluative claims as evidence in favour of his cognitivism. There is no reason to assume in advance that a non-cognitivist cannot be especially fervent in the expression of 'pro-attitudes'.

However, there is a way in which Nietzsche's rhetoric can be made sense of within a realist framework that is natural and does make ready sense of both the semblance of non-cognitivism and the forcefulness of his evaluative claims. Compare a utilitarian who regards the maximizing of pleasure (or preference-satisfaction) as good construed in terms of a realist metaethic. Utilitarians have historically been at some pains to oppose deontic, non-consequentialist accounts of duty. However, this need not be because the utilitarian has a different metaethics from the deontic theorist; both can agree that moral claims correspond to moral facts. Where they disagree is that the deontic theorist regards the fact that we have a duty as irreducible to any more basic normative fact; this is why the deontic theorist needs an intuitionist moral epistemology, for such facts will be 'queer' and require some sort of mysterious epistemic powers for their detection. The utilitarian, by contrast, insists that while we do have duties, and duty claims can be true or false, duty facts are reducible to complex facts about the consequences of acting in certain ways (or acting in accordance with certain rules). Such a utilitarian may rhetorically attack the deontic theorist's appeal to brute, irreducible facts of duty as peculiar, requiring peculiar modes of epistemic access, without offering in contrast a non-cognitivist metaethic. Rather, the utilitarian is saying that a duty is reducible to complex facts about the consequences of certain patterns of conduct, facts in principle ascertainable by empirical means. Indeed, as Sidgewick maintains, this is even compatible with the utilitarian belief that there are still basic, indemonstrable normative truths (that pleasure is better than pain) known by intuition. On such a view, the problem is not with cognitivism; the problem is that the deontic theorist does not see that there are no brute, irreducible duties.

Though there is some risk in drawing too close a comparison between Nietzsche and this sort of utilitarian, I think we can interpret his seemingly non-cognitivist rhetoric similarly. In the previous chapter, we suggested that the *Antichrist* axiology holds that power is objectively good. If that is correct, then normative theory ought to take a consequentialist form: things other than power can be assessed in terms of how they contribute to or thwart the production of power. A deontic theorist, however, regards duty claims as simply not subject to any deeper or more basic evaluative assessment. If Nietzsche is a consequentialist, then he can say that the deontic theorist is wrong in thinking that duty facts are basic and not subject to any more fundamental assessment, thus conveying the misleading impression that he is a non-cognitivist, since the deontic theorist targeted is likely to be (though need not be) a cognitivist. But he can also claim that we can evaluate duty claims by how much of some more basic good is realized by following them. Though Nietzsche stresses that the value of the exceptional individual is not dependent upon the consequences of his or her activity *for others* (*WP* §877), this does not alter the basic consequentialist thrust of his analysis; what is under discussion is the consequences of certain moral practices, where the promotion of exceptional individuals is the key consequence by which the practices are evaluated.

For if power is the only objective value, and the will to power is a universal psychological explanation, modern morality can be explained by the will to power just as much as Nietzsche's rival normative recommendations can. But matters do not end there. For after we have explained how modern morality, like its rivals, are attempts to increase or maintain power, we can then ask how successful they are in doing so. And it is here that the explanatory and normative inquiries intersect. For by specifying precisely how modern morality goes about the pursuit of power, we can then see the extent to which its strategies are successful. For example, in Nietzsche's discussion of 'the ascetic ideal' he characterizes certain ascetic practices as 'narcotics'. Suppose that I characterize all activities in a certain domain as medical, as attempts to respond to a health-related challenge, but I notice that some of these activities are surgical attempts to correct the underlying problem, while others are attempts to reduce suffering through anaesthesia while leaving the underlying source of the suffering untouched. I can say that everyone is engaged in the same fundamental enterprise, but that some are adopting a less efficacious strategy. The explanatory account (coming to understand how a certain activity can be likened to the use of a narcotic) at the same time suggests a normative assessment.

But why genealogy? What is the relevance of an essentially historical inquiry into these matters? In part, such an investigation will lend strength to the reducibility thesis: when we look at the origins of a particular moral practice or belief, if we can see its genesis in the needs and interests of its originators, this makes it less plausible that the belief emerged by way of recognition of a moral fact. But it is also true that the characteristic needs and interests that give rise to a belief or practice will tend to support it and later promote its prevalence to the extent that such needs and interests continue to exist in later generations. To be sure, Nietzsche is quick to stress that the utility of the practice at its origin need not be the same as its utility later. But when he says, for example, that the meaning of punishment is fluid, we can see this more as stressing that the interpretation of a practice changes over time. This need not imply that needs and interests served by the practice do not have some continuity. Part of Nietzsche's point is that even the original interpretation of the practice may have very little to do with the cause of its origin, if the originators' interpretation bears only a remote relationship to the way the practice originally serves their needs and interests. Thus their interpretation may have at most a diagnostic significance: it is a starting point for trying to ascertain what their needs and interests were.

One final point needs to be made that will be helpful in understanding the *Genealogy*. There is some temptation among recent philosophers to think that modern morality constitutes a coherent conceptual framework which it is the moral theorist's task to analyse and unpack.[2] Since Nietzsche is largely opposed to modern morality, it is tempting to see him as offering a critique that presupposes the unity and coherence of modern morality. If that were correct, one would expect that the *Genealogy*, Nietzsche's fullest discussion, would offer an account which is directed primarily at the conceptual commitments underlying modern morality, and that such an account would have to be exhaustive. Yet this is not how Nietzsche himself characterizes the enterprise. In *Ecce Homo* he calls the *Genealogy* '[t]hree decisive *preliminary* studies by a psychologist for a revaluation of all values' (*EH* III, '*Genealogy of Morals*', emphasis mine). The title itself suggests this incompleteness: *Zur Genealogie der Moral*. 'Zur' means 'towards', as in 'contributions towards a genealogy', thus underscoring the preliminary nature of the studies. '[D]er Moral', or 'of the moral', has been read and translated by commentators in various ways, but I think that the most literal, cognate translation captures Nietzsche's intentions best, better than 'morality', which suggests a degree of systematicity not to be expected. 'The moral' is a nominalized predicate, like 'the biological' or 'the linguistic', a construction more common in German than in English, suggesting a domain of objects to which a single predicate can be applied. A natural paraphrase would be 'moral phenomena'. The very content of the studies will show that moral phenomena are diverse and have no unifying essence other than the fact that they are human phenomena, to be explained by our best empirical theories. I think it is potentially misleading to assume that they all come together into a systematic account. What 'comes together' is that each of the phenomena in question plays some role, has some influence, on our contemporary normative commitments. Since Nietzsche doubts that historical formations evince anything more than a temporary and opportunistic unity, we should not suppose that modern morality is any exception.

THE STORY

Literature on the *Genealogy* typically follows Nietzsche's own division into three separate topics, covered by three separate essays. This approach is in accordance with the suggestions above. I think, however, that the intricacy of Nietzsche's account is obscured if we follow his exposition. Since these are historical narratives, it will be helpful if we try to disentangle as much as possible the sequence of events Nietzsche relates. In this way, we can achieve greater clarity about what is and is not involved in specific episodes. Some of this reconstruction may be controversial.

The earliest stage of Nietzsche's narrative is in Essay II, in which he discusses the emergence of guilt feelings. However, the emergence of guilt feelings is preceded by a long and complex development that begins, he claims, with the creditor-debtor relationship. Now it may seem odd to say that something suggesting a legal relationship, with a presumed legal order as its context and condition, would be the earliest phenomenon in the narrative. But Nietzsche's discussion makes clear that the basic relation of indebtedness that emerges from such a relationship is 'older even than the beginnings of any kind of social forms of organization [!]' (*GM* II, §8). This in turn is presupposed as a backdrop to the most primitive societies' experience of indebtedness to tribal ancestors (*GM* II, §19). What is more, the phase in which indebtedness to tribal ancestors occurs is contrasted with a later 'intermediate age, in which the noble tribes developed ...' (*GM* II, §19, ellipsis mine).

Nietzsche's first claim is that out of the debtor-creditor relationship, compensatory remedies emerged for defaulting debtors; the creditor's right to inflict pain upon the debtor is one of these. This arrangement, which is the origin of punishment, did not create the 'bad conscience', which he discusses later in Essay II, but rather the ability to remember one's debts and an incentive to repay them. What Nietzsche does not stress in the early sections of Essay II, though it is obvious on reflection, is that such practices will *terrify* the debtor. Indeed, the harsher the potential penalties of default, the more terrifying the state of being in debt would be. This practice, then, creates the terrified conscience. By contrast, confidence in one's ability to repay, which would manifest itself in part by the absence of terror, is what Nietzsche calls 'the good conscience'.

As Nietzsche later explains, the sense of debt, whether terrified or sanguine, is linked to the experience of advantages (as it were, the money in your pocket that you have borrowed). Because the most primitive tribal communities believe that they receive whatever advantages they possess by virtue of the tribal ancestor, this sense of debt comes to be transferred to the ancestor-as-creditor; as the advantages increase, the sense of debt increases, and with it the fear (transferred from the fear of punishment) of never being able to repay. Correlatively, the ancestor image grows into an increasingly fearsome one, eventually coming to be perceived as a god. It is noteworthy that Nietzsche's identification of the gods with tribal ancestors is one echoed by Freud, in *Totem and Taboo*.

Nietzsche also makes clear that this genesis of the gods applies to the later gods of 'the intermediate age, in which the noble tribes developed' (GM II, §19). Thus, the terrified conscience/good conscience phenomenon is one shared by the noble tribes, though Nietzsche points out that the Greeks, for example, were able to stay on the happier 'good conscience' side of this dual condition by various psychological expedients for reducing the sense of debt to the gods. At the same time that we see the emergence of noble tribes, we see the emergence of what, in *Beyond Good and Evil*, Nietzsche calls 'master morality'. This part of Nietzsche's account, with its associated contrast with 'slave morality', is perhaps the most famous part of his analysis and we can describe it briefly: the nobles, because of their success in the world and the comparatively free flow of their instinctual energies (in war, primarily) come to evaluate themselves and their traits (courage, self-assertion) as fundamentally good (*GM* I, §§1–5). Since other nobles they compete with on the battlefield possess similar traits, they perceive them as noble adversaries rather than as hated, despised or resented enemies.

Eventually, the nobles collide with a 'formless and nomad' population, conquering and enslaving them (*GM* II, §17). This has immediate, catastrophic consequences for the enslaved. Their own aggressive impulses are no longer able to express themselves outwardly, and become introjected or 'internalized'. Instead of acting aggressively against their adversaries, the now suppressed (out of prudence, presumably) aggression turns inward and becomes a desire for self-attack, a kind of masochistic cruelty. Nietzsche calls this 'the bad conscience' (*GM* II, §16). Presumably the nobles, now 'masters' (over the slaves), will not possess this bad conscience, because they are not enslaved. To the extent that settled life in a community inhibits the scope of expression for their aggression as well, this aggression never gets pent up entirely, since it can still be vented in war and in the 'management' of the slaves themselves.

With the cessation of outward hostility by the slaves, they come to acquire traits (caution, timidity, submissiveness) that strike the masters as radically distinct from their own traits or those of their noble adversaries. From this, the masters construct the concept of 'baseness' or ignobility as a contrast with their own traits. The slaves are now subject not only to the inconvenience of slavery, but to an evaluative interpretation of their typical responses to it: they are despised. Though Nietzsche does not discuss the point explicitly, there is no reason why the slaves would not 'buy into' the master evaluative scheme, for they have by now already developed the bad conscience, a propensity for self-hatred, and an evaluative scheme that regards them as worthy of contempt would fit quite naturally with a need to experience self-hatred. This alone should suggest that the creation of 'slave morality' is a bit more complicated and far later than might at first appear. Finally, the self-hatred of the bad conscience generates 'all ideal and imaginative phenomena ... This hint will at least make less enigmatic the enigma of how contradictory concepts such as selflessness, self-denial, self-sacrifice can suggest an ideal ...' (*GM* II, §18, ellipsis mine). In short, the bad conscience is a causal precondition of what in Essay III Nietzsche will call 'the ascetic ideal', available in principle to anyone whose aggressive energies are thwarted by social arrangements, though not only to them.

Next, the noble class splits itself into two subgroups: the 'knightly-aristocratic' and the 'priestly-noble'. Nietzsche makes clear that the priest is initially a dominating, noble position (*GM* I, §7), though he later says that 'he emerges from every class of society' (GM III, §11). But it is not a position based on martial success; the priests are constitutionally unfit for this, and their basic unhealthiness manifests itself in various ascetic practices and beliefs they adopt to reduce their discomfort (*GM* I, §6; *GM* III, §11). In their early form, they manifest two important traits. First, the priest displays 'an insatiable instinct and power-will that wants to become master not over something in life but over life itself' (*GM* III, §11). This can best be understood in terms of constitutional unfitness. Suppose that you have a functional disorder which causes you pain. The more vigorous, the more lively your basic bodily functions are, the more fuel is added to the fire of the disorder and the greater your suffering. This would create an incentive to reduce one's own vigour. For a more extreme example, suppose that the whole bodily constitution is so weak and depressive that merely existing is a source of discomfort. Even here, there is a linkage between one's vigour and suffering, for even a weak and depressive psychophysical constitution has some propensity to strive for survival. But if the most one can get from this propensity is to linger on in pain, the mere fact of existing in this state of minimal vigour will be a source of suffering. In any case, the priest, who like all people, is motivated by will to power comes to see his own vitality as an enemy to be defeated. As a result, he adopts various ascetic practices and beliefs which reduce his vigour and express his hostility towards concrete reality (see Chapter 3 above for a related discussion of the emergence of the contrast between a world of becoming and a world of being).

The ascetic priest, however, must initially make his way among the knightly-aristocratic. Since his basic stance is one of hostility towards vigour within himself, he will naturally generalize this hostility towards the vigorous, successful nobles. But there is one mechanism that will enable him to get on with the nobles, for they will feel (absent the special expedients Nietzsche says the Greeks developed) a sense of terrified indebtedness towards their ancestor gods as the one shadow over their otherwise successful existence. Here the ascetic priest can serve as a mediator between the community and the gods, by explaining the nobles' situation and the relevant sacrifices they need to make (in the earliest form, animal or even human sacrifices) (*GM* II, §19).

Most importantly for Nietzsche's moral psychology, the sense of terrified indebtedness becomes fused with the bad conscience by virtue of the slaves' adoption of the tribal deities of the nobles (*GM* II, §20). Again, it is presumably the priests who act 'as the herald and mouthpiece of more mysterious powers' (*GM* III, §15). It is only with this that we see 'the moralization of [the concepts "guilt" and "duty"] (their pushing back into the conscience ...)' (*GM* II, §21, ellipsis mine). This too is explicable in terms of the psychology of the bad conscience, for the basic self-attacking character of this faculty should be able to seize on any pretexts for self-criticism at hand. 'You have not paid your debts' is a natural basis for self-criticism. Since the idea of indebtedness to the gods is one that lends itself to grandiose interpretations, nothing else could provide as powerful a basis for self-attack. So with the onset of the bad conscience, at least receptivity to the moralization of indebtedness is present.

But at the same time, the slaves feel an intense *ressentiment* towards the masters for their condition. Part of the psychology of guilt, as Nietzsche explains it, is the propensity to assign blame. The natural form that blame assignment would take in the slaves is to assign blame to the masters. At this point the ascetic priest intervenes with a dual interpretative manoeuvre: the ascetic priest invents 'slave morality' as an expression of this *ressentiment*. He then exploits the bad conscience of those he dominates, changing the direction of their *ressentiment* so that the resentful blame themselves for their condition rather that the masters, interpreting it as punishment by God for their sins. This latter move can be seen either as a further development of the fusion of terrified indebtedness with the bad conscience, or as its principal cause.

It may come as something of a surprise to those accustomed to reading Nietzsche as attributing slave morality to the creativity of the slaves to find him attributing it to priests, hence aristocrats. Matters are complex, however, for Nietzsche says that it is 'the Jews, that priestly people' who devised slave morality, 'that with the Jews there begins the slave revolt in morality ...' (*GM* I, §7, ellipsis mine). How are we to understand this?

Nietzsche does not attribute slave morality to anyone else. As uncomfortable as it is for contemporary readers, the slave revolt in morals is squarely attributed to 'the Jews' and not to the abstract category of the socially subordinated wherever one finds them. Though it has become popular in recent Nietzsche scholarship either to stress the metaphorical nature of this attribution (which is in no way licensed by the text) or to emphasize the discontinuity between ancient Judaism and the modern Jewish community, while stressing the various favourable things that Nietzsche says elsewhere about the latter, the fact that Judaism occupies such a central role in his account of the genesis of values he considers anathema is surely troubling. But apart form being troubling, it is also perplexing: how can this be squared with the claims earlier in Essay I that the priestly is an aristocratic position, though one in conflict with the knightly? Though it is unclear within the *Genealogy* at what point Nietzsche thinks that the ancient Hebrews came to be dominated by their own priestly class, what is clear is that the ancient (if not the very earliest) historical experience of the Jewish people was one of collective subordination to foreign powers. Relative to the non-priestly tribes within ancient Israel, the priests would be dominant figures; in the context of the relationship with the succession of foreign powers (culminating in Rome) the status of totality of the Jewish people, even their highest priests, is one of 'enslavement'. This layered sense of multiple hierarchy is repeated in Nietzsche's complex account in *Antichrist* of the relations between the Romans, the Temple priests and the early Christians (*A* §27).

Here the psychological peculiarities common to priests everywhere move towards the social frustrations of the subordinated everywhere to form a unique intersection. It is from such a position that the Jewish priests invent slave morality as an ideological weapon against occupiers and a mode of self-esteem boosting for those whom the priests lead. Given Nietzsche's assumptions, this invention, tailored to the needs of a Jewish priestly aristocracy and Jewish common people alike, should have occurred almost simultaneously with the 'change in the direction of *ressentiment*' described in Essay III. For the natural tendency of a conquered people would be either to adopt the beliefs, values and practices of the conquerors, abandoning their prior commitments out of disappointment over their inefficacy, or rebel against the conquerors. But on Nietzsche's account, the Jews in antiquity did neither. Instead, they crafted slave morality as a normative justification for their moral superiority in the face of their social superiors, while clinging to their deity, who is understood not to have failed them, but to be punishing them for their moral shortcomings. It is difficult to resist the conclusion that the *ressentiment* that creates slave morality, the ascetic priest's interpretation of suffering as religious guilt, thus changing the direction of *ressentiment*, and the fusion of the bad conscience with the feeling of terrified indebtedness, all happen more or less simultaneously in the matrix of the military conquests and exiles suffered by the Jewish people. It is difficult to say what Nietzsche's own understanding of the actual history of the Jewish people in antiquity was, and contemporary scholars are also divided.

Two puzzles remain. First, it is crucial to the account of slave morality that it involves a characterization of the masters as wicked and blameworthy, while the slaves are redefined as good for having chosen to refrain from injuring others. Nietzsche thinks that the invention of the concept of free will as the basis for moral accountability occurs here. Yet it would seem that this is incompatible with the change in direction of *ressentiment*, which involves ceasing to blame the master and instead blaming oneself. Clearly *ressentiment* is the prior condition in both cases, but it is hard to see how one can simultaneously come to adopt a stance of moral superiority and moral worthlessness. Though Nietzsche never brings the two discussions together to answer this question, the experience of moral superiority in the slave upon adopting slave morality must be more complex than simply finding oneself good. It would also have to be to be compatible with finding oneself sinful.

On the slave moral interpretative scheme, hostile affects (among other things) are characterized as evil. The slave finds these hostile affects in himself; objectively, they should be even more prominent in himself than in the master, given the lack of appropriate discharge. Recall that Socrates' superior wisdom consisted in his knowing that he knew nothing, whereas his opponents' foolishness consisted in thinking they knew something while not knowing that they knew nothing. Perhaps the slavish sense of moral superiority can be fused with a sense of sin in a similar way. Hostile affects are evil, the slave says. I find hostile affects in myself. But at least I know that I am morally inadequate and am striving to overcome this. This makes me morally superior to the thoughtless master, who lacks even the slightest willingness to overcome his own depravity.

The second puzzle is a classic one in the Nietzsche secondary literature. How on earth did slave morality prevail? We know from the initial account of modernity that master morality did not simply go away, and presumably it had hosts which could transmit it. Nietzsche clearly thinks that the peculiar catastrophe of antiquity was the 'sale' of slave morality to the masters. How could this have occurred if the knightly-aristocratic class regarded the traits slave morality promotes as base and ignoble? More broadly, how could the whole cluster of ideas under discussion have found a foothold in people who, on the above account, should not even have possessed a bad conscience to any significant degree?

Though it is obvious that Nietzsche associates the turn of the masters towards slave morality with the Christianization of the Roman Empire, some specific mechanism for this must be at work. Nietzsche's own answer is at section eight of Essay I. First, he suggests that the essentially Jewish character of the values pushed by Christianity was concealed by the semblance of conflict between the Temple priests and Jesus. Of course this kind of cognitive error cannot even begin to explain such a tremendous reversal of perspective as that which Nietzsche is envisioning. Second, the Pauline doctrine of atonement coupled with the vividness of the Passion narrative has an 'enticing, intoxicating, overwhelming and undermining power ...' that joins 'love', 'cruelty' and 'salvation' together into a compelling unity (*GM* I, §8, ellipsis mine). It is not too difficult to see why the masters, given their enjoyment of cruelty, might be 'sold' on a movement which has a spectacle of cruelty as its centrepiece. However, this too seems insufficient. In the end, Nietzsche must think that the masters needed 'salvation'.

Helpfully, Nietzsche explains the psychology of this later. When the sense of terrified indebtedness is linked to the bad conscience, and interpreted as a relationship with the god (formerly the tribal ancestor) of the successful nobles, the greater the success the nobles experience, the greater the burden of guilt. In one stroke, the Christian doctrine of Atonement, vividly conveyed through the Passion narrative, offers the successful nobles a way out of accumulated guilt: all debts have been discharged (*GM* II, §21). If we link this account with the account of the crucifixion as 'bait' (*GM* I, §8), then the conversion to slave morality is clear. The self-sacrifice of God relieves the sense of obligation. Yet this incarnate God was also a teacher of slave moral values, which thus have the imprimatur of the outfit with which one must do business if the discharge is to be effective. In short, slave morality, otherwise distasteful to the nobles, was a package deal; if you wanted relief from guilt, you needed to buy the code as well.

Since this is the only coherent account that emerges from Nietzsche's texts of how slave morality could have prevailed against master morality, it suggests that the masters must have had a sense of indebtedness too. There are several ways we might understand this. First, we could suppose that the Romans, though lacking a bad conscience, nonetheless had what I called the terrified conscience, and as their ascendancy over the ancient world rose to unparalleled heights, this sense of debt (though not 'moralized' debt) rose to intolerable levels. Second, we could suppose that the Romans did have a moralized sense of debt – the fusion of indebtedness with the bad conscience – and try to explain how they could have acquired the bad conscience in the first place. Two subsidiary possibilities suggest themselves. First, the settled conditions of the Roman Empire may not have provided adequate scope for the expression of aggressive impulses, unlike the situation of the wilder nobles of prehistory, thus causing the Romans to develop internalized aggression after all. Second, given Nietzsche's Lamarckism, he may suppose that the bad conscience is inherited from those who first acquired it via the sudden trauma of socialization described in Essay II, and that the Romans had inherited this trait from ancient victims over the course of a tangled history. The text probably underdetermines any of these readings; it is far from clear that Nietzsche ever sought to synthesize and harmonize these 'preliminary studies' into a unitary account.

It is clear from Nietzsche's account that the various developments he charts come together in Christianity, which then goes on to become the dominant cultural force in western civilization for over a thousand years. Modernity has relinquished the specifically religious interpretation of the psychological factors at work in it, but continues to follow the psychological contours laid down by Christianity. Liberalism and socialism manifest the egalitarianism inherent in the slave-moral demand for equality between the masters and the slaves. If Nietzsche were with us today, he would no doubt say that the self-hatred of the bad conscience continues to manifest itself in the ways that recent conservatives mock as 'liberal guilt' over world hunger, capitalist exploitation, animal suffering, the mistreatment of criminals (though, to be sure, Nietzsche also allows that mercy towards criminals can be a manifestation of strength (*GM* II, §10)) and even global warming. The ascetic ideal shows up in the dispassionateness of modern science and the self-derogatory interpretation of the human condition that it has championed, whether mechanistic, Darwinian, Marxian or Freudian. Underneath it all, Nietzsche discerns a self-destructive tendency culminating in the enfeeblement of humanity and the progressive undermining of any prospects for human excellence and splendour. What does he propose in its place?

First, Nietzsche says that moving beyond the slave moral categories of good and evil 'does not mean "Beyond Good and Bad" ' (*GM* I, §17). This suggests that Nietzsche would like us to revive the master moral perspective if possible. To be sure, Nietzsche does say that he would have us move into an 'extra-moral' position (*BGE* §32), and this might seem to be in tension with an attempt to revive master morality. That appearance would be misleading, however. What is at issue in the contrast between 'moral' and 'extra-moral' in section 32 of *Beyond Good and Evil*, is the distinction between evaluating actions for the freely chosen, conscious intentions causing them instead of the character they express, which Nietzsche believes is a complex, unchosen and largely unconscious psychophysical totality. Though Nietzsche could distinguish himself from the original masters as far as the degree of penetration and insight he has into the determinants of character, nothing in master morality requires that people be evaluated by their conscious intentions as opposed to their character and its determinants. Indeed, though he says that the idea of the importance of intention has a master origin (*BGE* §32), the idea that this intention is freely chosen has a slave origin (*GM* I, §13). We can become 'extra-moral' by abandoning the slavish notion of free will and evaluating people instead by their character and its unconscious determinants, without abandoning the central categories of master morality.

That said, this may not have been Nietzsche's final word on the subject. In *Twilight* he seems to return again to the contrast between master and slave morality, this time using Hinduism as expressed in the law of Manu as an example of the former. Here he contrasts two types of morality, a morality of 'breeding' versus a morality of 'taming' with the latter clearly meant to refer to Christianity. Yet here Nietzsche stresses the failure of both sorts of morality to appreciate the 'no moral facts' thesis, which he takes as indicative of their dishonesty, and concludes that both types are 'entirely worthy of each other' (*TI* VII, §5). I think the solution to this problem rests on an ambiguity in the term 'master morality'. Recall that we distinguished above between the knightly master and the priestly master. The priestly master may or may not promote slave morality; there were priests before there were priests committed to slave morality. Clearly the law of Manu as Nietzsche describes it is not committed to slave morality, but by the same token it is a priestly phenomenon. What seems to distinguish the stance of the knightly master from the non-slavish priestly master is that the former is not committed to making people different. As much as the noble may disdain the base, they are only committed to using them as needed, and this use presupposes an acceptance of their character – their submissive nature, for example. By contrast, the priestly masters described in *Twilight* share with the priestly advocates of slave morality the belief that people ought to be different from the way that they are. When Nietzsche says sarcastically that both are worthy of each other, it appears to be this which they share in common, a trait which manifests itself by their common commitment to the existence of moral facts. A knightly master, by contrast, need not judge that anything fails to be as it ought. It is unclear, however, whether there is really an intelligible contrast here. Surely the knightly master judges that other knightly masters ought to be courageous? Or are we to assume that they never fail to be courageous? Is there no training regimen for bringing children up into master morality? Conversely, why can we not assimilate the priestly master's 'breeding programme' to a using of others, akin to the use that the knightly master puts his slaves to? If Nietzsche's only objection to the priestly master is that he is committed to the wrong metaethics, it is far from clear what metaethic the knightly master is committed to, and thus very difficult to see what this contrast really comes to. By the end of Nietzsche's authorship, however, he is willing to say that '[t]he problem I thus pose is not what shall succeed mankind in the sequence of living beings (man is an end), but what type of man shall be bred, shall be willed, for being higher in value, worthier of life, more certain of a future' (*A* §3). It would appear, then, that Nietzsche finally aligns himself with the non-slavish priestly master after all. Taken with the comment in *Twilight* above, this appears to mean that while he affirms the values that master morality expresses, he rejects the dishonesty involved in pursuing this goal while concealing its necessary means: the creation of social practices that bring it about. Though it is false to say that a person is morally blameworthy for failing to conform to such practices, it remains true that the higher types which such practices produce *are* more valuable than others.

Second, though the bad conscience is by now ineradicable, we can eliminate the association of it with indebtedness by abandoning theism. We can now dissociate it from the ascetic ideal by 'an attempt at the reverse ... that is, to wed the bad conscience to all the unnatural inclinations ...' (*GM* II, §24, ellipses mine). Third, science can be subordinated, not to the ascetic ideal, but to 'genuine philosophers' who command new values (*BGE* §211). The will to truth can become an invigorating test of strength instead of a will to self-denial as an end in itself, as Nietzsche suggests when he says that 'the strength of a spirit should be measured according to how much of the "truth" one could still barely endure ...' (*BGE* §39, ellipsis mine).

What are we to make of all this? First, it cannot be stressed enough how utterly speculative Nietzsche's psychological and historical claims are. Though seen from one angle the above narrative(s) are rather complex, one cannot resist the impression that Nietzsche has vastly oversimplified stretches of human, and western, experience, and has left us with stories so vague (especially the prehistory stories) as to put them beyond any meaningful empirical testing. Similarly, Nietzsche's psychological hypotheses suffer from this historical murkiness while adding the sins that Freud was heir to: not saying what people did, or said, but rather what they thought, or worse, what they did not realize they were thinking. Since these historical narratives tend to validate themselves by way of functional claims, they also generate the same dangerous attraction that sociobiological claims do. One can tell a surprising story about, for example, why men and women seem to behave differently, by appealing to differing reproductive strategies. But there will be many different possible strategies that would manifest themselves in the same conduct, even if we grant the basic explanatory approach. Conversely, are women attracted to strong men because they would make good breadwinners? Or to nurturing men because they would make good co-parents? It would help to have hard data on the attraction first, and then a careful survey of as many possible explanations as possible, and then some hard Popperian attempts at falsification and winnowing. But with Nietzsche we get comparatively little of that. It is not that he has no data at his disposal; it is that data, and plausible functionalist stories, are not remotely good enough. Given that at least for Nietzsche we have to ask what we are to do with our received moral practices, commitments and intuitions, the stakes could not be higher, and considerable methodological rigour is called for.

The comparison between Nietzsche and Freud is often made, given the essential identity between their two accounts of the bad conscience. But what is not often said is that we have now had several decades of methodological reflection on psychoanalysis behind us and the results are not encouraging. And yet Freud actually met the people he analysed! In Nietzsche's case, he read them, or about them, or just made them up. Second, Nietzsche and Freud share a dubious commitment to Lamarckism. It is often thought that this can simply be ignored and replaced with explanations dependent on learning and cultural transmission. But it remains to be seen whether such repair will always be effective. For example, the bad conscience is said to be the product a single, catastrophic event that redistributes psychic energies in a distinctive way. Unless this trauma is repeated in each generation, mere learning and cultural transmission cannot salvage the hypothesis. But while it may be that some analogous trauma does repeat itself in each life (as Freud might insist), this means that the historical hypothesis falls away as irrelevant. Finally, Nietzsche and Freud are both committed to what one might call a hydraulic account of the psyche. At crucial junctures, appeal is made to what Freud called 'economic' principles (the energy has to come from somewhere, the energy has to go somewhere, block discharge here, it spurts out there). Absolutely nothing in contemporary evolutionary biology, computational neurobiology, or molecular psychiatry suggests that the psyche works in anything like this way.

Though Nietzsche's critical distancing from our moral commitments is admirable and useful, these empirical concerns cast considerable doubt on how probative his psychological explanations really are. But there is one last objection. Nietzsche's entire project is driven by the sense that admirable human beings are lacking or are imperilled, and that the modern world is a breeding ground for mediocrity. Perhaps. But another possibility suggests itself. To use the example of a breeding ground for excellence closest to Nietzsche's heart, consider Grace. Was there some profound difference between mediocre modernity and excellent antiquity? Or it is merely that antiquity is exotic, alien and remote? Some features of their culture that impress us in retrospect may have seemed quite ordinary to them, and have only grown in our estimation by accumulated piety and the passage of time. Furthermore, whatever was not excellent about ancient Athens may not have been absent. It may simply be forgotten. But it takes centuries for the dross to fall away, for the excellent to grow in later estimation and understanding. It could be that the mediocrity of the modern is a trick of perspective. Perhaps all eras are suffused with mediocrity, and all eras, our own included, conceal hidden gems that come to light only gradually.

CHAPTER 6

HEIDEGGER'S NIETZSCHE

PRELIMINARIES

Heidegger's interpretation of Nietzsche is unusual in being that of another philosopher of the first rank. But this should also inspire caution, for Heidegger, we suspect, may not be concerned primarily with accurate interpretation of Nietzsche, let alone defending him as an advocate, but rather with competition. Most first-tier philosophers probably approach the task of interpreting the history of philosophy from the perspective of their interests in vindicating their own philosophical correctness and historical importance.

That said, the reception of Heidegger's Nietzsche has been peculiar among those not committed to championing Heidegger. I think we can pick out several reasons for this. First, the 'elephant in the living room': for many in the English-speaking world, Nietzsche is associated with Nazism, because the Nazi movement attempted to appropriate him to legitimize its policies. For those sympathetically disposed towards Nietzsche, this fact is remarkably easy to turn aside, because Nietzsche was not a contemporary of Nazism, and because Nietzsche says many things that are critical of both state power and German nationalism. Heidegger's relationship with Nazism is less easy to dismiss; he was, as the expression has it, a 'card carrying member'. While it is obvious enough that Heidegger distinguishes his own position from Nietzsche's as he understands it, and it is true (though less obvious) that Heidegger's own thought up to the end of the Second World War is subtly and importantly different from many prominent Nazi ideologues, the whole proximity to Nazism that contemplation of Heidegger creates in the reader is enough to make one want to make it all go away if possible.

This attitude is reinforced by certain confusions about the semantic structure and methodological features of Heidegger's interpretation. Heidegger's interpretation, like all interpretations, must distinguish between interpreted content, interpretative claims, explanations of interpreted content and evaluation. For example, if I were to say 'Sally thinks that robots are stealing her luggage, but that's ridiculous; perhaps this was caused by childhood trauma' it would be utterly irrelevant to note that Sally has never said 'childhood traumas make me say ridiculous things', and it is a terrible distortion of her views to foist such nonsense on her. Of course, nothing has been foisted upon her at all, unless of course Sally never even said 'robots are stealing my luggage'. The claim that Sally's views are ridiculous is an external evaluation, pre-supposing that 'robots steal people's luggage' is untrue, unwarranted and the like; it is not part of the propositional content of Sally's assertion. Similarly, appeal to her childhood experiences is an explanatory hypothesis about her utterance, and is again external to their content.

Heidegger makes claims about Nietzsche's thought which have inspired similar responses. For example, Heidegger claims that Nietzsche's thought bears a certain structural similarity to that of past western metaphysicians. The question is not whether Nietzsche thought this, but whether it is true. Heidegger, like Hegel, has a thesis about an overall narrative unity to the history of western philosophy according to which Nietzsche represents the culmination of certain tendencies and developments. It is beside the point to claim that Nietzsche did not think of himself as 'the last metaphysician'. He may not have understood his historical situation as well as Heidegger does (and the meaning of the term 'metaphysics' in Heidegger may have a broader scope than it does in Nietzsche, thus making Nietzsche's self-description on this point irrelevant). This logical point, of course, is independent of the plausibility of Heidegger's theses about metaphysics and the history of western philosophy. Furthermore, Heidegger characterizes Nietzsche as the philosopher of technology, an odd claim given that Nietzsche rarely discusses technology. Yet this discrepancy is wholly irrelevant to Heidegger's claim. According to Heidegger, each period of western history is characterized by a set of conceptual commitments which shape how we understand the world and how we go about living in it. These conceptual commitments tend to be largely unconscious or in some sense unavailable to those who share them. But when philosophers within a particular moment of history try to solve conceptual problems as philosophers, they too do so within the historical moment's commitments, and this is reflected in how they go about doing philosophy. Does the philosopher merely reflect changes in the conceptual framework, or does the philosopher in some sense originate them? Heidegger's account of major conceptual revolutions he associates with Plato, Descartes and Nietzsche seems to suggest that something ('being') other than the philosopher is responsible for radical conceptual change, and the philosopher tunes into this, perhaps in advance of the rest of the community. Now on Heidegger's view, there are certain features of our conceptual commitments that make it inevitable that we will adopt a stance of domination and control towards everything, and that technology in the ordinary sense, as it manifests itself today, is an especially apt but by no means the only expression of this. For reasons relating to the Greek etymology of the word 'technology', Heidegger characterizes this modern conceptual framework as 'technological'. Thus when Heidegger says that Nietzsche is the philosopher of technology, he means not that Nietzsche talks about technology in the narrow sense, but that Nietzsche talks about everything in a 'technological' way, thus manifesting the same tendency to see entities in terms of domination and control that we see manifested by current technological practices in the narrower sense. To continue with the analogy of Sally and the robots stealing her luggage, characterizing Nietzsche as a technological thinker is *diagnostic*, it is not meant to duplicate the propositional content of Nietzsche's thought, but to step outside it and explain it. It is also meant to be, in a sense reminiscent of Wittgenstein, *therapeutic* as well.

Many critics of Heidegger's approach are uncomfortable with its reliance on the unpublished writings. First, this is greatly overstated; of the four volumes of the English translation, only volumes three and four, the lectures of 1939–40, some essays written in 1941 and an essay written in 1944–46, show a partiality towards using the notes; the lectures of 1936–37 that make up the bulk of volumes one and two do not do this, despite Heidegger's methodological self-descriptions. Heidegger also from time to time reaffirms that *The Will to Power* is not a finished book, but an editorial construction from Nietzsche's notes. Why then does he use it? Because some of

Nietzsche's most interesting suggestions are found there. More to the point, why does he not refrain from using it? Is there no significance in the fact that Nietzsche allegedly rejected these notes, and at least did not see them through to publication?

It is difficult to see why. As Heidegger explains, he is not engaged in writing a biography. He is writing an exegesis of some philosophical texts. Nietzsche the human being has no particular authority to say that we should or should not examine a particular text. Suppose that a mathematician succeeded in proving Fermat's Conjecture, but in a fit of confusion, failed to see the significance of what he had done and falsely concluded that his attempted proof was a failure. He decides not to publish it, and it is found among his papers. Are we then by some unwritten rule forbidden to read and evaluate it?

Thus when Heidegger offers his interpretation, the word 'Nietzsche' is just a label he assigns to a body of texts, remarkable or not, not because some particular human being authorized their reading, but because of their propositional content. It is strange that a preoccupation with Nietzsche's personal authorization should loom large only among analytic and deconstructionist interpreters, both of whom for differing reasons, one might think, would take the point established long ago by New Criticism that authorial intention (including the intention to publish) counts for little. All this aside, there might be particular value nonetheless in focusing attention on unpublished materials, for it is here that we might be more likely to catch a thought 'in motion' as it were.

The final reason why I suspect that Heidegger's interpretation of Nietzsche is resisted is inertia. To understand Heidegger's Nietzsche, one has to know Heidegger, the development he passed through from being Husserl's student to being the author of *Being and Time*, the further development of his position in *Introduction to Metaphysics* in 1930, and the content of the Nietzsche lectures and essays of the 1930s and 1940s. This amounts to approximately a thousand pages of material, much of it written in an extraordinarily opaque style. Then it would be helpful if one had some independently conceived interpretation of Nietzsche that one could appeal to in evaluating Heidegger's claims. All this is difficult; it is far easier to focus on his methodological unsoundness for relying on the unpublished writings; in any case, one might think that Heidegger is obviously incapable of generating an adequate interpretation, given his agenda-driven characterization of Nietzsche as the philosopher of technology, when Nietzsche clearly never discusses technology in any sustained or important way.

Heidegger's *Nietzsche* was developed in a series of lecture courses and essays in the main written in the late 1930s and early to mid-1940s, subsequently published in two volumes in German in 1961 and published in four volumes from 1979 to 1987; I rely on the paperback edition of the latter, published in two volumes in 1991 (which, however, retains the separate four-volume pagination of the hardcover volumes). The English text contains the following materials: 'The Will to Power as Art', lectures from 1936–37; 'The Eternal Recurrence of the Same', lectures from 1937; 'The Will to Power as Knowledge', lectures from 1939; 'The Eternal Recurrence of the Same and Will to Power', an undelivered lecture manuscript from 1939; 'Nietzsche's Metaphysics', a manuscript from 1940; 'European Nihilism', lectures from 1940; 'Nihilism as Determined by the History of Being', an essay from 1944–46; 'Who is Nietzsche's Zarathustra?', a lecture from 1953. Since this last lecture is not included in the German edition, I do not consider it here. Three further essays from 1941, 'Metaphysics as History of Being', 'Sketches for a History of Being as Metaphysics', and 'Recollection of Metaphysics', have been translated and published separately by Joan Stambaugh in *The End of Philosophy*.[1] Though what I have called Heidegger's external explanation and assessment of Nietzsche's thought in terms of his own 'history of being' hypothesis intrudes periodically throughout the materials, it really only dominates the 'European Nihilism' lectures and the 'Nihilism as Determined by the History of Being' essay; the three further essays just mentioned are largely concerned with the 'history of being' hypothesis, so I do not consider them here.

THE WILL TO POWER AS ART

Heidegger's first lecture series ostensibly concerns Nietzsche's views on art; to anticipate Heidegger's ultimate concern, however – which emerges towards the end of the lecture series – is to make sense of Nietzsche's perspectivism as a metaphysical and epistemological doctrine. He summarizes Nietzsche's views in the form of five claims: (1) 'Art is the most perspicuous and familiar configuration of will to power', (2) 'Art must be grasped in terms of the artist', (3)

According to the expanded concept of artist, 'art is the basic occurrence of all beings; to the extent that they are, beings are self-creating, created', (4) 'Art is the distinctive countermovement to nihilism', and (5) 'Art is worth more than "the truth" '.[2] Heidegger's concern, as the claims indicate, is not primarily to develop Nietzsche's thought in aesthetics as it is commonly understood. Most philosophical theories in aesthetics are directed at spectator experience and the legitimation or delegitimation of aesthetic claims about art objects. For Nietzsche, according to Heidegger, the interest in discussing art is that the artist's creative activity is best conceptualized as will to power. Assuming that we accept a metaphysics of will to power, this will assist us in understanding in what sense things in general are 'creative'. Heidegger characterizes this creativity as 'form-engendering force'.[3] Since we have already discussed the reasons for taking a metaphysical reading of the will to power seriously in a previous chapter, we can set that issue aside here. In any case, Heidegger does not argue here for a metaphysical reading as opposed to other possibilities.

What interests Heidegger most is the relationship between our creative and cognitive interests, or as he calls them, 'art' and 'truth', and the 'raging discordance' between them.[4] In particular, he wants to clarify the relationship between this conflict, the two-world picture and perspectivism. If we begin with the two-world picture, which Heidegger often refers simply to as 'Platonism', it seems that we have a contrast between a sensuous world which is regarded as unreal, and a non-sensuous world accessible to reason which is real. If art is fundamentally concerned with the (devalorized) sensuous and philosophy with the (valorized) non-sensuous, then one possible construal of Nietzsche's repudiation of the two-world picture would be a simple reversal. This would have cognitive and evaluative implications: the sensuous is now regarded as the real and the proper object of our cognitive interests, and the non-sensuous is regarded as the unreal. Such a position would be nothing more than a form of empiricism. We could add that if what is to be regarded as real is what is to be valued, then reversal entails that we should value the sensuous world and not value the (unreal) non-sensuous world.

Heidegger recognizes, however, that this is too simple. The primary obstacle here is that it cannot be integrated with Nietzsche's 'untruth as a condition of life' rhetoric (*BGE* §4), the association of art with healthy illusion (*NCW*, Epilogue), and the connection of art so conceived with the sensuous. For if art is concerned with the sensuous, and has value because it shields us from harsh truths, we seem to have landed back in the two-world picture, with the non-sensuous as the realm of truth and the sensuous as the realm of illusion.

Matters are complicated still further by Heidegger's acceptance of some version of the panpsychist metaphysics described in Chapter 4. This implies that there is another sense in which the sensuous has priority over the non-sensuous: all beings are experiencers in some sense, which suggests that there are no non-sensory beings left over to be the denizens of a non-sensory realm. Furthermore, Heidegger also thinks that Nietzsche is committed to phenomenalism, the view that objects of experience become the sum of all experiencers' 'perspectives' on them, which also eliminates a non-sensory realm.[5] How can there be a 'raging discordance' between two terms if one of the terms drops out?

Heidegger's resolution is as follows. If we turn from Nietzsche's claims about art to his claims about cognition instead, then we see some prominent Kantian themes. Recall that on Kant's view the world of experience gives us neither direct access to mind-independent objects, nor indirect access to them by way of inner representations that correspond to them. Rather, the mind has various structures that it imposes on the manifold of sensation, thus creating stable objects that we can then explore with the resources of empirical science.[6] In a certain sense, these objects are 'in the mind'; what lies 'outside the mind' is unknowable. These structures, when properly employed, can generate some *a priori* knowledge about the empirical realm (because it is partly responsible for creating it). However, the mind is tempted to try to use these cognitive structures to generate *a priori* knowledge about the mind-independent world. This it cannot do, for there is no assurance of any isomorphism between these structures and a domain which they played no role in creating.

If a post-Kantian were to set aside what is 'outside the mind', the Kantian thing-in-itself, as an incoherent notion, then the sphere of the mind-independent becomes even more inappropriate as a target for *a priori* knowledge. Since there is literally nothing to know. Nietzsche often talks in these terms about rationalist metaphysics (*TI* III, §3). However, he also often seems to be saying that the very fact that the mind imposes structures on sensations to create a world of stable objects renders these objects somehow illegitimate or illusory. We think that there are stable objects but really there aren't, because we have created them. Of course Kant would not have been happy with this way of putting things, but it is understandable: we do tend epistemically to downgrade features of experiences which are artefacts of how we experience in more ordinary contexts.

The first thing we notice about this quasi-Kantian model is that it attributes to the mind in its epistemic modes something akin to artistic creativity: the mind takes sensations as raw materials and imposes a form on them to yield a product. For this reason, when Heidegger speaks of the mind's imposition of structure on experience, he calls this 'poetizing', both to indicate the parallel and to evoke the Greek sense of 'poetic', meaning 'productive'. Heidegger, noting this similarity, asserts that for Nietzsche art and knowledge are the same thing. If we regard Nietzsche's rejection of the thing-in-itself as involving some sort of phenomenalism, then this impression would be strengthened. The contrast between art as illusion and science as knowledge would only make sense if science transcends 'appearances' towards something beyond them, while art fails to deliver anything other than appearances. This line of thought can seem to suggest that the whole distinction between the truth and illusion has broken down, and with it any discordance.

To avoid this difficulty, Heidegger suggests that the discordance can be found in two ways. First, the scientist, unlike the artist, regards the appearance produced as 'the sole definitive appearance', while suppressing awareness of the (transcendental) creativity it involves. The scientist is a self-deceived artist, while the artist is not so afflicted. In this sense, science gives us expedient falsehoods but they are only falsehoods in the sense of this claim of exclusivity, since everything is creatively engendered appearance.

But more importantly, Heidegger sees a difference in the modes of creativity involved. Creativity involves an encounter with the world before form and structure have been imposed upon it. Think of this world as a kind of 'chaos'. In the quasi-Kantian account, the chaos in question is the chaos of sensation apart from categorial form.[7] Creativity is supposed to be life enhancing. The will to power in its cognitive mode requires that we interpret the world as a simplified, fixed stasis – this is the 'expedient falsification' – in order better to cope with what would otherwise be the overwhelming character of undigested chaos. This is 'empowering' in a sense, as it enhances our ability to cope pragmatically, but represents a fundamentally different tendency than the will to power as artistic creativity, for the dominant note of artistic creativity is to dissolve limits, to destroy barriers and to overcome resistance. By contrast, the cognitive impulse creates limits, erects barriers and 'permanentizes' resistance. 'Truth' seeks to contain chaos; 'art', to create new forms, must invite it.

But to contain chaos restrains the will to power as creativity, which wants to destroy these limits to expand power. For Heidegger, the cognitive interest and the aesthetic interest, though similar in source and epistemic result, both being expressions of will to power, and both generating nothing but perspectives, are fundamentally opposed in their direction and value. The cognitive interest gives us expedient *reifications* that help us cope by limiting us, while art gives us empowering dissolutions of precisely these expedient reifications. Though 'truth' and 'art' both involve appearance or perspective, the latter is liberating, loosens you up, gets your juices flowing, while the former is stultifying even if expedient. This is the sense that Heidegger attaches to 'untruth as a condition of life' – we need art (life-enhancing dissolutions) so that we do not perish of truth (stultifying reifications). In a sense, both 'art' and 'truth' are modes of combat, but 'art' is the courageous one and 'truth' is the cowardly one. This basic account would prove very influential for later French interpreters of Nietzsche.

But is it an accurate reading of Nietzsche's intention? Arguably not, for three reasons. First, while the presence of Kantian-constructivist themes in Nietzsche, especially in the late notebooks, is undeniable, it is far from clear what exactly Nietzsche is doing with these themes. An alternative reading would be that though late Nietzsche borrows Kantian cognitive psychology, he abandons the sort of transcendental idealism that Heidegger attributes to him. On this view, the Kantian apparatus is merely a helpful heuristic for generating empirical hypotheses in cognitive psychology, but that we can adopt a third-person point of view and assess the products of these cognitive processes by comparing them to what our best empirical theories tell us otherwise about the world. For example, Kant might be right in thinking that we are unable to imagine non-Euclidean space, and yet our best empirical theory might show that space is non-Euclidean. This would allow the 'falsification' rhetoric to proceed without any reliance on a contrast between the phenomenal world and some radically contrasting and inaccessible noumenal world, or with reliance on the notion of a pre-schematized, pre-reification experience as a privileged, chaotic truth contrasted with the falsified world or ordinary as well as scientifically regimented experience. Though such a view might make Nietzsche less philosophically interesting, it is a coherent one that helps to avoid some of the seeming paradoxes involved in Nietzsche's use of the Kantian model of perception. If an 'interesting' Nietzsche is an incoherent one, it is not clear that we should take him seriously.

Second, Heidegger's exceedingly abstract characterization of 'art' and 'truth' here conceal some homespun facts about both, even if a transcendental idealist account of them were accepted. Art may very well involve the dissolution of limits and the creation of new forms, and cognitive experience may very well involve transcendental processes that bear some resemblance to artistic creation. But ordinary artistic creation reworks materials found within the phenomenal world, objects already produced by these transcendental processes. And the reworking of objects that art involves has nothing to do with undoing these transcendental processes; rather, it presupposes them. Artistic creativity has to do with, say, reshaping a lump of clay into a differently shaped object, a sculpture. But both the lump and the sculpture are ordinary empirical objects, and per hypothesis, products of the transcendental processes of reification, synthesis and so on. All artistic materials are always already the products of such operations, and no artistic processes ever unwind them. If we see that the two kinds of fashioning occur at different levels, we can see that there is no discordance here at all. When I sculpt, I do not threaten to undo the metaphysical structure of the empirical world; and that structure, far from being an obstacle to my creativity, is a necessary condition of it.

Third, if we reject a transcendental idealist gloss on the reification theme, Heidegger has simply misidentified the 'terrifying truth' that we need artistic illusion to shield us from the pseudo-truth of stultifying reifications and rationalist flights of fancy. The terrifying truths Nietzsche is thinking of when sounding the discordance theme are claims like 'the world is a flux', 'all beings seek power', 'there is no God', 'there is no moral order' and the like. Not only are these terrifying truths different from the reification theme, they are in conflict with it. For these terrifying truths are the signs of chaos that we seek to shield ourselves from. A better character-ization would be, 'we need both art as illusion and cognition as reification to shield us from the terrifying truth of chaos that threatens to break in on us from without'. Heidegger's confusion on this score is probably best attributed to a tendency (not overtly manifested in his text, so this is somewhat speculative) to run together the art versus truth theme and the cognition as Kantian form-imposition theme, as articulated by the late Nietzsche, with the art versus truth theme in *Birth of Tragedy*. In *Birth of Tragedy*, there is also the notion that there are terrifying truths which Apollinian art especially shields us from. But these terrifying truths all point back to a terrifying basic truth: that the Kantian-Scho-penhauerian thing-in-itself is will. Similarly, the descriptions of Apollinian art, with their emphasis on balm and illusion, are often couched in terms reminiscent of phenomenality. Hence the contrast with the terrifying truth of the noumenal will. This might lead one to think that when late Nietzsche makes similar claims about art and truth, and discusses the experience shaping role of a quasi-Kantian subject, that the late writings must also somehow connect these themes. Since they cannot be connected in the same way as before, as late Nietzsche has no thing-in-itself to play the old role, they must be connected in some other way. Heidegger's solution to this problem is ingenious, but in the end distorts Nietzsche's posi-tion rather than illuminates it. Nietzsche does think that the will to power manifests itself as both art and cognition in much the way that Heidegger claims (with my caveat about how Nietzsche psy-chologizes the transcendental), and that there is a tension between art as illusion and terrifying truths. But since terrifying truths cannot be associated with a thing-in-itself and comforting illusions with a contrasting phenomenal world, the distinction between illusion and truth must be one which transpires within the phe-nomenal (that is, the only world). It is better to think that both art and cognitive reifications are phenomenal illusions in relation to some other phenomenal truth than to think of the reification pro-cess itself as the threat we should be terrified of.

THE ETERNAL RECURRENCE OF THE SAME

The second lecture series concerns the eternal recurrence doctrine. In terms of our prior discussion, Heidegger's account is a hybrid of an experiential and a metaphysical interpretation. The experiential aspect of the interpretation is in some respects indebted to Heidegger's own account of authenticity in *Being and Time*,[8] where he had presented a phenomenological description of what it is like to be a human being, a 'Dasein', from a first-person point of view. This description divided into two separate but interrelated accounts: what it is like to be inauthentic and what it is like to be authentic. Inauthenticity is described in terms of a human being's embeddedness in a cultural and pragmatic milieu in which the environment presents itself to Dasein as a holistic field of entities with functional characteristics (tools, in an extended sense), available for use in projects. Each functional entity not only has a particular use, but these uses are relationally interdependent (so a hammer's function cannot be specified without reference to a nail's function). The totality of these interdependent functions comprises a world of meaningful entities. The functional characteristics, in turn, are produced by social norms. Since social norms are only possible if there are human beings to sustain them through patterns of norm-governed activity, the world or environment as the totality of these functional characteristics is ultimately 'mind-dependent' (to use an expression Heidegger, with his resistance to Cartesianism, would object to). Similarly, Dasein finds itself embedded in such an environment with other Daseins, all of whom are subject to social norms as well (perhaps best thought of as norms that create roles and standards of role-appropriate conduct). These roles are similarly interdependent and bound up with the pragmatic meaning of non-human entities (a hammer is for hammering, a carpenter is one who hammers, a carpenter works with a plumber to build a house, and so on). On Heidegger's account, to regard one's role as obligatory is inescapable but inauthentic. Underneath it all, Daseins are free agents who choose to embrace a social role and the pragmatic projects that come with it, and the binding character of the norms stems ultimately from nothing more than Dasein's determination to regard them as binding.

As Heidegger focuses his description on the phenomenological character of agency itself, he observes that it has an intrinsically temporal aspect to it. The environmental milieu presents itself to Dasein as something Dasein is 'thrown' into, like coming into a movie in the middle: the roles, functions and norms all present themselves to Dasein as something that was there before, and thus contain an intrinsic reference to the past. Yet they are also given to awareness – I see a hammer before me, inviting me to take it up and hammer – and this givenness to awareness Heidegger regards as bound up with the sense of being in the temporal present. Finally, norms and the entities they govern make demands on Dasein in terms of what projects are to be pursued and what kinds of goal-orientated activities are appropriate. This awareness of the environment as making demands for goal-orientated activities contains within it an intrinsic reference to the future, towards which the completion of the goal-orientated activity is directed. Dasein does not confront this temporal structure of its experience, activity and environment with indifference. To be responsive to these temporally structured demands is to care about how things are to be and what is to be done. For this reason, Heidegger says that Dasein is essentially 'care'. So care is the heart of agency, and it is by virtue of agency that we have norms and norm-responsiveness, and thus have a meaningful environment or 'world' at all. Heidegger's more striking claim is that agency *produces* this temporal structure: if there was nothing to be done, there would be no such thing as the future at all. Furthermore, he claims that the experience of objective, non-pragmatic time of the sort referred to in scientific theories is the product of abstraction from the richer pragmatic temporality just described. Thus even the time of nature is in a sense 'mind-dependent'; Heidegger's metaphysics of time is both a 'tensed' and an 'idealist' one.

But thus far we have only seen Dasein in its inauthentic or 'fallen' mode, immersed in projects and work-teams, thoughtlessly subject to social norms and roles. Underneath this is an anxious awareness that acquiescence is a surrender of one's freedom. However, when we momentarily detach ourselves from the world and are aware of its arbitrariness, we do not experience the world atemporally, because even if we distance ourselves from projects by ceasing to regard anything as 'what must be done', we are still aware of another kind of temporality which we also create: the awareness that no matter what we do, and even if we did nothing, we are still hurtling towards our inevitable annihilation. In the face of death we cannot escape responsibility for choosing the sort of life we are to live. This kind of awareness of time is also tensed and mind-dependent, but as it does not involve immersion in socially defined projects and expectations, and persists even in the absence of others, Heidegger characterizes it as 'authentic temporality'.

The stripping away of one's thoughtless and immersed commitments, the awareness that one must nonetheless choose what kind of life to lead, all occurs in a 'moment'. Though one cannot in response simply create a life out of nothing, in this moment we become aware of the cultural possibilities available to us as an inheritance from the cultural past. We must choose 'resolutely' to embrace one of these possibilities and make it our own, henceforth aiming at future possibilities that are our own free choice and for which we can take full responsibility.

In the lecture series, Heidegger initially interprets the experience of coming to believe that eternal recurrence is true[9] and then affirming it despite one's sufferings as akin to the existential crisis in which one confronts the cultural legacy, freely chooses a role as one's 'destiny' and then projects oneself forward into the future in conformity with the lucidly chosen role. This existentializing of the eternal recurrence experience seems on the face of it entirely at odds with the elements of fatalism and repetition at work in Nietzsche's conception.[10] However, this experiential aspect of Heidegger's interpretation is important, since one might think that his account was entirely a metaphysical one, concerned only with an accurate interpretation of the cosmos as fated and recurrent. As we shall see, however, the existential and metaphysical aspects of his interpretation are connected in a surprising way.

The metaphysical aspect of the interpretation is presented in ten theses about the world. (1) The doctrine concerns the world in its collective (as opposed to pervasive) character; (2) The pervasive character of the world is force; (3) Force is intrinsically finite; (4) Given 2 and 3, the world is finite; (5) The play of forces never achieves any equilibrium or steady state; (6) The number of possible world states is finite; (7) Space is finite and imaginary; (8) Time is infinite and real; (9) The world, lacking any intrinsic, humanly significant order, is 'chaos'; (10) The world is nonetheless governed by 'necessity'.[11] From these theses, a 'proof' of sorts follows: if the world is finite in its range of possible states and cannot achieve any steady state, but time is infinite, then eventually the range of states is run through and the world must begin again with a previous state. If the transitions from state to state follow of necessity, then the world's history must eternally recur.

Heidegger's first point about the argument is that despite Nietzsche's image as a 'philosopher of becoming', the eternal recurrence gives us a picture of a world with a permanent, fixed structure of a sort. For though there is no permanent world of stasis beyond the world of flux, as would be the case if there were Platonic Forms, and the world of flux has no smaller-scale permanent structures within it, as would be the case if there were Aristotelian essences or natural laws, the world as a whole and each idiosyncratic event, process and configuration within it has become eternal by virtue of repetition. In this sense, Heidegger still discerns a Platonizing impulse in Nietzsche's thought.

Heidegger's second point about the preceding is that it cannot be construed as an empirical thesis; the claims hinge on what force *must* be like, what time *must* be like, given their natures, and the argument as a whole has a deductive character. It is thus a bit of rationalist metaphysics. Setting aside the question of how serious Nietzsche was about the argument, Heidegger's interpretation of the argument as rationalist metaphysics is surely correct. What is puzzling about this fact is that one would think Nietzsche would have known that it was rationalist argumentation. It is quite at odds with his own quasi-Kantian account of rationalist metaphysics as the product of the misuse of conceptual structures imposed on sensory experience, and the illusoriness of any attempt to characterize the world as it is in itself through arguments that presuppose structures of rationality that 'map onto' the real nature of the world. This is the puzzle that Heidegger sets out to solve.

Heidegger's response is surprising. Recall that Heidegger's Nietzsche pursues knowledge by imposing order on the chaos of experience, and that there is no thing-in-itself that can be contrasted with the world of experience by virtue of which we could regard it as inferior to any other form of cognition. Two consequences follow. First, the eternal recurrence is simply true. It is a feature of the world of experience, and the world of experience, though it can be impugned as stultifying, cannot be regarded as an illusion in the sense of not being isomorphic with a mind-independent world. Second, since the world of experience has the character that it does by virtue of the mind's imposition of order on the chaos of experience, it follows that the thinker of the thought of eternal recurrence *makes it become true* by virtue of thinking the thought. It is for this reason that Heidegger repeatedly quotes the passage, 'To impose upon becoming the character of being – that is the supreme will to power. Twofold falsification, on the part of the senses and of the spirit, to preserve a world of that which is, which abides, which is equivalent, etc. That everything recurs is the closest approximation of a world of becoming to a world of being: – high point of the meditation' (*WP* §617). But Heidegger has already repudiated talk of 'falsification' as hyperbole – there is no 'true world' in relation to which the structure we impose on experience could be said to be false. Thus the world eternally recurs, and we make it so. Furthermore, since the eternal recurrence doctrine does not reify individual entities or types, but rather eternalizes becoming in all its irreducible complexity, its projection is a purely creative act which does not stultify at all.

This 'transcendental' interpretation of the eternal recurrence in turn dovetails with the experiential account inspired by the choice of authenticity. If we think of the transcendental subject as spontaneous, both as agent and as source of the structure of the empirical world, then it would appear that we do not merely make the world eternally recur: we *choose* to make it eternally recur by authentically appropriating the past and authentically projecting ourselves towards a future. Thus the eternal recurrence turns out to be not about submitting to fate and ecstatically affirming life despite suffering, but about assuming responsibility for the world as a whole and bending it, even in its widest collective character, to our will. It is for this reason that Heidegger makes the otherwise mysterious claim that 'will to power' and 'eternal recurrence' mean essentially the same thing.

Though Heidegger seems to have characterized the logic of the argument correctly (he makes no attempt to evaluate its validity, however), and his impression that a Platonizing impulse is allied with it seems right as far as it goes, the larger claims he makes about it seem wide of the mark. First, there is no evidence that Nietzsche was aware of the rationalist character of the argument. This is because when Nietzsche talks about the mind's relationship to experience in a 'transcendental' vein, he only ever comments on our tendencies to (1) circumscribe and unify regions of 'chaos' as if they were *entities*, (2) classify entities, events, processes, etc. as if they were *types* (including classifying events as instantiating natural laws), and (3) project grammatical form on experience so that the 'chaos' has a substance/property structure isomorphic with language's subject/predicate structure. Yet certain propositions in the proof fit none of these. For example, when Nietzsche says that time is infinite, there is no indication that he regards this as a product of how we cannot help but think about time given the structure of our cognition. Indeed, it seems that the alleged facts about the world that need to be known in order to arrive at the conclusion that the world eternally recurs are precisely facts about the world as it is *in conflict with* the schematizing, form-imposing propensities of the mind. Nietzsche seems to have regarded these facts 'naively' or 'pre-critically'. This suggests that there are limits to how far one can push a transcendental idealist interpretation of Nietzsche. Though he uses notions borrowed from transcendental idealism opportunistically and naturalizes them into his own cognitive psychology, he seems to have thought that claims like 'the world is force', 'time is infinite' and so on are simply and discernibly true of the world apart from any order we might impose on experience. We even apprehend these truths more clearly the more we become aware of and set aside the distortive effects of our cognitive psychology.

Second, even if it were true that we make it the case that time, for example, is infinite by virtue of a structure we impose on experience the same problem mentioned above arises. It makes some sense to say that I choose to believe something, and it can even make sense to say that in choosing to believe something I make it true (in non-philosophical contexts, we call this 'self-fulfilling prophecy'). Furthermore, we can easily imagine a Kierkegaardian approach to eternal recurrence in which I choose to believe it without evidence or argument, thus transforming my life in the process. But whatever processes there may be of a Kantian character that impose form on my experience so that I can discover the 'metaphysics of experience', the body of necessary, *a priori* truths about the empirical world are not themselves subject to my choice. For Kant at least, if I chose not to impose them, I would cease to experience altogether. While Nietzsche did not regard these structures as necessary for empirical thought (at least we can imagine what the world is like without them), he did think them contingently inescapable, being the product of our evolutionary history and inheritance. We do not choose these structures: biological and linguistic history have already 'chosen' them for us.

Finally, the phenomenological description of willing eternal recurrence, which concerns the distinctive state in the agent's response to a world regarded as eternally recurring, seems to involve too much transposition of Heidegger's earlier existentialist account of authenticity to be fully convincing as an account of *Nietzsche's* experience. Though Nietzsche's 'affirmation' and Heidegger's 'resoluteness' in some sense share the adoption of a positive attitude towards one's own life, a sense of its finitude, and a refusal to squander it in the wrong sort of way, these very general similarities conceal large differences. The most obvious one, of course, is that Heideggerian resoluteness is *chosen*. It is one of Nietzsche's stable commitments throughout his authorship that there is no such thing as free will. Thus it is better to regard the life affirming experience Nietzsche is trying to capture as a matter of desiring rather than choosing; to 'will' eternal recurrence is a matter of being 'strong' enough to *want* it. Second, Heideggerian resoluteness contrasts with immersion in social norms. Nietzsche's own critique of morality cannot be assimilated to such a model, because his objections to modern morality are specific and substantive, whereas an existentialist critique of morality, rooted as it is in a notion of criterionless choice, is far more sweeping – it becomes a critique of all possible social norms when taken up in a certain way. Nietzsche's life affirming stance, by contrast, is not about repudiating immersion in social norms, but about celebrating life despite one's own and others' *suffering*. Failing to achieve the appropriate stance does not mean falling back into immersion in alien social norms and conferring on them an unreal authority; failing to achieve the appropriate stance means desiring that the world be different, or in the extreme case, that it not exist at all. This point dovetails with Nietzsche's rejection of free will, for the main reason we must affirm suffering is because every event in the world, including all events within one's own life, is *necessary*. Though it is interesting to see how far Heidegger can push a non-naturalistic reading of Nietzsche, in doing so he misses key phenomenological descriptions which presuppose a naturalistic, and thus for Nietzsche a deterministic, setting.

THE WILL TO POWER AS KNOWLEDGE

Thus far we have presented Heidegger's Nietzsche as if his epistemological commitments were to be understood as a kind of Kantianism. In the third lecture series, 'The Will to Power as Knowledge', Heidegger refines and transforms the Kantian theme of the mind imposing order on a chaos of sensations into a picture that owes more to his own earlier views. In *Being and Time*, Heidegger criticized the Cartesian picture of the mind as a substance or property-bearer, with representations as its properties, representations which when accurate correspond to another world outside the mind. Arguably, on traditional readings, Kant also presupposes some such picture, as if sensations are 'inside' the mind, and the mind can therefore reach out and touch them in the act of imposing form on them. Early Heidegger is determined to reject such a picture in favour of an embodied subject, embedded in a larger environment and in direct perceptual contact and pragmatic engagement with it. Yet he also wants to retain something of the Kantian notion that the orderliness of that environment is in some sense 'mind-dependent'. Heidegger's version of transcendental idealism instead regards this imposed order as a matter of how one interprets as meaningful the environment in which one finds oneself. Though this does not involve imposing a structure on sensations, the environment still displays the character and affordances it does by virtue of the pragmatic (and hence human-dependent) significance we attribute to what we find in it. If we did not orient ourselves in the environment in terms of these interpretive expectations, the environment would present itself to us as meaninglessly complex, impossible to orient ourselves in and, in a word, 'chaotic'. Heidegger now brings this notion of order-imposition to bear on his interpretation of Nietzsche: when Nietzsche speaks of imposing order on chaos, he means that we project 'horizons' of intelligibility on an otherwise meaningless environment. Heideggerizing Nietzsche in this way seems to be an application of interpretative charity on Heidegger's part: Nietzsche could not have seriously regarded the mind as a Cartesian container. Much of Heidegger's evidence for this reading draws on Nietzsche's frequent reference to the importance of the body as a philosophical starting point. It is not altogether clear, however, that Heidegger and Nietzsche mean the same thing by 'body' here. For Nietzsche, it seems that the notion of the body refers to the object of a third-person scientific inquiry, not a first-person phenomenological description. To be sure, given Nietzsche's panpsychism, he will then go on to characterize it as a social system composed of many 'souls'. But this too is quite alien to Heidegger's own anti-Cartesianism, and is not how my body presents itself to me phenomenologically anyway.

Ultimately, though, Heidegger will want partially to assimilate Nietzsche to Descartes in his epistemology, if not in his philosophy of mind. For he takes it that Nietzsche begins with the assumption, shared with every western philosopher from Plato to Descartes, that truth is correspondence. This is only the starting point, however, for according to Heidegger Nietzsche ends with a pragmatist conception of truth. In brief, if truth is conceived as some cognitive state in correspondence with reality, that means that there is a distinction between epistemically valued cognitive states and epistemically disvalued cognitive states. However, if there is no world beyond the world we create by our interpretative activity, then there are no truth conditions, and 'truth' can be nothing more than 'valued cognitive state'. If 'valued' boils down to nothing more than the result of an estimation of value by the will to power, then that is all truth will be as well. Heidegger even uses the term 'justification' in this connection, which suggests analogies between Nietzsche's and Peirce's conceptions of truth as idealized justification.

A similar pragmatist transformation is at work in Heidegger's comments about Nietzsche's conception of knowledge. Heidegger begins with the claim that since Descartes, knowledge is understood in terms of certainty, indubitability, incorrigibility and the like. But if a world independent of our cognition is eliminated, these too must be reduced to something inherently subjective. Thus for Heidegger's Nietzsche, objective certainty, a state of the subject's assurance combined with a guarantee of correct correspondence, becomes merely subjective certainty. Only the assurance remains. This assurance, in the end, comes from the success the subject has in navigating the environment whose interpretative significance it has conferred upon it.

The transcendental condition of the possibility of this success is that the subject produces a presupposed 'horizon' of background beliefs and concepts, especially formal concepts, through which it interprets and thus constitutes its environment. A central feature of this 'horizon' is commitment to the laws of logic. There is a link between the 'logic horizon' and the sense of subjective assurance because unlike other background expectations, the expectation that the world will be found to be self-consistent is one which cannot possibly fail to obtain. We therefore experience a kind of 'certainty' about the world at least in this respect. Reading Nietzsche's discussion of the law of non-contradiction in section 516 of *Will to Power*, Heidegger notes Nietzsche's claim that the law of non-contradiction involves a psychological incapacity. He rightly dismisses this as apparently absurd: people contradict themselves all the time. More promising, however, is the notion that the law of non-contradiction is a 'command'. Heidegger plausibly reads this as proposing that the laws of logic are normative and not descriptive, that we *shall* not regard as real anything which violates the laws of logic. Heidegger's concern here seems to be driven by his (and Husserl's) acceptance of Frege's critique of psychologistic theories of logic and mathematics, and his charitable determination not to find such a view in Nietzsche. However, if the law of non-contradiction is understood as normative rather than descriptive, it must obtain by virtue of the subject's responsiveness to the norm. Following the line suggested above in the discussion of the eternal recurrence, Heidegger attributes to Nietzsche the view that just as the transcendental subject's ethical capacities require spontaneity, so too does its 'world-constituting' capacities. Thus the law of non-contradiction obtains because we *choose* that it do so. We can see here that Heidegger's exegesis of Nietzsche's claim that 'logic would be an imperative' (*WP* §516) ends up characterizing it in terms reminiscent of Kant's ethics: the laws of logic are a species of self-legislation, laws the will gives to itself. As we said above in our criticism of Heidegger's interpretation of the eternal recurrence, this is to foist on Nietzsche a conception of agency that does not square with the texts.

Heidegger concludes that the known world is the product of the will choosing to impose interpretative norms on itself, and these norms are chosen because they promote pragmatic success. Thus the world is will to power, not just in the distributive, panpsychist sense, but also in that *our* world is the product of *our* will to power in a transcendental sense. As explained above, Nietzsche uses these seemingly transcendental themes in terms of a naturalistic cognitive psychology inspired by Kant's transcendental psychology, but not committed to any variation on the transcendental idealist metaphysics that Kant connected to it. This alternative to Heidegger's interpretation allows us to make sense of Nietzsche's continuing use of the expression 'falsification' to characterize the effects of our cognitive-psychological apparatus. For now the falsification in question is quite literal, but metaphysically innocuous, akin to the sort of falsification involved in optical illusions. Optical illusions by themselves do not force us to adopt a transcendental idealist metaphysics that makes the world (which can be experienced in part with the eyes) the product of the eyes.

NIHILISM AGAIN

The most interesting and controversial aspect of Heidegger's account of Nietzsche is what we called an external explanation and criticism of it in terms of the 'history of being' hypothesis. It is important to repeat here the caveat expressed above: whether Heidegger's interpretative hypothesis (in essence that Nietzsche is a sort of transcendental idealist) is correct or not is separate from any attempt to explain or criticize Nietzsche so interpreted. Heidegger's 'history of being' might be a good general account of the history of western philosophy, but Nietzsche might not fit into his story in quite the way he thinks he does. Nietzsche may not have thought what Heidegger says he did. Conversely, Heidegger may be right in characterizing Nietzsche as a kind of transcendental idealist, while the speculative account of the history of western philosophy might be wrong in fundamental ways. Finally, even if both the interpretation and the history of being hypothesis are correct, the use Heidegger puts them to, which is to criticize Nietzsche for being internal to and the culmination of this history, depends upon a separate evaluative stance towards that history. In many ways, Heidegger makes it very difficult to see any of these points. First, the interpretative claims become difficult to separate from the historical hypothesis. As we saw, Heidegger explains Nietzsche's conception of truth by comparison with Descartes'. But his way of communicating this point draws on the historical hypothesis that Nietzsche is a further development in a narrative in which Descartes occupies a key role. Second, the evaluative claims Heidegger wants to make are couched in descriptive language laden with far from value-neutral terminology. For example, Heidegger characterizes Plato's metaphysics as involving 'forgetting of being'. In ordinary

contexts, forgetting is a bad thing. It is part of Heidegger's rhetorical strategy to persuade the reader that there is a meaningful
narrative unity to western history, intimately connected with the
development of western philosophy, culminating in a nihilistic crisis
which we can escape from only by making profound changes in
how we conceptualize the world (though he also suggests that these
changes are not, ultimately, up to us). One way of approximating
Heidegger's point is to see him as proposing a kind of reverse
Hegelianism, in which the history of thought and the history of
social practices are in harmony with each other and develop over
time. But while Hegel's story is a story of progress, Heidegger's is a
story of decline.

To understand fully how this narrative is supposed to work, we
must return to *Being and Time*. As we saw above, early Heidegger
portrays the human condition in terms of pragmatic subjects
embedded in a meaningful environment, pursuing projects with
entities imbued with functional properties, traceable ultimately to
social norms which are themselves ultimately sustained by and
dependent upon the subjects' choice to take them seriously. Heidegger's critique of Cartesianism, however, is broader than a mere
antipathy towards the representationalist theory of mind. For not
only Descartes' thought, but most modern scientific thinking,
regards the world outside the mind as possessing only those properties which can be captured in the net of scientific theory ('primary
qualities' susceptible to mathematical representation). All other
properties are regarded as in some sense not fully real, 'subjective',
projected on the real objects science treats of ('secondary qualities'
like colours, sounds, tastes, smells and so on). Heidegger seeks to
destroy this privileging of the scientific account of the world by
arguing that it is an abstraction from (really a subtraction from) the
richer content of the pragmatic environment. If we regard the
content of the pragmatic environment as fully real in the first place,
then the scientific account will be seen not as demystifying, but as
merely partial. But how can Heidegger claim that the pragmatic
character of the world is fully real if it is a product of the 'horizons'
we project? Here Heidegger follows Berkeley, just as Kant did
(though neither of them would be happy with this way of characterizing things!): if the world that science is concerned with is the
'internal' rather than the 'external' world, then there is no contrast
to be made between the world of experience and the world of

science by virtue of which the richer experiential world could be said to be subjective in a pejorative sense when contrasted with the objective world of science. Of course, the sphere into which science gets pulled is not 'the mind' as in Berkeley, but the pragmatic environment. In Heidegger, as in Berkeley and Kant, we can discern an anti-sceptical motive: if I am in direct contact with whatever is 'inner' in the relevant sense, and we identify what is real with that instead of with some contrasting 'outer' world, then no sceptical gap can open between inner and outer. (As we already saw in a previous chapter, this strategy is of limited usefulness in combating scepticism.)

For Descartes, functional properties are 'subjective' in the pejorative sense, because they are mind-dependent. It is only by virtue of our preferences and goals that entities have functions at all. In a word, entities only have *ascribed* functions. Interestingly, Heidegger agrees with this, with two caveats. First, it is the community which does the ascribing. Second, there is no reason to view this pejoratively, since the world in which we find functions is the *same* world we study scientifically. When we study it scientifically, however, we must subtract or put out of play the functions that the entities we study possess. So the first narrative element in early Heidegger's history of metaphysics is that Descartes inaugurates a transformation of how we think about the world, by abstracting away functional properties in the pragmatic environment and denigrating them as not real in the same way that mathematical properties are. This abstraction occurs at the subject-pole as well: if we abstract away the subject's pragmatic engagement in the environment, all that remains is the subject as a purely contemplative entity: that which observes objects and thinks about the mathematical properties they possess.

Aristotle, by contrast, is viewed more favourably as someone who takes seriously the reality of functional properties in the world. However, Aristotle is guilty of a different error. Recall that the functional properties of entities are due to social norms, and when we are inauthentic, we are immersed in these norms in a way that obscures how the collective choices of subjects sustain them in existence. Since these choices are themselves criterionless, it is a mistake to think that they are simply there to be found; they are *made to be*. Our motivation for inauthenticity hinges on our unwillingness to accept our mortality. For Heidegger this is linked to our unwillingness to see temporality as mind-dependent (the primordial experience of temporality as hurtling towards our own non-existence). Had Aristotle been authentic in Heidegger's sense, he would have recognized that functional properties are always ascribed (though no less real for all that, as long as the ascription occurs).

Late Heidegger accepts this basic account in broad outline.[12] With this, he adds a particular account of the pre-Socratics' fundamental experience of reality as 'physis', which he characterizes as 'upsurgent presencing'. Though this notion is somewhat murky, the general idea seems to be that the world contains entities which are initially hidden in some sense, but which can unfold and manifest themselves, becoming available to human awareness (though the role of human awareness in this becoming available is suppressed or passed over). The real is both that which is hidden before it becomes manifest, that which is manifest and that which is no longer manifest. However, given the failure to appreciate the nature of time as a tensed, mind-dependent unity stretching from past through the present towards the future, there is a temptation to regard the present tense as peculiarly associated with the real. It is as if past and future were not real as well, because they do not manifest themselves to us as the present does. This privileging of the present as somehow more real than the past and the future is rooted in the failure to recognize the three tenses' unity, a failure itself rooted in a failure to appreciate time's mind-dependence and its relationship to our experience of hurtling towards the future out of the past.

With Plato, these failures come to fruition in the conception of Platonic Forms. The origin of the idea of Platonic Forms comes from the conception of things as radiantly manifesting their character in the present and thus 'presencing'. Heidegger's notion of a thing radiantly manifesting its character seems indebted here to Husserl's notion of eidetic intuition, which presupposes that things have abstract structural features we are capable of intuiting. This radiant manifesting in the present *ought to be* understood as a temporal process. But by identifying the real with the present, a single tense detached from the triple unity of the tenses, Plato ends up thinking of the temporal as unreal, and the real as atemporal. This paves the way for thinking of the manifest character of an entity as timeless. Since concrete entities themselves are obviously temporal, and come and go through time, the manifest character of the entity must be something *other than* the entity. This timeless manifest character then becomes conceptualized not as the entity itself in its manifestness, but as a separable item distinct from it: the Platonic Form. This is Heidegger's version of the two-world picture. Like Nietzsche, Heidegger regards it as pernicious and lasting in its effects.

The faulty distinction between the concrete entity and its manifest character brings with it several other pernicious distinctions. First, as we have already seen, the Platonic Form is regarded as atemporal in contrast with the concrete: thus we have a distinction between 'being' and 'becoming'. Second, the Platonic Form comes to be seen as a separable repository of value (this is why I characterized 'manifest character' as 'radiant'). According to Heidegger, in the pre-Socratic vision of the world, there is no distinction made between seeing things as real and seeing them as valuable. After the distinction between Platonic Form and concrete entity, since the 'radiance' is associated with the Form, we come to see a distinction between fact and value. Third, because the Platonic Form is regarded as real, the concrete entity must be thought of as unreal, which gives us a distinction between appearance and reality. Fourth, since the manifest character of an entity was originally presented to perception-cum-eidetic-intuition as a unitary encounter with it, when this manifest character becomes detached from the concrete entity given in perception, eidetic intuition becomes separated from perception and becomes mere 'thinking' which is done properly when it establishes an isomorphism with the abstract character. Thus truth changes from manifestness to correspondence. From the standpoint of the diagnosis of nihilism, however, it is the identification of value with Platonic Form and the simultaneous separation of Platonic Form from concrete entity that is decisive.[13]

With Descartes, the Platonic ontological interpretation acquires a new, subjectivist twist. By re-interpreting the real as that which can be captured by a mathematical interpretation, the association of value with the real as Platonic Form becomes impossible. The subject can no longer be conceived as that which intuits this value either in the concrete entity (as the pre-Socratics did) or in a realm beyond it (as Plato did). Accordingly, value-intuition becomes mere value-estimation by the subject of the concrete entity. But this can only be understood as preference-satisfaction or 'desire', because

NIETZSCHE: A GUIDE FOR THE PERPLEXED

nothing about the concrete entity as valuable shows up in the mathematical interpretation. At most the concrete entity has various scientifically representable, value-neutral properties which can come to be taken as valued given the preferences of the subject. Its 'radiant' character thus completely disappears.

According to Heidegger, Nietzsche simply radicalizes this development. For Nietzsche, there is no isomorphism between the subject's mathematical interpretation of entities and the independently real mathematical character of the entities themselves, because the seeming independence of the entities is an illusion, a product of the subject's mathematization, conceived as a quasi-Kantian ordering of the chaos of the subject's environmental milieu. Thus nothing remains except subjects, their mathematizing interpretation in the service of their desires, and their desires themselves. In this sense, the world is now will to power and nothing else. However, on Heidegger's reading, this is tantamount to nihilism, since value and even the valued drop out of the picture completely. Note that when I use the word 'value' here, I am using it in a slightly different sense than Heidegger would; for Heidegger the very concept of value is an artefact of the separation of the concrete entity from the manifestation of its 'radiant' character. Thus it would be for him inappropriate to refer to the primordial, pre-Socratic interpretation as fusing perception of the concrete entity with an eidetic intuition of both its abstract character and its value, since characterizing all this in terms of a fusion of disparate elements already commits the sin of separating them, even if only for analytical purposes. Heidegger arguably has a point here: when I encounter an entity – for example an orange – I encounter it as present, coloured, beautiful, potentially delicious and akin to other oranges in its fruity orangeness. None of this should be characterized phenomenologically as involving mental acts of abstraction, comparison or reflection. Nonetheless, it is extremely difficult to articulate Heidegger's view without analysing it in just this way.

Since Heidegger regards any interpretation of reality which presupposes the various distinctions described above as 'metaphysical', it is fair given his terminology to characterize Nietzsche as a 'metaphysician'. Given an understanding of the term 'technological' as concerning production, fashioning or shaping in any sense, Heidegger's characterization of Nietzsche's view as a 'technological' one seems fair as well; for Heidegger's Nietzsche, there is nothing *to* life except the taking up of otherwise chaotic and intrinsically meaningless materials and refashioning them to produce something desired. That Nietzsche does not regard machinery and management as the 'highest' expression of this is beside the point.

Beyond this, Heidegger also sees Nietzsche as the 'last' metaphysician. In part this is nothing more than a completeness claim: given the basic Platonic move, there are a finite number of permutations of it possible, and with Nietzsche, the one remaining permutation gets expressed. Thus after Nietzsche, any western metaphysical position by a philosopher will be a variation on one of the positions already entertained. This kind of claim is almost impossible to evaluate, for it depends upon how abstractly one pitches the claim that two metaphysical positions are fundamentally the same position. For example, I suspect that if Heidegger were with us today, he would say that Quine and Nietzsche are 'basically' saying the same thing; this would no doubt have startled them both! But there is another, even more speculative sense in which Heidegger claims that Nietzsche is eliminated, what we might call the 'neo-Hegelian' sense.[14]

As mentioned above, according to Heidegger metaphysical interpretations are not simply the result of private episodes of thinking by specific individual thinkers. Rather, philosophers 'tune into' the implicit interpretative scheme taken up by the larger culture at a moment in history. These interpretative schemes manifest themselves not only in metaphysical thinking, but in how the era conceptualizes the 'regional ontologies' presupposed in its scientific pursuits, and how it orders itself ethically and politically. These interpretative schemes just happen, though they happen according to a kind of successive narrative logic; the philosopher merely articulates them (and typically regards his doing so as expressing a timeless metaphysical truth). As we shall see, this neo-Hegelian theme was an important influence on Michel Foucault, and affected his own reception of Nietzsche. According to this conception, Nietzsche is not only 'tuning into' the current conceptual framework, the way being gives itself out to us now, but is at the end of a narrative that begins in the framework articulated by Plato. A 2,500-year-old story is drawing to its conclusion in him and in us. We can either live in this last chapter, or begin a new story. It is Heidegger's hope that by illustrating the unsavoury aspects of the common commitments of our culture from Plato to Nietzsche that he can inaugurate, or at least foreshadow, a new story. This sort of claim is also almost impossibly difficult to evaluate.

If we step back and reflect, we can see that both Nietzsche and Heidegger have a certain account of the trajectory of western thought in terms of a two-world picture that culminates in nihilism and demands a response. What is more, they both root that history in a fundamental dissatisfaction and misinterpretation of temporality. For Nietzsche and Heidegger both, it is the inability to accept the transitoriness of the real which generates the relocation of the valuable into an atemporal dimension, and which ultimately leads to a devaluation of the concrete world. Yet their characterization of this differs in subtle but crucial respects. For Nietzsche, the concrete world is essentially a world of contest and competition; this is just a brute fact about how things are. Given that such a world generates winners and losers, it is only natural that the losers fantasize about another, Platonic world in which threats to their equipoise are erased. But the character of this fantasy world is essentially compensatory and contemplative. If we succeed in overcoming nihilism, the 'weak' are left back where they started, as losers in the *agon*. Not only is the Platonic world a beautiful illusion but its very beauty, its character as an object of passive contemplation, is a part of its illusory nature; getting back in touch with the concrete world means renouncing the contemplation of beautiful illusion in favour of energetic activity.

Heidegger's picture is subtly different. For Heidegger, the Platonic mistake consists, not in inventing an imaginary world of passive, contemplative beauty as compensation for failure in the harsh world of competition, but rather in mislocating the very real, radiant character of the concrete world as an object of contemplation somewhere outside it. Though it is easy to focus one's attention on the ways in which Heidegger thinks of Plato being half wrong, there is an underlying sense in which Heidegger thinks Plato is half right: value really does reside in and imbue that which is radiantly manifest, and we really should reverently contemplate it. The mistake consists in thinking that it is atemporal (permanent) and separate from the concrete world.

Where does that leave us? Nietzsche would say that Heidegger is still standing in judgement over those who successfully engage in the *agon* of life, by insinuating that his contemplative stance is superior, even if he declines to connect that contemplative stance with something otherworldly. Heidegger, by contrast, would say that Nietzsche is wilfully blind to the splendour of the ordinary concreteness of things, and hastens past them to refashion them, to bend them to his will, failing to see that they are already perfect as they are. Nietzsche would say that Heidegger is fantasizing in thinking that there is a manifest abstract character of concrete things, while Heidegger would say that Nietzsche is wilfully blind to it. Absent separate argument on the 'technical' questions here, both positions seem to be fundamentally question-begging. It is worth broaching here, delicately, a lesson contained in this: much Continental philosophy involves such explanatory (Marxian, Nietzschean, Freudian, Heideggerian) hypotheses about why philosophical opponents think as they do. The more unattractive the traits the hypotheses posit, the more one becomes motivated to address them (or, more likely, counter them with analogous hypotheses of one's own about those who express them) while ignoring the underlying questions about the cogency of the philosophical positions being dealt with by such explanatory hypotheses. Apart from the interesting questions about the cogency of Heidegger's more specific interpretative claims about Nietzsche, and his more speculative claims about the development of western thought and culture, no adjudication seems possible between their two positions. Readers will no doubt respond to them according to the inherent attractiveness they find in 'tough-minded' versus 'tender-hearted' ways of thinking about life.

CHAPTER 7

A DIFFERENT NIETZSCHE

DERRIDA

Derrida's interpretation of Nietzsche in *Spurs: Nietzsche's Styles* is an attempt at a critical engagement with Heidegger's interpretation. Derrida registers two complaints against Heidegger. First, Heidegger's use of Nietzsche's posthumously published notes is methodologically suspect. He treats these notes as fragments, and the notion of a semantic fragment implies a complementary semantic whole of which these fragments are parts, thus suggesting that the task of the interpreter is to fill the gaps to restore the missing wholeness. However, this missing wholeness may be nothing more than an illusion of the interpreter and unrecoverable in any case. Derrida's notorious example is a passage in the Nietzsche corpus, 'I have forgotten my umbrella'.[1] It should be noted here that this objection speaks as much against any unitary interpretation of the published works as well.

The second objection is that Heidegger misses a crucial psychoanalytic dimension to Nietzsche's texts. Taking the two-world picture as his focus, Derrida notes that in the central discussion of this in *Twilight of the Idols*, 'How the "True World" Became a Fable', Nietzsche's second stage of his six-stage narrative says that the idea of the true world 'becomes female, it becomes Christian' (*TI* IV). This comment, along with Nietzsche's remark elsewhere, 'Supposing truth is a woman – what then?' (*BGE*, Preface) suggests that Nietzsche's reflections on truth and reality have a gendered dimension that may yield insights if approached psychoanalytically.[2]

The psychological phenomenon that Freud analysed, which

Derrida thinks will shed light on Nietzsche's thought about truth, is *fetishism*, the tendency to find sexually attractive some non-sexual body part or inanimate object associated with the body. Freud's account, in 'Fetishism' (1927) is described in the *Abstracts of the Standard Edition* as follows:

> The fetish is a substitute for the penis: the woman's (the mother's) penis that the little boy once believed in and does not want to give up. The fetish achieves a token of triumph over the threat of castration and serves as a protection against it. It also saves the fetishist from becoming a homosexual, by endowing women with the characteristic which makes them tolerable as sexual objects. Because the fetish is easily accessible, the fetishist can readily obtain the sexual satisfaction attached to it. The choice of the fetish object seems determined by the last impression before the uncanny and traumatic one. In very subtle instances both the disavowal and the affirmation of the castration have found their way into the construction of the fetish itself. In conclusion, Freud says that the normal prototype of fetishes is a man's penis, just as the normal prototype of interior organ is a woman's real small penis, the clitoris.[3]

The philosopher's desire for the truth is a desire to connect with reality as a kind of plenitude, and this plenitude is just a cipher for the fetish object. Thus the desire for truth amounts to a male desire to possess woman by way of the fetish. This means to possess a simulated replacement for the woman, because real possession of the fully disclosed woman would reveal her to be castrated, terrifying the male, triggering his own castration anxiety and recoil. But if that is right, then the truth the dogmatic philosopher obtains cannot be the real truth, but a fetishistic replacement for it that perpetuates the illusion of being able to possess woman without experiencing castration anxiety. This basic complex of ideas, Derrida claims, suffices to explain the various contradictory comments Nietzsche makes about truth (that truth is terrifying, that there is no truth).

As Derrida explores the psychoanalytic dimension of Nietzsche's texts, he discerns a sixfold structure, generated by two axes.[4] First, Nietzsche is ambivalent about whether he wants to identify with the female or differentiate himself from it. This is suggested by

Nietzsche's characterization of creativity as a sort of male pregnancy, a favourable way in which a man can be like a woman. By contrast, Nietzsche's critique of Christianity, which seeks to extirpate the (male) passions, is not only 'female' itself, but seeks to 'castrate' the male, presumably rendering him 'female' as well. The second axis distinguishes between regarding elements as passive, active or neither. Thus the six spaces in the two-by-three chart are:

1. Nietzsche regards himself as castrated.
2. Nietzsche regards woman as castrated.
3. Nietzsche regards himself as castrating.
4. Nietzsche regards woman as castrating.
5. Nietzsche regards himself as life.
6. Nietzsche loves life.

This list also has a 'Hegelian' dimension, in terms of negation, double negation and affirmation: point 2 and point 4 are Hegelian negations that differentiate self from other, where 'woman' is not-(male)-self; point 1 and point 3 are (male) self-negations; point 5 and point 6 are self- and other-affirmation. Since self and other must be appropriately coupled with activity and passivity to generate coherent castrating/castrated dyads, this gives us three fundamental positions:

> First position: point 2 plus point 3 has Nietzsche castrating woman.
> Second position: point 1 plus point 4 has woman castrating Nietzsche.
> Third position: point 5 plus point 6 transcends the whole castration dialectic.

Derrida characterizes the first position as Nietzsche the truth-speaking philosopher criticizing woman as the locus of illusions. The second position has Nietzsche the creative artist criticizing woman as the Christian advocate of a true world of being as a ploy to persuade him to renounce his creative-yet-illusion-generating passions. The third position transcends this contest in favour of life affirmation.

In some broad sense, there is something to this. Nietzsche's rhetoric on all sorts of subjects appeals to gender stereotypes in a way that evinces a profound ambivalence towards femininity. As a map of Nietzsche's thought, however, the distinction between the first two positions is too simple; the scheme presupposes too clear a distinction between Nietzsche in his 'philosopher' and 'artist' modes. When Nietzsche criticizes Christianity as passion-extirpating, he also stresses the role that cognitive illusions play in its operations, thus occupying a position of 'truth-teller' about Christianity in the very act of deploring its ethical effects. To be sure, Nietzsche is quick to note the connection between the will to truth and asceticism, which would seem to reinforce the link between a protest against the extirpation of the passions with a high value placed on the illusoriness of art. But this brings other difficulties in its wake. For that would mean that the will to truth is self-castrating, not other-castrating, which conflicts with the account of the first position. The better way to think about the will to truth in Nietzsche is not to decide whether it is essentially self-fulfilling or self-denying, but to notice a *gradient* in the way Nietzsche conceptualizes the desire for truth and illusion. For Nietzsche, strength and weakness form a continuum. In the weak, the will to truth is a manifestation of a self-destructive impulse, ultimately explicated in terms of the 'ascetic ideal'. But weakness also manifests itself in the desire for comforting illusions. By contrast, the strong can meet the prospect of threatening truths not by embracing them self-destructively or eschewing them in a celebration of illusion, but by using them *athletically*, as a challenge that strengthens. This is arguably a masculinist notion, if we presuppose gender stereotypes which associate the athletic with the masculine. But by virtue of its gradient character, it defies the simple binary character of any conceptual model couched in terms of castration, which (one would think) is rather an all or nothing affair! The difficulty in making sense of Nietzsche's thought in terms of binary oppositions at all casts some doubt on the viability of making sense of it in this quasi-Hegelian way as well: the binary oppositions have to be there in the first place if they are to be transcended, and they may not be. Finally, one suspects that Derrida's tendency exclusively to align masculine protest against castration with the position of 'artist' involves too close an association between the notion of sensuousness as a locus of artistic activity and production, on the one hand, and sensuousness as pleasure, *while setting aside the relationship between truth-telling and sensuousness*. In short, like Heidegger,

Derrida has simply missed the empiricist in Nietzsche, the Nietzsche who would stay close to the *testimony* of the senses in an attempt to speak the truth.

Having criticized Heidegger for failing to come to grips with the psychoanalytic dimension of Nietzsche's texts, he then reverses himself, suggesting, somewhat opaquely, that Heideggerian resources may be useful for understanding Nietzsche after all.[5] These are not exactly the resources of Heidegger's interpretation of Nietzsche, but rather of Heidegger's own views about how to think about, and ultimately how to think beyond, the 'history of being' as metaphysics. Derrida, however, seems to vacillate between seeing such recourse as a way of shedding light on Nietzsche and a way of shedding light on Heidegger. First, recall Heidegger's thesis that the history of western thought and practice is a succession of conceptual frameworks for interpreting the world. One possible way of bringing this idea into relation with Derrida's psychoanalytic reading of Nietzsche is to suggest that the various unconscious processes which Freud describes are conditioned by prior ontological commitments traceable to such a framework. Thus Nietzsche's various thoughts about truth and illusion, creativity and asceticism, suffering and life affirmation, inspired as they seem to be by gender stereotypes, can be seen as the inescapable product of a conceptual framework that determines how we think about gender in the first place. In the absence of such a framework, there is no such thing as gender. On this view, the conceptual framework gives us background concepts, assumptions and expectations about what masculinity and femininity are, which in turn shape our sexuality, including our unconscious sexual thoughts, and thus serve as a deeper explanation for the processes that psychoanalysis describes.

Second, and in tension with that suggestion, is Derrida's attempt to rethink Heidegger's own history of being hypothesis in gendered terms. Though we have not discussed this aspect of late Heidegger's thought, his view is not merely that there are a succession of conceptual frameworks which have a certain narrative logic to them, but rather that these frameworks come from some deeper source, which Heidegger calls 'being'. In this connection, the frameworks and the 'worlds' they constitute for us can be seen as a kind of gift from being. What is more, this process of gifting frameworks is one that cannot be conceptualized within any framework. Attempting to do so necessarily obscures this fundamental phenomenon. In

Heidegger's own reading of Nietzsche, part of the pejorative point of characterizing Nietzsche as a metaphysician is to say that his thinking of the world as will to power and eternal recurrence is to think within a framework. This obscures the fact that it *is* thinking within a framework, that this framework is given to us by being, and that what is important about being is its very generosity and self-effacing nature. Derrida's second suggestion then is that Nietzsche's use of gendered stereotypes in thinking about truth and illusion is not merely an illustration of his being trapped in a gender-constituting framework, but reveals deeper insights of his own into the meta-framework situation we find ourselves in. Crudely, Derrida seems to be insinuating that there is something feminine about the late Heidegger's conception of being and something masculine about humanity as recipient, so that there may be something to Nietzsche's gendered metaphysical discourse after all. Or, less crudely, Nietzsche's use of these gender stereotypes may point us beyond them to fundamental truths about our ontological situation that the later Heidegger himself has tried to articulate, though in non-gendered language.

The first suggestion – that gender concepts are the artefacts of conceptual frameworks – is one that has proved to have enormous influence. There are two ways in which this could be understood. One is that there is a real environment which we might again think of as displaying an irreducible, 'chaotic' complexity, which we then go on to classify in various ways. On this view, it is not that there are no differences between male and female, but that our partial and limited classifications highlight some while rendering others comparatively invisible. The other way of thinking about this is to suggest that the very act of classification reshapes its social material and makes sexual and gender phenomena exist in the first place. Since we are already far afield from Nietzsche, it needs only to be said that empirical (biological and historical) investigations would be highly relevant to any such discussion. However, if one thinks of these frameworks in a transcendental way, as constituting the world of empirical objects in the first place, then empirical investigation could only serve to re-assert the '*a priori*' of our own framework's assumptions about gender, and thus would seem pointless.

The second suggestion suffers from two difficulties. First, there are serious objections to be made to the very idea of an ontological framework in the sense intended, even if we set aside the highly metaphorical character of talking about being as giving us these frameworks. It is not clear that Derrida agrees with Heidegger that there is a plurality of these frameworks, with a successive narrative logic to them. On the contrary, one gets the impression that Derrida seems to think, in a quasi-transcendental manner, that there is only one framework that is gifted to us. This may be due to Derrida's complex debt to Husserl's conception of the history of European culture as the growth of a community committed since the ancient Greeks to a unitary ideal of pure, disinterested theoretical knowledge.[6] However, whether we conceive of frameworks as singular or plural, the very idea of a framework would seem to imply some sort of meaningful contrast with that which is not (one's own) framework.

Donald Davidson has argued that any such notion nonetheless requires a distinction between framework and the facts generated by it. The ability to individuate a framework in turn requires that some sense be made of a plurality of (at least possible) frameworks. A priori constraints on linguistic interpretation will always yield the result that where the notion of there being two such frameworks seems plausible, this will be because of the possibility of translation between them. Thus there was really only one framework in two different dialects in the first place. By contrast, where the impression of genuine diversity is supported by a genuine impossibility of translation, this is evidence that the alleged alien framework user is not speaking or thinking at all. Davidson's suggestion is not that the facts that lead to talk of rival conceptual schemes do not exist. It is that they are grossly overstated, and better understood as local differences in theoretical commitments (Aristotle thought the sun revolved around the earth, Galileo thought the earth revolved around the sun) rather than global differences in ontology (Europeans think that the world consists of substances, the Hopi think that the world consists of processes).[7] Davidson's entire discussion here is highly relevant to much recent French philosophy, since the quasi-Kantian image of a duality of scheme and content has become such a common one.

The suggestion that Derrida thinks we might find that there is 'something to' Nietzsche's gender-inflected remarks after all must be made quite tentatively, for his text is elliptical and obscure on this very point. Supposing he did, however, one is tempted to respond as Norman O. Brown once did to Joseph Needham's celebration of Taoism: 'An organism whose own sexual life is as disordered as man's is in no position to construct objective theories about the Yin and the Yang and the sex life of the universe'.[8] That is to say, if we take psychoanalytic interpretation seriously – and the late Heidegger's post-metaphysical reflections on the relationship between being and beings evinces a gendered component – the response should be to psychoanalyse this as well. It is noteworthy that the idea that there is something right about psychoanalytic explanation, if it is regarded as a provisional account of deeper ontological issues, was previously made by Sartre in *Being and Nothingness*.[9] Lastly, echoing a remark made in Chapter 5 above, Derrida's most interesting suggestions about Nietzsche in *Spurs* all have an unstated premise: supposing psychoanalytic theories can be taken as a given, what follows? Dogmatic commitment to psychoanalytic modes of explanation is not unusual in recent French thought, and one wonders what could possibly justify it in light of the large body of critical literature on psychoanalysis and subsequent developments in psychology and evolutionary biology in the twentieth century.

FOUCAULT

Foucault's relationship to Nietzsche and Heidegger is complex. First, Foucault also offers his own interpretation of Nietzsche, in his essay 'Nietzsche, Genealogy, History'.[10] But more important than his account of Nietzsche's thought – which focuses almost entirely on methodological issues for the study of history – is Foucault's own emulation of Nietzsche, inflected by a criticism of themes from Hegel and the late Heidegger. Foucault's importance for Nietzsche scholarship is largely the result of post-Foucauldian readers seeing Nietzsche, not as Foucault saw him when explicitly engaged in Nietzsche interpretation, but seeing Nietzsche *as* Foucault. The tendency to regard Nietzsche as similar to Foucault is an example of what Borges called the invention of predecessors.[11] We should therefore look not only at what Foucault says about Nietzsche, but at what Foucault himself does when engaged in what he also calls 'genealogy'.

The essay on genealogy is meant not only to articulate what Nietzsche's methodology is, but to signal Foucault's endorsement of it. The essay is divided into seven sections. In the first section, Foucault indicates that one of his central targets is Hegel's (and by extension, both Marx's and Heidegger's) conception of history as a linear narrative with a teleological unfolding towards a particular goal. History, Foucault insists, is simply not like that. The second section is more specifically directed at the late Heidegger. Just as history has no goal, it has no origin if origin is conceived in a certain way. Foucault contrasts origin as '*Ursprung*' (the Heideggerian conception) with origin as '*Herkunft*' (the Nietzschean conception). Origin in the former sense posits that at the beginning of a meaningful historical sequence (like Heidegger's 'history of being'), there is some sort of essence or necessary structure. This essence is a repository of value. Finally, the essence is most clearly revealed at the moment of origin. Subsequent developments can be seen as under the persisting sway of the original essence or as a deplorable falling away from it. One helpful way (for American readers at least) to think about the target of Foucault's criticism here is American constitutional originalism. On this view, there are certain timeless truths about the nature of individual liberty and good government that were revealed at the moment of the ratification of the US Constitution. These timeless truths thus become an ultimate law for the American community, which it is the task of jurists and finally the US Supreme Court, to attend to, preserve and apply. To apply the law properly in a current case, according to an originalist, one must try to discover the sacred thoughts of the Founders and conform one's rulings to them. Correlatively, when post-Founding rulings are correct, they are under the continuing sway of the sacred founding, and when they are not, we have fallen away from the sacred origin. The genealogist, by contrast, insists that there is no point of origin in this sense: the founding is not a unity and it does not embody any revelatory truth. It is, instead, simply a moment in which a variety of historical forces happened to come together in a particular configuration. All subsequent moments, including bad faith attempts to speak with the authority of the founding (or to wriggle away from it, to adapt or transform it) are nothing but contingent moments in which the historical forces at work come into a particular configuration. The alleged essence is merely 'fabricated' from 'competition' between various forces and factions.[12] The implicit dig at Heidegger is that we were not in touch with some revelation of being during the era of the pre-Socratics, nor is the current age of technology an unfolding of or a falling away from that revelation.[13]

The third section continues the criticism of Heidegger. If there is no original essence or decisive falling away from one of these ages, then neither of them can control history or constitute a destiny in relation to which real historical actors (very much including ourselves) must be passive. Both the past and the present are revealed as more or less arbitrary and 'up for grabs'. This very indeterminacy not only facilitates normative criticism but political action as well: we see that nothing has to be the way it is; if we do not like what there is, we can change it. Foucault also stresses the concreteness of genealogical inquiry and its possible focus on the body as both subject and agent of historical events; nothing about an alleged timeless human nature can be presupposed.

In the fourth section, Foucault returns to Hegel. There is also a surprising allusion to Deleuze's criticism in *Nietzsche and Philosophy* of Hegel's account of the master/slave relation. In Hegel's *Phenomenology of Spirit*, Hegel had argued that the struggle for recognition leads to the master/slave relation in which the master obtains recognition at the slave's expense. Ironically, this causes the master to become dependent upon the slave, both psychologically and materially. The slave then becomes the vehicle for further dialectical developments towards the self-actualization of freedom (initially through his control of nature and his cultivation of rationality).[14] Deleuze, by contrast, insists on the Nietzschean activity, primacy and independence of the master's self-affirmation, as opposed to the reactive, secondary and dependent character of the slave. Oddly, in a section largely devoted to criticism of Hegel, we see Foucault claim that Deleuze has missed that 'the concept of goodness is not specifically the energy of the strong or the reaction of the weak, but precisely this scene where they are displayed superimposed of face-to-face'.[15] Though the Hegelian notion of recognition has dropped out, there still seems to be some allusion to an interdependence here that echoes Hegel. But the dominant note is a rejection of Hegel's Whiggish approach to history as the inevitable growth of rationality-as-freedom. He singles out social contract theory for particular criticism, which sees government, law or community as arising out of a rational renunciation of asocial conflict. Rather, whenever such systems emerge historically, they will be in the furtherance of conflict, the war of all against all prosecuted by other means. In this remark, Foucault shows a surprising debt to Rousseau, who, in the *Discourse on Inequality*,[16] made essentially the same point about the state. More to the point, the re-interpretation of an on-going conflict as the institution of law shows that history is just a succession of re-interpretations of ever-shifting conflicts.

In the fifth section, Foucault continues the theme of the absence of essence. Just as there is no essential origin which reveals itself at the beginning of history, there are no 'great men' who play crucial roles at crucial junctures. Instead of focusing on dramatic episodes in the history of politics or the history of thought, the genealogist focuses on small facts which reveal the development of (and sudden shifts in) underlying or permeating practices. These are precisely the sorts of things that tend to escape the attention of the traditional historian with his more dramatic image of history. Attention to these practices is crucial, for they constitute the character of human life in a particular moment. Just as there is no essence revealed at the origin or at crucial junctures, there is no essential human nature which is constant throughout history and immune to the shaping force of quotidian practices. Foucault then returns to the normative importance of genealogy, characterizing it as revealing the changing and hence changeable character of human life; if the conditions of life at a particular moment are changeable and unsatisfactory, genealogy can serve a diagnostic function, leading the way to therapeutic action. This medical analogy underscores the pragmatic character of genealogical inquiry. It is not geared towards the dispassionate discovery of value-neutral truths, but pursues its inquiries with a 'curative' interest. Foucault suggests that genealogy is hence perspectival, a claim that often generates a certain degree of epistemological anxiety. Are the claims of the genealogist true? At least within the bounds of this essay, Foucault does not appear to be making claims that would entail either a self-referential paradox or any sort of conceptual relativism (though as we shall see, these issues do suggest themselves in reading Foucault's writings). Rather, the claim here is that every inquiry expresses pragmatic interests, including the genealogist's. The stance of detached, neutral inquiry is dishonest where found, unattainable in any case, and need not be embraced by the genealogist. To follow the analogy, the physician need not pretend that the health of the patient is a matter of indifference to her and does not shape what is and is not investigated. But this does not mean that there are no facts as to symptoms and causes.

The sixth section is peculiar and in some tension with points made earlier. Foucault criticizes the 'demogogic' character of history as it is traditionally conceived, where it debunks the great episodes of the past and stands in judgement over them. His point seems to be that such a mode of doing history (for example, in political biography) serves to assimilate an alien past to a familiar present, the better to adopt a self-congratulatory stance towards it. Foucault is not taking back his strictures against 'great man' and 'great events' history, but rather stressing the alienness of the past and the questionableness of the present which emerges from it.

In the final section, Foucault returns to Nietzsche's second *Untimely Meditation* on history, to show how Nietzsche's mature view departs from his earlier thoughts. In the earlier essay, Nietzsche had contrasted monumental, antiquarian and critical modes of historical inquiry, seeing each as possessing some pragmatic interest but also certain dangers 'for life'. Though Nietzsche himself never directly addresses the differences between his earlier account of historical inquiry and the mature view in *Genealogy*, Foucault suggests that we can discern a triple transformation. He identifies monumental history with 'reminiscence' (echoing both the Platonic notion of knowledge as recollection and the Heideggerian quest for the origin). Monumental history is to give way to 'parody'. One of the examples used to illustrate what he means by this is Nietzsche's use of the historical Zoroaster as a parodic mask; it is not altogether clear what this has to do with genealogical method. Antiquarian history is concerned, on Foucault's account, with the discovery of essences, which he associates with 'identity'. However, these identities are revealed by genealogy to be artificial syntheses, false unities to be dissolved by 'dissociation'. Finally, he associates critical history with 'knowledge' as detached, impersonal, non-perspectival inquiry. By contrast, he proposes his model of engaged, risky, pragmatic inquiry, which he calls 'sacrificial' because of the risk it poses for the inquirer. Though all these points shed some light on both Nietzsche's and Foucault's intentions, it is not clear that he has quite understood the earlier essay. He may be missing continuities in Nietzsche's thought that are obscured by his determination to see a reversal or inversion from the early to the late Nietzsche. Nonetheless, the essay is of considerable interest and shows great sympathy with and not a little insight into Nietzsche's approach, despite the polemical asides aimed at Hegel and

Heidegger, whom Nietzsche either did not or could not have defined his position in relation to.

Very late in his career, Foucault offered a retrospective account of his own work in relation to his conception of genealogical method. Genealogy can be applied to three different domains or 'axes' as he calls them: truth, power and ethics. He explains his architectonic conception as follows:

> First, a historical ontology of ourselves in relation to truth through which we constitute ourselves as subjects of knowledge; second, a historical ontology of ourselves in relation to a field of power through which we constitute ourselves as subjects acting on others; third, a historical ontology in relation to ethics through which we constitute ourselves as moral agents.[17]

However, it is not clear that this retrospective account does justice to Foucault's own development viewed *ex ante*. Foucault's orientation towards Nietzsche and genealogy came late in his career. In his earlier, 'archaeological' works, Foucault analysed medicine, the human sciences economics, linguistics, biology and philosophy. According to Foucault, structured codes organize scientists' perception, discourse and social practices at a level unknown to them. Such codes, or 'epistemes', play a quasi-Kantian role, as 'conditions of the possibility' of knowledge. Foucault's conception of episteme thus makes the work of scientists subject to a cultural force beyond anyone's conscious control. His conception of these epistemes and their historical succession is indebted to the later Heidegger's conception of a 'history of being' as well as to the work of the structuralists (such Althusser, Lacan and Levi-Strauss). The debt to Heidegger (indicated in part by the quoted passage above, in which he calls his various projects 'historical ontologies') is complex. In *Birth of the Clinic*, he had argued that a certain conception of death is peculiar to our current episteme; this appears to be a dig at the early Heidegger for thinking that there was some trans-historical experience of death which could provide the underpinnings of 'fundamental ontology's' account of authenticity and temporality.[18] In *Order of Things*, Foucault broadened this critique, suggesting that not only the quasi-Kantian commitments of early Heidegger, but also the very idea of a history of being as a falling away from an essential origin was an artefact of the same episteme.[19] These earlier works do not show much of Nietzsche's influence, either substantively or methodologically. A common complaint against them is that the notion of epistemes is itself quasi-Kantian, and involves Foucault in either a self-referential paradox or a pernicious conceptual relativism. After all, his own historical inquiries are presumably generated by his own episteme, about which he must be as unconscious as the thinkers he studies. Foucault's implicit response to this in his later works seems to involve backing off of the more dramatic formulations involved in the notion of an episteme, thus rendering them accessible to empirical inquiry. That said, his later turn to genealogy would inherit both the culturalism and the epistemological interests of his earlier work.

Foucault's claim that epistemes – which are abstract conceptual or linguistic structures – governed social life became associated in his mind with an undue reification. To address this, he added the notion of regimes of power, which coerce people into following specific norms. We see here both a debt to the early Heidegger's conception of 'worldhood' being shaped by social norms, and Nietzsche's conception of norms as expressing power relations. The mechanisms which maintain this coercion are micro-practices demanding specific kinds of behaviour in specific contexts (the use of time cards and clocks in factories, for example). Though these micro-practices in effect subordinate some people to the benefit of others, they need not be the products of any deliberate design. Perhaps more important is a point that Foucault seems to owe to Nietzsche: power so conceived, even when it is the object of social criticism, should not be understood as essentially negative, restrictive or prohibitory, as contrasted with a freedom conceived in opposing terms. Rather, power is creative. It does not prevent people from being what they are: it makes people be as they are.

Foucault's analysis of society in these middle works often seems to jump from detailed concrete descriptions of micro-practices to more impressionistic claims about the common style of the micro-practices.[20] This common style betrays a pervasive, invisible, impersonal force: power. Power structures behaviour; at the same time, it structures the perception, discourse and practices of scientists who want to understand human behaviour scientifically. Foucault's account of the relationship between power and knowledge echoes Nietzsche's in *Genealogy*, Essay III. However, where Nietzsche's analysis of the will to truth depends on psychological explanations, in Foucault's micro-sociology and a broad cultural thematics replace psychology.

Foucault's genealogical method echoes Nietzsche's concern with power. Both philosophers' historical inquiries are directed at practices whose character bears on philosophical concerns. Furthermore, Foucault's analyses, like Nietzsche's, portray historical processes with an emphasis on their contingent, non-teleological character. He is sensitive to how alien even something as recent as the Enlightenment can appear, if viewed through historicist lenses. What connects him most decisively with Nietzsche, however, is his commitment to demystifying accounts of the historical processes that most concern him. We easily ignore our 'disciplinary' practices in their institutional home, the prison, because our ideological commitments interpret such practices as just. Once we see the practices described in coolly non-ideological terms and in concrete detail, we clearly perceive their outrageousness. What is more, the presence of similar 'carceral' practices in other social domains can then be more clearly perceived. Foucault wants his readers to transfer their outrage from the one setting to the other. His work thus shares Nietzsche's critical intent: Nietzsche wants to use his critique as a tool to reanimate 'noble' values, whereas Foucault places his critique in the service of radical politics.

Foucault had intended to continue his genealogy of modernity. He meant to supplement his account in *Discipline and Punish* of the growing 'carceralization' of modernity (which in many ways echoes, on a much more concrete level, Heidegger's account of modernity as 'technological') with a parallel account of its growing 'sexualization' in the projected multi-volume *History of Sexuality*. However, after one promising introductory volume, *The Will to Knowledge*, Foucault turned his attention away from the historical processes that culminated in contemporary society. He instead turned towards the genealogy of western ethical ideals and their relationship to sexual self-mastery. This project begins with an analysis of Greek ethics in *The Uses of Pleasure*, and continues with an account of Roman ethics in *The Care of the Self*.[21] A final volume was to deal with medieval ethics and the 'hermeneutics of the self'. In these final works, Foucault relegates his political passion – so reminiscent of Rousseau – to the background. Instead, we see the beginnings of work much closer in subject and spirit to Nietzsche.

DELEUZE

Even more than Foucault's interpretation, Deleuze's interpretation of Nietzsche is couched in terms of a response to Hegel. But whereas Foucault is primarily concerned with articulating a non-Hegelian conception of history, Deleuze's approach sees in Nietzsche a much broader, systematic response to Hegel. Though we cannot do justice to the entirety of Hegel's thought here, two themes are especially important. First, Hegel regards all phenomena, both conceptual and concrete, as manifesting a rational 'dialectical' pattern. Michael Inwood has illustrated the notion of a dialectical process with the following example.[22] Suppose that you are taught a system of natural arithmetic which involves only natural numbers (0, 1, 2, 3, etc.), simple syntactical rules for forming equations, and the operations of addition and subtraction. All goes smoothly until you form a subtraction equation in which the first term is smaller than the second ('3–4 = ?'). At this point, you are lost, in a state of conceptual 'cramp', unable to proceed further. This condition is the sort that Hegel calls, somewhat misleadingly, a 'contradiction'. There are only two ways to proceed, since you cannot return to the earlier state of not being aware of these kinds of equations. Either you construct a restrictive rule forbidding the formation of such equations (the 'Kantian' approach), or you rethink your concept of what a number is so that it now includes and differentiates itself into both positive and negative integers, allowing the equation to be solved, '3–4 = –1'. This process thus has three stages: a 'naive' stage in which the simpler system works smoothly, a 'troubled' stage in which the limits of the system are apprehended and one cannot go forward (unless a restrictive rule is added) and a third 'higher' stage in which the original concept of number is enriched and revised to allow new forms of arithmetic without 'contradiction'. This general pattern appears again and again in Hegel's thought in a vast variety of different contexts.

Hegel's characterization of these kinds of processes involves appeal to three features. First, to continue with Inwood's example, the process has only one 'good' outcome, the transformation of the concept of number that allows subtraction to proceed unhindered; these processes thus have a peculiar kind of necessity and normativity that Hegel identifies with rationality itself. Hegel is here indebted to Aristotle's conception of coming-to-be as a teleological process and the manifestation of essence as it passes from potentiality to actuality. However, the essence as potential is not a kind of blueprint or anticipatory copy of the final product, but rather a kind of self-organizing and self-differentiating system. Second, these sorts of processes involve an inescapable traffic with 'negation' in some broad sense: our imaginary arithmetical system cannot grow in the right sort of way until it undergoes a kind of preliminary failure, and this temporary negativity is justified or vindicated by the favourable outcome of the process. In Hegel's descriptions of these processes, the three stages are characterized in terms of an initial unity, a separation of that unity due to 'self-negation' into a subject/object polarity, and a subsequent overcoming of this polarity into a new unity. Third, concrete mathematicians, the 'you' in the story above, in a certain sense drop out because they can only be passive in relation to the process. You do not create a new conception of number in any real sense because there is only one rational way for the process to develop; in a sense the simpler conception of number simply passes over into a richer sense of number and drags the mathematician along with it. To the extent that the mathematician is just a living embodiment of the arithmetical system, the system transforms itself. Thus there is a kind of passivity built into this model when we think about concrete persons in a rational-dialectical process.

The second theme is Hegel's peculiar relationship to Christianity. When Hegel's philosophical system is complete, it presents itself as a total rational account of the world. Religions could also be said to provide us with a total *picture* of the world. One of Hegel's concerns was to address the conflict between Christian religious conservatism and Enlightenment anticlericalism, both of which struck him as partial and inadequate. His resolution of this tension was to claim that religions provide the believer with the same content as a philosophical system; if the philosophical system that corresponds to the religion is true, the religion is also true if taken as a non-literal presentation of the philosophical insights it expresses. The opposition between Christianity and Enlightenment is only a real or 'troubled' opposition if we take the claims of each literally. If we take the claims of Christianity non-literally, then the literal meaning of these non-literal claims can also be true or, indeed, identical to the non-religious philosophical account of the world. Thus 'properly understood' there need be no conflict between the two at all.

Since Hegel thinks that the plurality of world religions form a dialectical sequence culminating in Christianity, and the plurality of philosophical systems form a dialectical sequence culminating in his own system, he can then claim that Christianity, 'the absolute religion', is true in a sense. It expresses metaphorically the metaphysical truths that are only properly and literally apprehended in Hegelian philosophy. For example, Hegel will identify the rationality manifested by dialectical sequences in history with the idea of Providence in Christianity. One could encapsulate all this by saying that in a certain sense, for Hegel, Socrates equals Jesus.

This last remark helps to set up Deleuze's approach to Nietzsche, for Deleuze finds in Nietzsche a comprehensive alternative to Hegelian thought. First, consider the idea of the three-stage process where we passed from the idea that a number is the same thing as a natural number, through a perplexed stage where the system could no longer operate, to a conception of number that embraced both positive and negative integers. Though Hegel is famous for his insistence on the pervasiveness and unavoidability of 'negation', if we look at this pattern we see that negation serves an instrumental role in getting us to a higher stage in which it is absent. Negation remains a bad thing, to be superseded in favour of a richer concept from which it is absent. But why is this so? It can only be because the incoherence or instability of the intermediate stage is a bad thing by virtue of its incoherence. The very idea of the dialectical process thus privileges coherence over incoherence, stability over instability, and negation in Hegel's sense only gains its peculiar character as negation in light of its contrast with unity, coherence, stability and the like.[23]

Deleuze's somewhat opaque suggestion here is that this privileging of coherence over incoherence, unity over disunity, stability over instability, whether that privileging is metaphysical (regarding the coherent as more real or the only truly real) or normative (regarding it as more valuable), flies in the face of the pervasive incoherence of the world, its 'multiplicity' and instability. Once we have made that commitment, we end up passing judgement on the world because it fails to live up to our expectations of coherence. And it is only for this reason that incoherence comes to be thought of as negative, that 'negation' comes into play at all. If we could regard incoherence, disunity, instability and the like as the fundamental character of the world to be affirmed, then there would be

NIETZSCHE: A GUIDE FOR THE PERPLEXED

no flaws to be overcome and consequently no dialectical progressions. Everything would be perfect just as it is.

This critique of the 'Socratic' dimension of Hegel is paralleled by a critique of the 'Christian' dimension of Hegel. In Christianity as well, interpreting the world as standing in need of redemption (whether conceived literally or non-literally) rests on a prior refusal to affirm the world as it is. Deleuze sees Nietzsche as attacking both dimensions of Hegel's thought. He reminds us that in *Birth of Tragedy*, Nietzsche contrasted the Dionysian art of tragedy with Socratism, while in his later work the opposition is not 'Dionysus versus Socrates' but 'Dionysus versus the Crucified'. Rationality and Christian world-denial are of a piece.[24]

Though one may doubt that this is quite what is going on in Nietzsche, Deleuze's interpretative strategy focuses on the topic in Nietzsche that lends the most credibility to it: Nietzsche's account of the master/slave relation in *Genealogy of Morals*. For here is a topic which (as we have already noted in passing) lends itself to a direct comparison with a crucial episode in Hegel's *Phenomenology of Spirit*, the discussion of 'Lordship and Bondage'.[25] In Hegel, we begin with a conflict between two subjects, each of which wants to affirm its essence as a consciousness, which it can only do by pushing itself to the limit and being willing to risk bodily death to receive it. But because consciousness is unable simply to affirm itself, it must look to another consciousness to do this affirming for it, by becoming the object for that other subject. Here again we see the typical Hegelian pattern of an initial unity which cannot sustain itself, and which therefore divides into a subject/object polarity. The earthier description of this process is to say that each consciousness fights out of a need for prestige, for other-validation, or, in Hegel's term, 'recognition'. Eventually, one must give way to the other and give it the recognition it seeks. The recognized consciousness then becomes the master, the recognizing consciousness becomes the slave. But the result is perverse or ironic: the master is now dependent upon the slave's continuing submission for his bodily existence and social prestige, while the slave needs nothing from the master in return. Furthermore, the slave, since he must deal with both fear of the master and the recalcitrant processes of nature as he works according to the master's bidding, acquires a stoical self-discipline and the beginnings of a rational understanding of nature. The master, by contrast, is a dead end. Looking ahead, we know that it will be from the slave's dialectical descendants that Christianity, and ultimately 'philosophical science', the Hegelian system itself, will spring.

Nietzsche by contrast characterizes the master, not as seeking recognition from the slave, but as simply working his will on the world while affirming his uniqueness. He does not *need* the slave for anything; he is completely self-sufficient. The master expresses an 'active force'. In his purely affirmative stance, he affirms himself and his difference from everything else. Crucially, the master does not define himself primarily in terms of his relations with the slave. He merely notes the slave's difference and disdains it as an aspect of his unqualified self-affirmation. The slave, by contrast, begins by defining the master as evil, and only secondarily defines himself as good by contrast. The slave expresses 'reactive force'. The anti-Hegelian point, then, is that the Hegelian dialectic of master and slave is nothing more than how, in Nietzsche's terms, the slave views things. The slave imagines that the master seeks recognition because the slave seeks recognition, but this is not the case. The master is always totally independent of the slave. Most importantly, the characteristic slave move as Nietzsche describes it – 'you are evil, I am not like you, therefore I am good' – is a classic Hegelian negation relation between subject and object and its supercession in favour of a higher unity. But if there is no analogous phenomenon on the master side, then Hegelian thinking is defectively slavish and needlessly negative. There is an alternative to it which is purely positive, is in no interdependent relation with it and which demands no supercession in favour of anything else: the master's perspective.[26]

If we take these competing accounts of the master/slave relation as emblematic of a larger, systemic contrast between Nietzschean and Hegelian thought, Deleuze's suggestion is that it is only from a Hegelian perspective that any problem of negativity arises to be solved at all; from a Nietzschean perspective, there just is no such thing as negation at all. How can this be possible? We suggested that negation only arises by way of a contrast with incoherence, a failure to cohere, a failure to achieve or sustain a valuable unity. But if coherence and its value are illusory and purely symptomatic of the slave's failure to affirm his own inescapable incoherence, then the world in all its 'disparateness' is not failing to live up to some higher standard. There is no failure, no negation, and nothing to

NIETZSCHE: A GUIDE FOR THE PERPLEXED

overcome. Much of the difficulty in making sense of Deleuze's texts stems from his pursuit of a language in which he can characterize this pervasive incoherence of the world which does not contain an implicit 'dig' at it, as if it were something that should not be the case. For this reason, he prefers the expression 'difference' for what I have called incoherence.

In any case, Deleuze's chief concern is with articulating in his own language Nietzsche's spirit of life-affirmation. For example, Deleuze's account of the doctrine of the eternal recurrence seems to be nothing other than an alternative formulation of this to-be-celebrated incoherence of the world, rather than a cosmological account. He explicitly rejects the latter sort of interpretation, claiming that the proofs of the eternal recurrence in Nietzsche's notes are casuistic, akin to Pascal's wager, which should not be regarded as expressing the meaning of Christian salvation so much as a rhetorical trick to persuade us to accept it.[27] These proofs could only be accepted if we first accept a conception of temporality which reifies individual temporal moments thus permitting cross-cycle identification of moments as recurring. Deleuze, by contrast, seems to attribute to Nietzsche a Bergsonian conception of time as flowing duration, which is a tensed theory of time.[28] If we add to this a denial of ontological identities of any sort, then literal recurrence will make no sense. Deleuze, reading Nietzsche charitably by his own lights, instead understands the doctrine as a practical conception with two aspects. First, he accepts as a provisional characterization the 'Kantian test' reading in which the doctrine is an idea by which we judge our actions as fit or unfit for unconditional affirmation.[29] Second, in what he calls the 'esoteric' sense of the doctrine, its importance consists in its selective, life transformative character. The reactive person who embraces the doctrine by affirming their incoherence instead of judging it and trying to escape from it, finds that their negativity ceases to be other-directed, becomes self-directed instead, and transforms itself into pure (self-destructive) activity. In this sense, Deleuze says that reactive forces do not return.[30] This is enough to show that Deleuze cannot understand the eternal recurrence in any literal sense. (One also suspects that it also shows a certain residual affection for Hegelian patterns of thought, since we see in this last instance examples of other-negation, self-negative and consequent self-affirmation.)

Deleuze's celebration of incoherence finds expression outside his Nietzsche interpretation, in his ethics and politics (which are contained in his *magnum opus*, co-authored with Felix Guattari, *Capitalism and Schizophrenia*). In the first volume, *Anti-Oedipus*, Deleuze and Guattari argue – starting from the given of Jacques Lacan's structuralist reformulation of psychoanalysis – that the typical psychological structure that Freud and Lacan find in an allegedly universal Oedipus complex is actually a construction from initially chaotic materials.[31] Once 'Oedipalized', the subject (itself a kind of fiction constructed by the Oedpialization process) is doomed, and whether one responds by sublimation, neurosis or its cure, an Oedipalized subject can only find its way in the world in various modalities of renunciation, suffering and despair. The schizophrenic, by contrast, destroys the psychic structure, liberating the bound energy within and becomes a 'desiring machine', which is another version of the Nietzschean, self-affirming, creative master. This too connects with the critique of Hegel, for what could be emblematic of a more profound departure from rationality than psychosis? Similarly, in the second volume, *A Thousand Plateaus*, Deleuze and Guattari criticize the idea of the subject as a coherent, functionally articulated system.[32] In its place they urge that we become 'bodies without organs', a metaphor for repudiating functional structure in favour of a kind of de-differentiated state in which nothing within oneself is *for* anything, and hence there are no limits on what kinds of creative activity are now possible.

We must pass over the vast amount of detail in Deleuze's thought, including his often perspicacious monographs on individual thinkers such as Hume, Spinoza, Kant and Leibniz. However, some conclusions can be drawn. Though Deleuze's interpretation of Nietzsche is thoroughly grounded in textual citation and seems to be animated by an intuitive sympathy with the spirit of Nietzsche's thought, the suggestion that Nietzsche is best understood as a radical critic of Hegel seems to be an illusion fostered by the popularity of post-war French discussions of Hegel's account of the master/slave relation (perhaps most famously appropriated by Sartre's in his discussion of 'the Other' in *Being and Nothingness*) and Nietzsche's prominent but quite different discussion of a parallel master/slave relation in *Genealogy*. There is minimal textual evidence that Nietzsche knew Hegel well or cared much about Hegel's thought and influence, which had been in eclipse in

Germany for more than a generation at the time Nietzsche wrote. This does not mean that the two accounts cannot be fruitfully contrasted, but at the least one can say that Deleuze makes too much of it. Perhaps worse, however, is that for Nietzsche the master/slave relation plays a role in an empirical hypothesis about the genesis of a specific moral code as an historical phenomenon. Ironically, Deleuze borrows the seemingly timeless and abstract quality of Hegel's account and transfers it onto Nietzsche, so that Nietzsche's master/slave relation becomes detached from its larger strategic purposes and becomes a generalized ahistorical critique of two timeless ways of approaching life: the noble and the base. In the process, much of the complexity of Nietzsche's account gets lost, replaced by an almost Manichean contrast between the two modes of existence, one perfectly good, the other perfectly bad: master and slave, active and reactive, become the unifying categories that impose a pervasive dualism on Nietzsche's texts that is not really there.

Though one cannot blame Deleuze's own, separate philosophical efforts for failing to coincide fully with Nietzsche's intentions (if they do not coincide, perhaps Deleuze is right and Nietzsche is wrong!), because Deleuze identifies himself so closely with Nietzsche, it is tempting to read his own separate work as continuing the commentary on Nietzsche as well. And yet, if we do so, one cannot resist the impression that Nietzsche would not have found himself much in sympathy with Deleuze's celebration of schizophrenia as an ethic and anarchy as a political ethic. For Nietzsche, creativity involves giving form to chaos, or at the very least re-organizing what one finds organized in some other fashion. Thus order has a certain value for Nietzsche, since it is the upshot of a creative activity. Second, the ability to be creative depends upon the construction of various skills and abilities, itself an ordering of the self. Finally, in many places Nietzsche characterizes the highest activities as involving the imposition of an order on oneself (making the self a work of art, a theme Foucault echoes in his last writings and interviews), and even imposing order on communities, as if the mass of humanity were raw material to be reshaped by an artist's intent and skill. Whatever we may think of this, it is all quite alien to Deleuze's intuition that order always obstructs, that destruction of order is always good. Though this intuition to some extent fits Deleuze's alliance with radical politics, and his often acute interpretations of modern art, it reflects a sensibility quite alien to Nietzsche's, for whom a specific instance of destruction can be affirmed because it opens possibilities of creative orderings, not because it is a step on a path to total destruction as an absence of any and all limitations. One even senses, to play the rhetorical game too, that Nietzsche would sense too much 'slavishness' in such a preoccupation with the elimination of all constraints.

NOTES

1 INTRODUCTION

1 Scott Turow, *The Laws of Our Fathers*, New York: Farrar, Straus and Giroux, 1996, p. 79.
2 The earliest letters from Nietzsche date from 1850. The earliest notes date from 1852.
3 '[T]here is perhaps as much as 25% more material-excluding Nietzsche's letters, letters to him, and personal effects – than exists in even the very best edition of Nietzsche's works, the monumental Colli-Montinari edition ... The reasons for this ... may include the following facts ... Montinari, often did not produce the pages and the notations Nietzsche himself crossed out in his handwritten manuscripts ... Montinari ... excluded ... matters he considered "personal" ... and many editors have excluded all marginalia ...' Bernd Magnus, 'How the "True Text" Finally Became a Fable: Nietzsche's Weimar Literary Estate', *Nietzscheana* 6 (1997): 14, ellipses mine.

2 NIETZSCHE'S WRITINGS

1 Patricia Easterling, 'A Show for Dionysus', *The Cambridge Companion to Greek Tragedy*, Patricia Easterling (ed.), Cambridge: Cambridge University Press, 1997, pp. 36–53.
2 Gerald F. Else, *The Origin and Early Form of Greek Tragedy*, Cambridge, MA: Harvard University Press, 1965.
3 In part this is simply another manifestation of his break with Wagner's romanticism, but it may reflect another related shift. Early Nietzsche had placed great hopes in the reform of music and theatre. These are enterprises requiring a fairly high level of institutional support, and thus broad social acceptance. By the late 1870s, Nietzsche had not only given up on Wagner but had also given up on himself as a musician for the most part. His model of cultural achievement now is the *writer*, and while writers need an audience, they do not need a *large* audience, supporting orchestras, theatres and so on. A network of free-spirited

friends devoted to reading and writing can subsist in the modern world
without large-scale institutional support and the broader social assent it
presupposes. Pen, ink, paper, envelopes, stamps – these are cheap. Thus
cultural reform of the sort Nietzsche had come to care about could
happen invisibly, in our midst, while both the non-cultural institutions
and the cultural ones are left to go on their soul-stultifying way.
4 Julius Wellhausen, *Prolegomena zur Geschichte Israels*. Edinburgh,
   1885. Reprinted, Gloucester, MA: Peter Smith, 1973. For a contemporary account of the Documentary Hypothesis, see Richard Elliott
   Friedman, *Who Wrote the Bible?*, Upper Saddle River, NJ: Prentice
   Hall, 1987.
5 Robert W. Funk, *Honest to Jesus: Jesus for a New Millennium*, Santa
   Rosa, CA: Polebridge Press, 1996; Robert W. Funk and Roy W.
   Hoover, *The Five Gospels: The Search for the Authentic Words of Jesus*,
   Santa Rosa, CA: Polebridge Press, 1993.
6 Donald Harmon Akenson, *Saint Saul: A Skeleton Key to the Historical
   Jesus*, New York: Oxford University Press, 2000.

3 NIHILISM, WILL TO POWER, AND VALUE

1 Richard Schacht, *Nietzsche*, London: Routledge, 1983, chapter 3.
2 Bernard Reginster, *The Affirmation of Life: Nietzsche on Overcoming
   Nihilism*, Cambridge, MA: Harvard University Press, 2006, chapter 3.
3 The following account is indebted to Ruth Millikan, *On Clear and
   Confused Ideas: An Essay About Substance Concepts*, Cambridge:
   Cambridge University Press, 2000, chapter 4.
4 Contrast the account in Maudemarie Clark, *Nietzsche on Truth and
   Philosophy,* Cambridge: Cambridge University Press, 1990, chapter 7.
5 Ibid.
6 For the classic discussion of 'the myth of the given', see Wilfrid Sellars,
   Empiricism and the Philosophy of Mind, Cambridge, MA: Harvard
   University Press, 1997.
7 Robert Nozick, *Philosophical Explanations*, Cambridge, MA: Harvard
   University Press, 1981, chapter 1.

4 PERSPECTIVISM

1 Clark, op. cit., chapter 2.
2 The original debate over antirealism was modelled on the debate about
   mathematical intuitionism. One common method of proof is to show
   that a particular mathematical proposition is true by showing that its
   negation is false, on the assumption that every proposition is one or the
   other. Intuitionists reject the law of the excluded middle, and thus insist
   that we cannot prove mathematical propositions by *reductio*. In effect,
   they replace the concept of truth with the concept of proof. Thus for an
   intuitionist it makes no sense to say that a particular mathematical

proposition may be true, but we do not know that it is. By contrast, a 'Platonist' insists that this does make sense. Since we tend to think of truth in terms of correspondence, we can read the Platonist as saying that there is a world of mathematical fact, waiting to be discovered. For the intuitionist, there is only a body of possible proofs, waiting to be constructed. If we call the Platonist a 'mathematical realist' and the intuitionist a 'mathematical antirealist', this suggest a broader distinction between realism and antirealism which might turn up in other domains. Unfortunately, it became common for people to use the expression 'mind-dependent' to characterize the antirealist's view of the objects of his discourse, because of expressions like 'there is no fact of the matter as to what the billionth digit in the expansion of pi is until some mind actually expands it to that point'. This is a very different sense of 'mind-dependent' than what we mean when we say that dreams are mind-dependent; we mean merely that dreams inhere in dreamers and have no independent existence. We do not mean that there is no fact of the matter as to whether I have dreamed or not until I complete a dream-verification procedure.

5 CRITIQUE OF MORALITY

1 G. W. F. Hegel, *Phenomenology of Spirit*, trans. A. V. Miller, Oxford: Clarendon Press, 1977, pp. 104–38.
2 I also succumbed to it. See R. Kevin Hill, *Nietzsche's Critiques*, Oxford: Clarendon Press, 2003, pp. 196–229.

6 HEIDEGGER'S NIETZSCHE

1 Martin Heidegger, *The End of Philosophy*, trans. Joan Stambaugh, New York: Harper and Row, 1973.
2 Martin Heidegger, *Nietzsche, Volume I: The Will to Power as Art*, trans. David Farrell Krell, New York: Harper and Row, 1979, pp. 71–5.
3 Ibid., p. 115.
4 Ibid., p. 142.
5 Ibid., p. 239.
6 This interpretation of Kant is both philosophically and historically untenable. See my *Nietzsche's Critiques*, chapter five, for a different account.
7 As we shall see, Heidegger later offers a somewhat different account of what chaos and order mean here that is more indebted to Husserl and his own position in *Being and Time* than to Kant.
8 Heidegger, *Being and Time*, trans. Joan Stambaugh, Albany, NY: State University of New York Press, 1996, pp. 213–306.
9 This way of putting things will subsequently have to be severely qualified. We both believe it true and make it true.
10 The reason why Heidegger thinks there is a connection between his

reading of eternal recurrence as resoluteness and Nietzsche's fatalism has to do with Heidegger's characterization of resoluteness in *Being and Time* as a matter of assuming one's 'destiny'. There seems to be at most a verbal similarity here.

11 Heidegger, *Nietzsche, Volume II: The Eternal Recurrence of the Same*, trans. David Farrell Krell, New York: Harper and Row, 1984, pp. 84–96.

12 It is unclear whether he continues to regard temporality as mind-dependent; some have argued that late Heidegger rejects this thesis. See William Blattner, *Heidegger's Temporal Idealism*, Cambridge: Cambridge University Press, 1999, pp. 230–310.

13 Heidegger, *Introduction to Metaphysics*, trans. Gregory Fried and Richard Polt, New Haven, CT: Yale University Press, 2000, chapter 4.

14 Following here Herman Philipse's account of the 'neo-Hegelian theme' in his *Heidegger's Philosophy of Being*, Princeton, NJ: Princeton University Press, 1998, pp. 151–72.

7 A DIFFERENT NIETZSCHE

1 Jacques Derrida, *Spurs: Nietzsche's Styles*, trans. Barbara Harlow, Chicago: University of Chicago Press, 1979, pp. 123–39.

2 Ibid., pp. 55–63.

3 *Abstracts of the Standard Edition of the Complete Psychological Works of Sigmund Freud*, ed. Carrie Rothgeb, Nortvale, NJ: Jason Aronson Publishers, Inc., 1973, p. 153.

4 Derrida, op. cit., pp. 95–101.

5 Derrida, op. cit., pp. 109–23.

6 Edmund Husserl, *The Crisis of European Sciences and Transcendental Phenomenology: An Introduction to Phenomenological Philosophy*, trans. David Carr, Evanston, IL: Northwestern University Press, 1970.

7 Donald Davidson, 'On the Very Idea of a Conceptual Scheme', *Inquiries Into Truth and Interpretation*, 2nd ed., Oxford: Oxford University Press, 2001, pp. 183–98.

8 Norman O. Brown, *Life Against Death: The Psychoanalytic Meaning of History*, Middletown, CT: Wesleyan University Press, 1959, p. 317.

9 Jean-Paul Sartre, *Being and Nothingness*, trans. Hazel E. Barnes, New York: Philosophical Library, 1956, pp. 712–84.

10 Michel Foucault, 'Nietzsche, Genealogy, History', in *Language, Counter-memory, Practice: Selected Essays and Interviews*, Donald F. Bouchard (ed.), Ithaca, NY: Cornell University Press, 1977, pp. 139–64.

11 Jorge Luis Borges, 'Kafka and His Precursors', in *Labyrinths: Selected Stories and Other Writings*, Donald A. Yates and James E. Irby (eds), New York: New Directions, 1964, pp. 199–201.

12 Foucault, op. cit., p. 142.

13 It is unclear whether Foucault's practice conforms to his admonition. Much of his account of modern 'carceralization' and 'sexualization' seem inspired by Heidegger's notion of the technological. See Foucault,

Discipline and Punish: the Birth of the Prison, trans. Alan Sheridan, New York: Pantheon Books, 1978, and *The History of Sexuality, Volume I: An Introduction*, trans. Alan Sheridan, New York: Pantheon Books, 1978.
14 Hegel, op. cit.
15 Foucault, 'Nietzsche, Genealogy, History', p. 150.
16 Jean-Jacques Rousseau makes the same point about the state. See 'Discourse on Inequality,' Second Part, in *Rousseau's Political Writings*, ed. Alan Ritter and Julia Conway Bondanella, trans. Julia Conway Bondanella, New York: W. W. Norton and Company, 1988, pp. 34–57.
17 Foucault, 'On the Genealogy of Ethics: An Overview of Work in Progress', in *The Foucault Reader*, ed. Paul Rabinow, 1984, p. 351.
18 Foucault, *Birth of the Clinic*, trans. A. M. Sheridan Smith, New York: Pantheon Books, 1973, pp. 195–9.
19 Foucault, *Order of Things*, New York: Pantheon Books, 1971, pp. 328–35.
20 See Foucault, *Discipline and Punish*, and *The History of Sexuality, Volume I: An Introduction Will to Knowledge*.
21 Foucault, *The Use of Pleasure: Volume 2 of The History of Sexuality*, trans. Robert Hurley, New York: Pantheon Books, 1985, and *The Care of the Self: Volume 3 of The History of Sexuality*, trans. Robert Hurley, New York: Pantheon Books, 1986.
22 Michael Inwood, *Hegel*, London: Routledge, pp. 19–22.
23 It is important to realize that the 'coherence' in question is not *logical* coherence in the sense of absence of propositional contradiction, either in Hegel or Deleuze. Otherwise Deleuze's suggestion that we should accept the incoherence of the world would suffer from fatal objections.
24 Gilles Deleuze, *Nietzsche and Philosophy*, trans. Hugh Tomlinson, New York: Columbia University Press, 1983, pp. 10–19.
25 Hegel, op. cit.
26 Deleuze, op. cit., pp. 111–45.
27 Deleuze, op. cit., p. 202.
28 Deleuze, op. cit., pp. 47–9.
29 Deleuze, op. cit., pp. 68–9.
30 Deleuze, op. cit., pp. 69–72.
31 Gilles Deleuze and Félix Guattari, *Anti-Oedipus: Capitalism and Schizophrenia*, trans. Robert Hurley, Mark Seem and Helen R. Lane, Minneapolis, MN: University of Minnesota Press, 1983.
32 Gilles Deleuze and Félix Guattari, *A Thousand Plateaus*, trans. Brian Massumi, Minneapolis, MN: University of Minnesota Press, 1987.

SELECT BIBLIOGRAPHY

SUGGESTIONS FOR FURTHER READING

The simplest way to get into Nietzsche's texts is to read them in chronological order (see 'Abbreviations (pp.vii–viii) for dates). Two anthologies taken together, *The Basic Writings of Nietzsche* and *The Portable Nietzsche*, contain all the books except *Untimely Meditations* and the middle works. From there, one can explore the early and middle works in more depth by reading *Untimely Meditations, Human, All Too Human, Daybreak*, and *Gay Science*. The best secondary source on Nietzsche's thought is arguably Richard Schacht's *Nietzsche* (London: Routledge, 1983).

BIOGRAPHY

Hayman, Ronald, *Nietzsche: A Critical Life*, New York: Penguin, 1982.
Safranski, Rüdiger, *Nietzsche: A Philosophical Biography*, trans. Shelley Frisch, New York: W. W. Norton, 2002.

BACKGROUND AND RECEPTION

Aschheim, Steven, *The Nietzsche Legacy in Germany 1890–1990*, Berkeley: University of California Press, 1992.
Köhnke, Klaus Christian, *The Rise of Neo-Kantianism: German Academic Philosophy between Idealism and Positivism*, trans. R. J. Hollingdale, Cambridge: Cambridge University Press, 1991.
Smith, Douglas, *Transvaluations: Nietzsche in France 1872–1972*, Clarendon Press, 1996.
Thatcher, David S., *Nietzsche in England 1890–1914: The Growth of a Reputation*, Toronto: University of Toronto Press, 1970.

COMPREHENSIVE INTERPRETATIONS

Deleuze, Gilles, *Nietzsche and Philosophy*, trans. Hugh Tomlinson, New York: Columbia University Press, 1983.

Heidegger, Martin, *Nietzsche, Volume I: The Will to Power as Art*, trans. David Farrell Krell, New York: Harper and Row, 1979.

____, *Nietzsche, Volume II: The Eternal Recurrence of the Same*, trans. David Farrell Krell, New York: Harper and Row, 1984.

Kaufmann, Walter, *Nietzsche: Philosopher, Psychologist, Antichrist*, Princeton, NJ: Princeton University Press, 1974.

Nehamas, Alexander, *Nietzsche: Life as Literature*, Cambridge, MA: Harvard University Press, 1983.

Reginster, Bernard, *The Affirmation of Life: Nietzsche on Overcoming Nihilism*, Cambridge, MA: Harvard University Press, 2006.

Richardson, John, *Nietzsche's System*, Oxford: Oxford University Press, 1996.

Schacht, Richard, *Nietzsche*, London: Routledge, 1983.

EARLY NIETZSCHE

Hollinrake, Roger, *Nietzsche, Wagner and the Philosophy of Pessimism*, London: George Allen & Unwin, 1982.

Silk, M. S. and J. P. Stern, *Nietzsche on Tragedy*, Cambridge: Cambridge University Press, 1981.

MIDDLE NIETZSCHE

Abbey, Ruth, *Nietzsche's Middle Period*, Oxford: Oxford University Press, 2000.

ZARATHUSTRA

Lampert, Laurence, *"Nietzsche's Teaching, An Interpretation of 'Thus Spoke Zarathustra,"* New Haven, CT: Yale University Press, 1989.

OTHER SECONDARY LITERATURE ON NIETZSCHE

Ansell-Pearson, Keith, *An Introduction to Nietzsche as Political Thinker: The Perfect Nihilist*, Cambridge: Cambridge University Press, 1994.

Clark, Maudemarie, *Nietzsche on Truth and Philosophy*, Cambridge: Cambridge University Press, 1990.

Derrida, Jacques, *Spurs: Nietzsche's Styles*, trans. Barbara Harlow, Chicago: University of Chicago Press, 1979.

Foucault, Michel, 'Nietzsche, Genealogy, History', in *Language, Counter-memory, Practice: Selected Essays and Interviews*, Donald F. Bouchard (ed.), Ithaca, NY: Cornell University Press, 1977, pp. 139–64.

Green, Michael, *Nietzsche and the Transcendental Tradition*, Urbana, IL: University of Illinois Press, 2002.

Hill, R. Kevin, *Nietzsche's Critiques*, Oxford: Clarendon Press, 2003.

Hunt, Lester H., *Nietzsche and the Origin of Virtue*, London: Routledge, 1991.

Irigaray, Luce, *Marine Lover of Friedrich Nietzsche*, trans. Gillian C. Gill, New York: Columbia University Press, 1991.

Leiter, Brian, *Routledge Philosophy Guidebook to Nietzsche on Morality*, London: Routledge, 2002.

Magnus, Bernd, 'How the "True Text" Finally Became a Fable: Nietzsche's Weimar Literary Estate', *Nietzscheana* 6, 1997.

Poellner, Peter, *Nietzsche and Metaphysics*, Oxford: Clarendon Press, 1995.

Solomon, Robert, *Living with Nietzsche: What the Great 'Immoralist' Has to Teach Us*, Oxford: Oxford University Press, 2003.

Wilcox, John, *Truth and Value in Nietzsche*, Ann Arbor, MI: University of Michigan Press, 1974.

OTHER BOOKS AND ARTICLES

Abstracts of the Standard Edition of the Complete Psychological Works of Sigmund Freud, Carrie Rothgeb (ed.), Nortvale, NJ: Jason Aronson Publishers, Inc., 1973.

Akenson, Donald Harmon, *Saint Saul: A Skeleton Key to the Historical Jesus*, New York: Oxford University Press, 2000.

Berkeley, George, *Berkeley's Philosophical Writings*, David M. Armstrong (ed.), New York: Macmillan, 1965.

Blattner, William, *Heidegger's Temporal Idealism*, Cambridge: Cambridge University Press, 1999.

Borges, Jorge Luis, 'Kafka and His Precursors', in *Labyrinths: Selected Stories and Other Writings*, Donald A. Yates and James E. Irby (eds), New York: New Directions, 1964, pp. 199–201.

Brown, Norman O., *Life Against Death: The Psychoanalytic Meaning of History*, Middletown, CT: Wesleyan University Press, 1959.

Davidson, Donald, 'On the Very Idea of a Conceptual Scheme', *Inquiries Into Truth and Interpretation*, 2nd ed., Oxford: Oxford University Press, 2001, pp. 183–98.

Deleuze, Gilles and Félix Guattari, *Anti-Oedipus: Capitalism and Schizophrenia*, trans. Robert Hurley, Mark Seem and Helen R. Lane, Minneapolis, MN: University of Minnesota Press, 1983.

____, *A Thousand Plateaus*, trans. Brian Massumi, Minneapolis, MN: University of Minnesota Press, 1987.

Dostoevsky, Fyodor, *The Idiot*, trans. Richard Pevear and Larissa Volokhonsky, New York: Vintage, 2003.

Easterling, Patricia, 'A Show for Dionysus', *The Cambridge Companion to Greek Tragedy*, Patricia Easterling (ed.), Cambridge: Cambridge University Press, 1997.

Else, Gerald F., *The Origin and Early Form of Greek Tragedy*, Cambridge, MA: Harvard University Press, 1965.

Foucault, Michel, *Order of Things*, New York: Pantheon Books, 1971.

___, *Birth of the Clinic*, trans. A. M. Sheridan Smith, New York: Pantheon Books, 1973.

___, *Discipline and Punish: The Birth of the Prison*, trans. Alan Sheridan, New York: Pantheon Books, 1978.

___, *The History of Sexuality, Volume I: An Introduction*, trans. Alan Sheridan, New York: Pantheon Books, 1978.

___, 'On the Genealogy of Ethics: An Overview of Work in Progress', in *The Foucault Reader*, Paul Rabinow (ed.), 1984.

___, *The Use of Pleasure: Volume 2 of The History of Sexuality*, trans. Robert Hurley, New York: Pantheon Books, 1985.

___, *The Care of the Self: Volume 3 of The History of Sexuality*, trans. Robert Hurley, New York: Pantheon Books, 1986.

Frazer, James George, *The Golden Bough: A Study in Magic and Religion*, New York: Macmillan, 1963.

Freud, Sigmund, *Totem and Taboo: Some Points of Agreement Between the Mental Lives of Savages and Neurotics*, trans. James Strachey, New York: W. W. Norton, 1962.

Friedman, Richard Elliott, *Who Wrote the Bible?*, Upper Saddle River, NJ: Prentice Hall, 1987.

Funk, Robert W., *Honest to Jesus: Jesus for a New Millennium*, Santa Rosa, CA: Polebridge Press, 1996.

Funk, Robert W., and Roy W. Hoover, *The Five Gospels: The Search for the Authentic Words of Jesus*, Santa Rosa, CA: Polebridge Press, 1993.

Gardner, Sebastian, *Kant and the 'Critique of Pure Reason'*, London: Routledge, 1999.

Hegel, G. W. F., *Phenomenology of Spirit*, trans. A. V. Miller, Oxford: Clarendon Press, 1977.

Heidegger, Martin, *The End of Philosophy*, trans. Joan Stambaugh, New York: Harper and Row, 1973.

___, *Being and Time*, trans. Joan Stambaugh, Albany, NY: State University of New York Press, 1996.

___, *Introduction to Metaphysics*, trans. Gregory Fried and Richard Polt, New Haven, CT: Yale University Press, 2000.

Husserl, Edmund, *The Crisis of European Sciences and Transcendental Phenomenology: An Introduction to Phenomenological Philosophy*, trans. David Carr, Evanston, IL: Northwestern University Press, 1970.

Inwood, Michael, *Hegel*, London: Routledge, 2002.

Kant, Immanuel, *Critique of Pure Reason*, trans. Werner S. Pluhar, Indianapolis, IN: Hackett Publishing Company, 1996.

Locke, John, *An Essay Concerning Human Understanding*, Peter H. Nidditch (ed.), Oxford: Oxford University Press, 1979.

Millikan, Ruth, *On Clear and Confused Ideas: An Essay About Substance Concepts*, Cambridge: Cambridge University Press, 2000.

Nozick, Robert, *Philosophical Explanations*, Cambridge, MA: Harvard University Press, 1981.

Philipse, Herman, *Heidegger's Philosophy of Being*, Princeton, NJ: Princeton University Press, 1998.

Rousseau, Jean-Jacques, *Rousseau's Political Writings*, Alan Ritter and Julia Conway Bondanella (eds), trans. Julia Conway Bondanella, New York: W. W. Norton and Company, 1988.

Sartre, Jean-Paul, *Being and Nothingness*, trans. Hazel E. Barnes, New York: Philosophical Library, 1956.

Schopenhauer, Arthur, *The World As Will and Representation*, 2 vols., trans. E. F. J. Payne, New York: Dover Publications, 1966.

____, *Parerga and Paralipomena: Short Philosophical Essays*, 2 vols., trans. E. F. J. Payne, Oxford: Oxford University Press, 2001.

Sellars, Wilfrid, *Empiricism and the Philosophy of Mind*, Cambridge, MA: Harvard University Press, 1997.

Stendhal, *Love*, trans. Gilbert and Suzanne Sale, New York: Penguin, 1975.

Strauss, David Friedrich, *The Life of Jesus Critically Examined*, trans. George Eliot, London: Thoemmes Continuum, 2006.

____, *The Old Faith and the New*, reprint ed., Amherst, NY: Prometheus Books, 1997.

Thomson, Iain D., *Heidegger on Ontotheology: Technology and the Politics of Education*, Cambridge: Cambridge University Press, 2005.

Turow, Scott, *The Laws of Our Fathers*, New York: Farrar, Straus and Giroux, 1996.

Wellhausen, Julius, *Prolegomena zur Geschichte Israels*, Edinburgh, 1885. Reprinted, Gloucester, MA: Peter Smith, 1973.

Wittgenstein, Ludwig, *Philosophical Investigations*, 3rd ed., ed. and trans. G. E. M. Anscombe and Elizabeth Anscombe, London: Blackwell, 2001.

Yalom, Irvin D., *When Nietzsche Wept: A Novel of Obsession*, New York: Basic Books, 1992.

INDEX

ability, abilities 21, 28, 54, 61, 64, 69–72, 76, 87, 106, 111–12, 123, 144, 172, 188
aesthetics 19, 21, 35, 141
agency 41, 67, 69, 80, 148, 156
Alcibiades 109, 116
alienation 28, 33, 111, 116
appearance 18–22, 51, 54, 62–3, 83, 97, 141–4
asceticism 19, 21, 47, 51, 53, 117, 120, 125–6, 128, 131, 133, 169, 170
Althusser, L. 178
Anaxagoras 35
Anaximander 35
antirealism 101, 118
Apollo, Apollinian 20–2, 25, 146

Bauer, B. 6
Bayreuth 13, 31
Beethoven, L. 109–111
Bergson, H. 186
Berkeley, G. 82–3, 101, 158–9
Bismarck, O. 5
Bizet, G. 53
Borges, J. 173
bourgeoisie 7, 112
Bowie, D. 3
Brahms, J. 54
Brown, N. O. 172
Buddhism 55–6

Caesar, J. 109
Carmen (Bizet) 53
castration 167–9
categories 1, 25, 131–2, 188
catharsis 17
causality 3, 11, 24, 31, 36, 42, 44, 67–9,

73–4, 79–81, 83–6, 101–3, 114, 116, 118, 121, 125, 127, 130–1, 137, 175–6
certainty 81, 155
chaos 66, 117, 143–4, 146, 150–151, 154, 162, 188
Christianity 2, 4, 10, 23–4, 28, 42, 45, 47, 50–1, 55, 57–9, 62, 95, 115–16, 127, 129, 130–2, 166, 168–9, 182–6
cognitivism 119–20
Colli, G. 12
consciousness 22, 80, 82–3, 184
consequentialism 120
Cornford, F. 23
Critique of Pure Reason 89

Darwin, C., Darwinism 24–5, 51, 87, 131
Dasein 147–8
Davidson, D. 172
deconstruction 13
déjà vécu 9
déjà vu 95
Deleuze, G. 175, 181, 183–8
Democritus 35
Derrida, J. 166–73
Descartes, R. 2, 6, 51, 84, 86–7, 94, 138, 147, 154–5, 157–9, 161
desire-qualia 82–5, 87
desire-satisfaction 74, 77
determinism 18, 27, 41, 67, 81, 153
Deuteronomist 56
dialectic, dialectical 17, 168, 175, 181, 183–5
Diderot, D. 6
Diogenes Laertius 11
Dionysus, Dionysian 10, 14, 20–3, 25, 53, 184